Yaser Chaaban

Robustness of Hybrid Central/Self-Organising Multi-Agent Systems

Yaser Chaaban

Robustness of Hybrid Central/Self-Organising Multi-Agent Systems

in Intersections without Traffic Lights

Südwestdeutscher Verlag für Hochschulschriften

Impressum / Imprint

Bibliografische Information der Deutschen Nationalbibliothek: Die Deutsche Nationalbibliothek verzeichnet diese Publikation in der Deutschen Nationalbibliografie; detaillierte bibliografische Daten sind im Internet über http://dnb.d-nb.de abrufbar.

Alle in diesem Buch genannten Marken und Produktnamen unterliegen warenzeichen-, marken- oder patentrechtlichem Schutz bzw. sind Warenzeichen oder eingetragene Warenzeichen der jeweiligen Inhaber. Die Wiedergabe von Marken, Produktnamen, Gebrauchsnamen, Handelsnamen, Warenbezeichnungen u.s.w. in diesem Werk berechtigt auch ohne besondere Kennzeichnung nicht zu der Annahme, dass solche Namen im Sinne der Warenzeichen- und Markenschutzgesetzgebung als frei zu betrachten wären und daher von jedermann benutzt werden dürften.

Bibliographic information published by the Deutsche Nationalbibliothek: The Deutsche Nationalbibliothek lists this publication in the Deutsche Nationalbibliografie; detailed bibliographic data are available in the Internet at http://dnb.d-nb.de.

Any brand names and product names mentioned in this book are subject to trademark, brand or patent protection and are trademarks or registered trademarks of their respective holders. The use of brand names, product names, common names, trade names, product descriptions etc. even without a particular marking in this works is in no way to be construed to mean that such names may be regarded as unrestricted in respect of trademark and brand protection legislation and could thus be used by anyone.

Coverbild / Cover image: www.ingimage.com

Verlag / Publisher:
Südwestdeutscher Verlag für Hochschulschriften
ist ein Imprint der / is a trademark of
OmniScriptum GmbH & Co. KG
Heinrich-Böcking-Str. 6-8, 66121 Saarbrücken, Deutschland / Germany
Email: info@svh-verlag.de

Herstellung: siehe letzte Seite /
Printed at: see last page
ISBN: 978-3-8381-3821-3

Zugl. / Approved by: Leibniz Universität Hannover, LUH, Diss., 2014

Copyright © 2014 OmniScriptum GmbH & Co. KG
Alle Rechte vorbehalten. / All rights reserved. Saarbrücken 2014

Dedication

This dissertation is dedicated to my beloved:

    Ebtisam Shaban,
        Ebraheem Al.Zahran,
            Sohib Al.Zahran.

Hannover 2014   Yaser Chaaban

Abstract

The Organic Computing initiative aims to build robust, flexible and adaptive technical systems. Future systems shall behave appropriately according to situational needs. But this is not guaranteed in novel systems, which are complex and act in dynamically changing environments.

The focus of this thesis is to investigate the robustness of coordination mechanisms for multi-agent systems in the context of Organic Computing. As an application scenario, a traffic intersection without traffic lights is used. Vehicles are modelled as agents.

An interdisciplinary methodology called "Robust Multi-Agent System" (*RobustMAS*), has been developed and evaluated regarding different evaluation scenarios and system performance metrics.

The new developed methodology (*RobustMAS*) has the goal of keeping a multi-agent system running at a desired performance level when disturbances (accidents, unplanned autonomous behaviour) occur. The result is an interaction between decentralised mechanisms (autonomous vehicles) and centralised interventions. This represents a robust hybrid central/self-organising multi-agent system, in which the conflict between a central planning and coordination algorithm on one hand and the autonomy of the agents on the other has to be solved.

The *hybrid coordination* takes place in three steps:

1. A course of action with no disturbance: central planning of the trajectories without deviation of the agents.
2. Observation of actual trajectories by an Observer component, identifying deviations from plan.
3. Replanning and corrective intervention.

In the *scenario* of this work, an intersection without traffic lights, the participants are modelled as autonomous (semi-autonomous) agents (Driver Agents) with limited local capabilities. The vehicles are trying as quickly as possible to cross the intersection.

An intersection manager is responsible for *coordinating tasks*. It performs first a path planning to determine collision-free trajectories for the vehicles (central). This path planning is given to vehicles as a recommendation. In addition, an observation of compliance with these trajectories is done, since the vehicles are autonomous (decentralised) and thus deviations from the plan in principle are possible. Of particular interest is the ability of the system, with minimal central planning intervention, to return after disturbances to the normal state. Here, different coordination and replanning mechanisms as well as the capability of the system to operate under real time conditions have to be investigated.

For the *path planning*, common path search algorithms are investigated. Particularly interesting here is the A*- algorithm. The path planning is considered as a resource allocation problem (Resource Allocation Conflict), where several agents move in a shared environment and have to avoid collisions. The implementation should be carried out under consideration of virtual obstacles. Virtual obstacles model blocked surfaces, restricted areas (prohibited allocations of resources), which may arise as a result of reservations, accidents or other obstructions. In addition, virtual obstacles can be used for traffic control.

Different types of *deviations* of the vehicles from the plan have been investigated. The controller is informed by the Observer about the detected deviations from the plan, so that it can intervene in time. The controller selects the best corrective action that corresponds to the current situation so that the target performance of the system is maintained.

The *evaluation* of the concept has been carried out based on the basic metrics: throughput, waiting time and response times. Simultaneously, an appropriate metric for the quantitative determination of the robustness has been developed. The required experiments were carried out based on a MAS simulation (Repast framework).

The evaluation of the new methodology "Robust Multi-Agent System" (RobustMAS) demonstrated the benefit of applying this methodology to build robust hybrid central/self-organising technical systems. In this context, analytical considerations of the experiments showed that RobustMAS provides a high level of robustness. RobustMAS ensures an acceptable level of reduction of the system performance as long as the disturbance is not increased beyond a certain threshold (robustness).

Keywords: Organic Computing, Robustness, hybrid coordination.

List of Abbreviations

AA	Autonomous Agents
AAA	Adaptive Agent Architecture
AACN	Advanced Automatic Collision Notification
ABC	Avoid, Build and Correct
ABS	Anti-lock Braking System
AC	Autonomic Computing
ACC	Adaptive Cruise Control
ACID	Atomicity, Consistency, Isolation and Aurability
ACN	Automatic Collision Notification
ACS	Adaptive Computing Systems
ANRA	Autonomous and Non-Rational Agents
ANRV	Autonomous and Non-Rational Vehicles
ANTS	Autonomic Nano-Technology Swarm
APLR	Agent Programming Language for Robustness
ARA	Autonomous and Rational Agents
ARV	Autonomous and Rational Vehicles
ATAM	Architecture Tradeoff Analysis Method
ATT	Agents in Traffic and Transportation
AV	Autonomous Vehicles
AWD/4WD	All Wheel Drive/ Four Wheel Drive
BDI	Belief–Desire–Intention
C2C	Car-to-Car communication
CACC	Cooperative Adaptive Cruise Control
CAM	Content Addressable Memory
CD	Collision Detector
CDF	Cumulative Distribution Function
CICA	Cooperative Intersection Collision Avoidance
CICAS	Cooperative Intersection Collision Avoidance Systems
CNP	Contract Net Protocol
CVHS	Cooperative Vehicular Highway System
DBMS	Data Base Management Systems

DD	Deviation Detector
DFRA	Distributed Field Robot Architecture
DM	Decision Maker
DMUC	Decision Making Under Certainty
DMUU	Decision Making Under Uncertainty
DRG	Dynamic Route Guidance
DSR	Dynamic Steering Response
DSRC	Dedicated Short-Range Communications
EBA	Emergency Braking Assistance
ESC	Electronic Stability Control
ESP	Electronic Stability Program
ET	Emergency Threshold
EU	Expected Utilities
EUT	Expected Utility Theory
EVP	Emergency Vehicle Preemption
FDA	Food and Drug Administration
FORM	Framework for Self-Organization and Robustness in Multi-agent systems
FOT	Field Operational Test
GPS	Global Positioning System
HEDS	Human Exploration and Development of Space
IC	Integrated Circuit
ICA	Intersection Collision Avoidance
IMU	Inertial Measurement Unit
IS	Information Systems
ISA	Intelligent Speed Adaptation
ITS	Intelligent Transportation Systems
IVI	Intelligent Vehicle Initiative
KISS	Keep It Simple, Stupid
KRASH	Karlsruhe Robust Agent SHell
LDWS	Lane Departure Warning System
LIDAR	Light Detection and Ranging
MAS	Multi-Agent Systems
MWT	Mean Waiting Time
NAA	Non-Autonomous Agents

NAV	Non-Autonomous Vehicles
NOW	Network On Wheels
O/C	Observer/Controller
OC	Organic Computing
OCCS	Observation and Control of Collaborative Systems
OSU	Ohio State University
OTC	Organic Traffic Control
OTCC	Organic Traffic Control Collaborative
PP	Path Planning
PPC	Production Planning and Control
RADAR	Radio Detection and Ranging
RAVON	Robust Autonomous Vehicle for Off-road Navigation
RePast	Recursive Porous Agent Simulation Toolkit
RT	Response Time
SD	situation Descriptor
SFX	Sensor Fusion Effects architecture
SoC	Systems on Chip
SuOC	System under Observation and Control
SWIS	Swarm-Intelligent Systems Group
TCS	Traction Control system (TCS)
TL	Traffic Level
TM	Trajectory Memory
TR	Tolerance Range
TRIAD	Trustworthy Refinement through Intrusion-Aware Design
TRS	Trust and Reputation Systems
TSP	Transit Signal Priority
V2V	Vehicle-to-Vehicle communication
VANET	Vehicular Ad hoc Network
WAVE	Wireless Access for Vehicular Environments

Contents

Contents ix
List of Figures xiii
List of Tables xvii
1 Introduction 1
   1.1 Objectives of the thesis 2
   1.2 Background 2
      1.2.1 Robustness 3
      1.2.2 Organic Computing 3
   1.3 Scientific focus and contribution 4
   1.4 Outline of the thesis 5
2 Scenario and required technology 7
   2.1 Application Scenario "Autonomous cars in a traffic intersection without traffic lights" 7
   2.2 Required technology 9
3 State of the art 11
   3.1 Organic Computing (Observer/Controller architecture) 11
   3.2 Architectures for technical systems 12
   3.3 Robustness of systems 15
      3.3.1 Robustness in general 15
      3.3.2 Robustness of OC systems 29
      3.3.3 Robustness in multi-agent systems (MAS) 31
      3.3.4 Metrics for robustness 37
      3.3.5 Faults and fault tolerance 42
   3.4 Intelligent Transportation Systems 46
   3.5 Agents in Traffic and Transportation 47
   3.6 Adaptive traffic control systems 50
   3.7 Autonomous driving and autonomous cars 51
      3.7.1 Intersections for autonomous cars 53

- 3.8 Comparison of the RobustMAS concept with related work 57
- 3.9 Summary 60
- 4 **Design and architecture for robust multi-agent systems** 63
  - 4.1 Robust system with disturbance 63
  - 4.2 Goals (contributions) of RobustMAS 65
  - 4.3 Objectives of RobustMAS 66
  - 4.4 Concept and architecture 67
    - 4.4.1 Distribution possibilities 67
    - 4.4.2 Hybrid central/self-organising concept for multi-agent systems 67
    - 4.4.3 Approach of RobustMAS 69
    - 4.4.4 Approach of RobustMAS in a special problem domain: "RobustMAS Traffic" 78
    - 4.4.5 Measurement of robustness and gain 81
  - 4.5 Summary 87
- 5 **Realisation of RobustMAS** 89
  - 5.1 First step: Path planning 89
    - 5.1.1 A*-algorithm 91
    - 5.1.2 Trajectories 92
    - 5.1.3 An adapted A*-algorithm 92
    - 5.1.4 Virtual obstacles 95
    - 5.1.5 Summary: Path planning 95
  - 5.2 Second step: Observation 96
    - 5.2.1 Deviation classes 96
    - 5.2.2 Detection of deviations 97
    - 5.2.3 Detection of deviations (an example) 100
    - 5.2.4 Situation Parameters 102
    - 5.2.5 Summary: Observation 105
  - 5.3 Third step: Controlling 105
    - 5.3.1 Decision making 106
    - 5.3.2 Controller algorithm 106

- 5.3.3 Action table of the controller 108
- 5.3.4 Decision making (under certainty & under uncertainty) 109
- 5.3.5 Uncertainty of sensor values 110
- 5.3.6 Tasks of the decision maker 111
- 5.3.7 Summary: Controlling 111
- 5.4 Summary 112

6 Evaluation 113
- 6.1 Experimental setup and the simulation environment 113
- 6.2 System performance metrics 115
  - 6.2.1 Modes of the reservation algorithm for trajectories 116
- 6.3 Test situations 117
  - 6.3.1 First test situation: Si1 (Plan) 118
  - 6.3.2 Second test situation: Si2 (Deviation) 133
  - 6.3.3 Third test situation: Si3 (Plan, Disturbance) 139
  - 6.3.4 Fourth test situation: Si4 (Deviation, Disturbance) 140
- 6.4 Summary 146

7 Conclusion and future work 149
- 7.1 Conclusion and final words 149
- 7.2 A peek at future trends 151

8 Bibliography 153

Contents

List of Figures

Figure 2-1: The intersection without traffic lights "RobustMAS Traffic" 8
Figure 3-1: Concept of the Observer/Controller architecture [13] 12
Figure 3-2: Robustness requirements for API's [22] 15
Figure 3-3: Robustness with relation to other concepts [66] 22
Figure 3-4: The wide definition of robustness of software architecture according to [66] 23
Figure 3-5: The ABC design methodology [24] 25
Figure 3-6: The dependability tree [59] 26
Figure 3-7: Types of Faults in self-organising Systems [51] 28
Figure 3-8: Properties of self-organising systems [51] 28
Figure 3-9: System state spaces model [23] 30
Figure 3-10: Layered agent implementation architecture [80] 34
Figure 3-11: Proposed robust MAS architecture [82] 35
Figure 3-12: The general FePIA procedure [24] 39
Figure 3-13: Characterising the robustness of a system according to the statistical approach [24] 41
Figure 3-14: The elementary fault classes [59] 43
Figure 3-15: Failure modes [58] 43
Figure 3-16: Traditional Fault-Tolerance Techniques [63] 45
Figure 4-1: Robust system with disturbance occurrence 64
Figure 4-2: The methodologies integrated within (RobustMAS) 65
Figure 4-3: Distribution possibilities of the generic observer/controller architecture [17] 67
Figure 4-4: The hybrid central/self-organising concept 68
Figure 4-5: The conflict between a central planning algorithm and the autonomy of the agents (The general flow plan proposed by RobustMAS solving the conflict) 69
Figure 4-6: The paradigm of the proposed solution consisting in an Observer/Controller architecture 70

List of Figures

Figure 4-7: System architecture 72

Figure 4-8: Simplification of a shared environment, example for planning of trajectories (resulting resource allocations) 73

Figure 4-9: A shared environment as a 12 x 12 grid of reservation cells (tiles) 73

Figure 4-10: Detailed RobustMAS system architecture 77

Figure 4-11: Comparison of cumulative system performance (throughput) for three situations 82

Figure 4-12: Measuring robustness and gain using cumulative system performance 83

Figure 4-13: Comparison of system performance (throughput per time unit) for three situations 84

Figure 4-14: The disturbance strength (the accident size) in three cases: 1, 2, and 4 cells in the traffic intersection 86

Figure 4-15: The evasive action of autonomous vehicles that check the possibility (right or left) to avoid the accident by pulling into another lane 87

Figure 5-1: The traffic intersection without traffic lights 90

Figure 5-2: Rational paths of vehicles with respect to the travel direction 93

Figure 5-3: An adapted A*-algorithm used for the problem of path planning in the three- dimensional configuration time-space. 94

Figure 5-4: Blocking surfaces (virtual obstacles) used by RobustMAS 95

Figure 5-5: Detection of deviation 97

Figure 5-6: The used neighbourhood in RobustMAS 99

Figure 5-7: The 1-step neighbourhood (direct or first neighbourhood) in RobustMAS 100

Figure 5-8: Detection of deviation (Example) 101

Figure 5-9: Deviation and disturbance (accident) specification 103

Figure 6-1: The traffic intersection as cells 113

Figure 6-2: The traffic intersection without traffic lights 114

Figure 6-3: The structure of the AllTrajectoriesVector mode 116

Figure 6-4: The structure of the PhotoOfGrid mode 117

Figure 6-5: The cumulative system throughput (# Vehicles) for each evaluation scenario (I, II, III, and IV) in an interval between 0 und 3000 ticks 122

List of Figures

Figure 6-6: The system throughput (# Vehicles/tick) for each evaluation scenario (I, II, III, and IV) in an interval between 0 und 3000 ticks 124

Figure 6-7: The throughput of system in the four evaluation scenarios after 3000 ticks 125

Figure 6-8: The throughput of system in the four evaluation scenarios including the extreme case after 3000 ticks 125

Figure 6-9: The mean waiting time for each evaluation scenario (I, II, III, and IV) in an interval between 0 und 3000 ticks 127

Figure 6-10: The mean waiting time in the extreme case (1000 vehicles) 129

Figure 6-11: The mean response times of system in scenario I (Equal-Equal) after 3000 ticks using the reservation mode AllTrajectoriesVector 131

Figure 6-12: The comparison of the system throughput after 3000 ticks between the first and second test situations 135

Figure 6-13: The comparison of the mean waiting times between Si1 and Si2 136

Figure 6-14: The comparison of the mean waiting times and the standard deviation of all vehicles that left the intersection after 3000 ticks between the first and second test situations 136

Figure 6-15: The comparison of the mean response time after 3000 ticks between the first and second test situations 138

Figure 6-16: The "Disturbance occurrence time" adjusted to the tick 1000 and the simulation length is 3000 ticks (upper figure is cumulative throughput; lower figure is throughput per time unit) 142

Figure 6-17: The system throughput per time unit (lower figure) and the cumulative system throughput (upper figure) using different values of the disturbance strength (size of the accident) 144

List of Figures

List of Tables

Table 3-1: RobustMAS in comparison with selected related work 61

Table 5-1: The actions table of the controller 108

Table 6-1: The four test situations with the three used metrics 118

Table 6-2: The four evaluation scenarios 119

Table 6-3: The four evaluation scenarios with the three used metrics 119

Table 6-4: The four evaluation scenarios (two traffic flows with orthogonal directions) 120

Table 6-5: The mean waiting time and the standard deviation of all vehicles that left the intersection after 3000 ticks in the extreme case (1000 vehicles) 129

Table 6-6: The mean response times after 3000 ticks comparing both reservation ways 130

Table 6-7: The comparison of the system throughput after 3000 ticks between the first and second test situations 134

Table 6-8: The comparison of the mean waiting times and the standard deviation of all vehicles that left the intersection after 3000 ticks between the first and second test situations 136

Table 6-9: The comparison of the mean response time after 3000 ticks between the first and second test situations 137

Table 6-10: The robustness and the gain of the system for various values of disturbance strength 144

List of Tables xviii

1 Introduction

Behavioural intelligence can be seen as a mixture of flexibility, robustness and adaptiveness of behaviour. This mixture is however the key idea of developing today's technical systems, which use the Organic Computing (OC) concept. The Organic Computing initiative uses life-like properties such as self-organisation, self-optimisation and self-configuration towards building these systems as flexible, robust, and adaptive systems.

The ever increasing complexity of today's technical systems embodies a real challenge for their designers. This complexity can be regarded as the major source of unexpected system failures. Organic Computing is concerned with this complexity. It deals with reasonable certainty that most requirements of current technical systems are able to be satisfied in analogy with organic systems in nature [9] [10]. Organic Computing equips technical systems with life-like properties to realise self-x properties such as self-organising, self-configuring, self-healing, self-protecting, and self-explaining. In such systems, many reasons could cause strong deviations in the system behaviour from the expected one. Consequently, the system's performance may deteriorate considerably putting the system into an inacceptable state.

In this context, the design of the system architecture plays a main role in achieving a robust system so that its performance has to remain acceptable in the face of deviations or disturbances occurred in the system (intern) or in the environment (extern). That means, the development of robust systems needs to take into account that degradation of the system's performance in the presence of such disturbances should be limited in order to maintain a satisfying performance. Therefore, a robust system has the capability to act satisfactorily even when conditions change from those taken into account in the system design phase. Nevertheless, this capability has to be retained, because of the increasing complexity of novel systems where the environments change dynamically. As a result, fragile systems may fail unexpectedly even due to slightest disturbances. Thus, a robust system will continue working in spite of the presence of disturbances by counteracting them with corrective interventions.

Considering the system design paradigm, it should be decided whether the system architecture will be centralised or decentralised. A centralised approach is the paradigm where the system is based on a central controller and the components of the system are not fully autonomous. On the other hand, a decentralised approach means that the system has a distributed (there is no central controller and all components of the system are autonomous) or a hierarchical architecture (the components of the system are semi-autonomous in which they are locally centralised) [4]. Based on this, distribution possibilities of the system architecture have important implications for system robustness.

Although the decentralised approach would have some advantages over the centralised one, especially scalability, the hybrid approach containing both centralised and decentralised elements at the same time is applicable and even may be much better than the use of each one separately. The hybrid approach should be robust enough against disturbances, because robustness is an indispensable property of novel systems. Additionally, it represents the interaction between decentralised mechanisms and centralised interventions. In other words, the hybrid approach exhibits the central/self-organising traits simultaneously. This means that a conflict between a central controller (e.g., a coordination algorithm) and the autonomy of the system components must be solved in order to achieve the robustness of the system.

During the last years, the progress in communication and information technologies was significant. Consequently, a lot of investigations were done aiming to improve transport systems so that the area of "Intelligent Transportation Systems (ITS)" was developed. ITS have several applications in traffic and automotive engineering. According to ITS, numerous notions were distinguished such as, among others, intelligent vehicles, intelligent intersections, and autonomous vehicles. In this context, a traffic intersection without traffic lights was chosen as a main testbed to apply the hybrid approach, where autonomous agents are autonomous vehicles, and the controller of the intersection is the central unit. However, the basic idea of a hybrid approach is applicable for other systems as well.

1.1 Objectives of the thesis

This thesis aims to investigate the creation of a robust hybrid central/self-organising multi-agent system using the Organic Computing (OC) concept. The hybrid architecture has to solve the conflict between a central unit (an observer and a controller) and decentral autonomous agents. Thus, the coordination problem for hybrid (central and decentral) multi-agent systems should effectively be solved. It has to demonstrate that such architectures will be able to play a positive role in building robust multi-agent systems in presence of disturbances.

1. The first challenge towards the realisation of this vision is to develop a system architecture that exhibits a hybrid form (a combination of central and self-organising). This architecture should have mechanisms for planning, but only as recommendation, and control decisions. These recommendations are a key element in both the minimisation of the individual travel times of agents across the environment and consequently in avoiding congestions. Accordingly, the autonomous agents may follow this plan or may violate it. Therefore, such hybrid architectures permit that agents behave autonomously.

2. The second challenge is to support the multi-agent system with mechanisms to keep the system at a desired performance level when disturbances and deviations from plan occur (robustness). Furthermore, a new method is necessary to measure the robustness of such hybrid multi-agent systems.

3. The third challenge is to solve the resource sharing problem (resource allocation problem) for the special case of a traffic system. This problem appears wherever multiple agents act in a common shared environment. As a result, such solutions allow agents to move reliably avoiding collisions in their environment.

4. Additionally, this thesis deals with the traffic problem as a special problem domain. A traffic intersection without traffic lights was chosen as application scenario, which is a suitable field for applying the hybrid central/self-organising approach. An intersection controller has to be developed that is equipped with the capabilities to observe the system and to intervene if necessary. In this scenario, vehicles will be driven by agents.

1.2 Background

The research in this thesis was conducted in the context of: (1) Organic Computing (OC) considering (2) robustness as an essential property of OC systems. Therefore, this section will discuss briefly these research fields. A more detailed discussion will be given in the state-of-art section 3.

1.2.1 Robustness

As mentioned above, the Organic Computing Initiative aims to build flexible, adaptive, and robust systems. Thus, it investigates robustness of distributed self-organising systems. This robustness demonstrates a crucial property of OC systems. As a result, robust systems have the capability to continue working in spite of disturbances so that their major tasks can be carried out.

Robustness of a system can be defined in very diverse ways according to the context. Effective control mechanisms for modern systems are desired in order to attain such systems with a better performance and higher robustness. It is very familiar that robustness will be considered with respect to disturbances. The disturbances affect the robustness of the system and may lead to the suspension of the system in the worst case or may constrain, at least, the functionality of the system (the system works but with a reduced degree of robustness). Therefore, variations of the disturbance size are needed in order to study the degree of the system robustness. The disturbance size affects the length of the recovery phase which is required by the system to work robustly again. Briefly, if a system is provided with self-healing properties, this system will be robust against failures or disturbances which may occur.

Because environments of complex systems may change dynamically, self-organising systems should be provided with some degrees of autonomy so that they can adapt their behaviour to new environmental situations. This autonomy as well as disturbances and other reasons may cause an unwanted emergent behaviour [146] or the whole system may fail unexpectedly. Therefore, the system should be observed (e.g., by an observer) and controlled (e.g., by a controller) so that this emergent behaviour or the complete system failure can be prevented. Consequently, the system performance remains effective and will not deteriorate significantly or at least the system will not fail completely.

The main point here is that using a fully centralised approach to design systems is not sufficiently robust, because this design form has a single point of failure. On the contrary, a decentralised approach exhibits more robustness than a centralised approach in many situations; however it often requires overhead costs (e.g., a high overhead in terms of communication). In accordance to this, a hybrid approach including both centralised and decentralised elements will provide a certain degree of robustness, which is one of the main issues of this thesis.

It is noteworthy that the definition of system robustness varies according to the context in which the system is used. Therefore, manifold meanings of system robustness were introduced in literature. Additionally, various formal measures and metrics were presented to achieve the system robustness. For more details see section 3.3.4 (Metrics for robustness) in this thesis.

1.2.2 Organic Computing

The Organic Computing initiative introduces an OC system as follows [152]: An OC system is "a technical system which adapts dynamically to the current conditions of its environment. It is self-organizing, self-optimizing, self-configuring, self-healing, self-protecting, self-describing, self-explaining and context-aware". Therefore, the goal of this initiative is to develop systems that are robust, flexible and adaptive at the same time utilising the advantage of the organic computing properties. In other words, OC has the objective to use principles that are detected in natural systems. The technical usage of these principles is expected to support the development of information processing systems so that they can operate as self organising systems. Moreover, by means of such principles of natural systems biologically inspired life-like computer systems will be created [152]. In this case, nature can be considered as a model for technical systems aiming to cope with the increasing complexity.

Organic systems or autonomic systems [153] [154] try to realise quality in several aspects of system engineering including: functional correctness, safety, security, robustness/reliability, credibility, and usability [48] [49]. This wide range of properties of organic systems can be used to establish the vital concept of "controlled self-organisation". Also, organic systems use the "controlled self-organisation" design paradigm, in which the unwanted behaviour should be prevented, whereas the desired behaviour should be rewarded. In this regard, the robustness of OC systems is a key property, because the environments of such systems are dynamic.

Since OC systems are self-organising systems that exhibit some degrees of autonomy, the behaviour of these systems should be observed in order to take an appropriate intervention timely if necessary. Therefore, OC uses an observer/controller (O/C) architecture as an example in system design. Using the O/C design pattern proposed in [10], the behaviour of OC systems can be observed and controlled (for details see section 3.1). In this regard, a generic O/C architecture was introduced in [13] so that this architecture is able to be applied to various application scenarios. Additionally, the suggested O/C architecture has different distribution possibilities (from fully central to fully distributed), where designers have to select between them according to the applied scenario (for details see section 4.4.1). With that in mind, these possibilities of the generic architecture were studied and then implemented in [3] (for details see section 3.2).

Within the Organic Computing initiative many projects were completed. Some of these projects that are more closely related to this thesis are: Organic Traffic Control (OTC) [92] [93] (For details see section 3.6), Organic Traffic Control Collaborative (OTCC) [94] [95] (For details see section 3.6), Observation and Control of Collaborative Systems (OCCS) [144] [145] (For details see section 3.8) and OC-Trust (For details see section 3.3.1.5).

1.3 Scientific focus and contribution

The main contribution of this thesis is the integration of concepts from different research areas into a practically applicable methodology "Robust Multi-Agent Systems" (RobustMAS). According to the previously introduced theoretical background, the scientific focus of this thesis and the contribution to the state of the art can be summarised as follows:

• **System architecture:** This thesis presents a system architecture, which is a hybrid form of a central/decentral (central/self-organising) solution of the coordination problem for multi-agent systems. This means that the agents are (semi-) autonomous, because the central components of the system observe the agents and endow them with a plan as recommendation. Consequently, such hybrid architectures permit that agents behave autonomously. An O/C (Observer/Controller) architecture adapted to the traffic intersection without traffic lights application scenario has been designed using the Organic Computing concept.

- **Hybrid coordination:** RobustMAS addresses the conflict between a central controller (e.g., a central planning algorithm) and the autonomy of the agents. Thus, RobustMAS introduces a hybrid coordination of a multi-agent system (central and decentral) to solve this conflict. This hybrid coordination happens over the following three steps: path planning, observation and controlling. Here, the autonomy of the agents is considered as a deviation from the central plan (desired behaviour) when the agents violate this plan.

- **System aspect:** As a system aspect, the focus of RobustMAS is the robustness of the multi-agent system, so that RobustMAS keeps the system at a desired performance level when disturbances and deviations from plan (desired behaviour) occur. RobustMAS proposes a novel concept towards building robust hybrid organic systems. Additionally, a new appropriate method has been developed to measure the robustness of such hybrid multi-agent systems.

- **General problem domain:** The general problem domain of RobustMAS is the resource allocation problem (resource sharing problem). This is a dynamic coordination problem. RobustMAS tries to solve the question how agents move reliably in a common environment. In addition, RobustMAS gives a solution for the special problem domain, the traffic problem.

- **Traffic Control:** The application scenario of RobustMAS is a traffic intersection without traffic lights. The problem of this application scenario is the coordination of autonomous vehicles. This application scenario is very interesting for the intelligent transportation system, which utilises autonomous vehicles. In this application scenario, RobustMAS tries to solve the question how vehicles move reliably in the intersection area in order to cross it as quickly as possible.

1.4 Outline of the thesis

This thesis is structured as follows. Chapter 2 presents the application scenario used in this thesis, a traffic intersection without traffic lights. This scenario serves as a testbed for the evaluation of the RobustMAS concept. Moreover, it introduces the required technology for autonomous vehicles needing to meet a wide range of requirements and safety standards.

Chapter 3 presents a survey of related work that was published in the domain of robust systems. It gives an overview of many approaches or architectures, which were introduced concerning the construction of robust systems. Apart from related solutions, the generic Observer/Controller architecture will be explained in section 3.1, which serves as basis for this thesis. Afterwards, section 3.2 presents diverse architectures for technical systems presented in the literature. Subsequently, section 3.3 discusses several research fields that investigate the robustness of systems. This investigation contains: robustness in general, robustness of Organic Computing (OC) systems, robustness in MAS and measures for robustness. Afterwards, the current state-of-the-art will be given about the most closely related approaches to the scenario "traffic intersection without traffic lights" in section 3.4, 3.5, 3.6 and 3.7. It contains also autonomous driving and autonomous cars and intersections of autonomous cars. Section 3.8 introduces the comparison between the RobustMAS concept of this thesis and the most closely related work.

Chapter 4 is the main part of this thesis. It presents the new developed methodology (RobustMAS), which serves as a basis for design of robust multi-agent systems. It describes the concept, architecture and objectives of RobustMAS. Furthermore, it highlights the hybrid central/self-organising concept as a main issue of RobustMAS. The general problem domain of RobustMAS, the resource sharing problem, is presented in section 4.4.3.2 together with the proposed solution to cope with it. Subsequently, the measurement of robustness and gain of a multi-agent system will be introduced in section 4.4.5. This measurement is based on the RobustMAS concept, where a new appropriate method is proposed.

In Chapter 5 the realisation of RobustMAS will be discussed. This realisation has three steps: path planning, observation and controlling. These steps will be explained in section 5.1, 5.2 and 5.3 respectively.

The suggested RobustMAS concept was evaluated in Chapter 6. It explains the experimental setup and the simulation environment needed to verify the performance of RobustMAS in section 6.1. The three metrics: throughput, waiting time and response time used in the empirical evaluation will be explained in section 6.2. Additionally, section 6.3 discusses the four test situations proposed to perform the evaluation, where the robustness and gain of RobustMAS are measured in section 6.3.4.1.

Finally, Chapter 7 draws the conclusion of this thesis and gives a peek at future trends for follow-up research projects.

2 Scenario and required technology

This section describes the application scenario of this thesis, a traffic intersection without physical traffic lights, where autonomous vehicles attempt to cross the intersection as fast as possible. Additionally, it presents diverse capabilities (required technology) that autonomous vehicles should possess so that they can move safely on roads.

2.1 Application Scenario "Autonomous cars in a traffic intersection without traffic lights"

Since the coordination of autonomous vehicles is a key point in this thesis, an application scenario has to be selected, which has a very strong relationship with autonomous vehicles. Therefore, the application scenario used in this work is a traffic intersection without physical traffic lights. For this reason, an intersection control algorithm based on virtual traffic lights is used. Such scenarios contain and assemble the required concerns that can be used to build robust multi-agent systems.

In this scenario, a resource sharing problem (resource sharing conflict) arises, which has to be resolved in order to avoid collisions within the intersection (a shared resource). Thus, the coordination of autonomous vehicles is the problem of this application scenario, which will be used later for the evaluation of the RobustMAS concept. A trajectory-based approach will be used where dynamic replanning of trajectories will be investigated in the presence of disturbances.

In this context, fully autonomous vehicles are considered, because autonomous vehicles promise huge benefits for the safety and efficiency of transportation. Recent advances in technology [15] suggest that modern vehicles will be controlled in the near future without direct human involvement, as well as recent advances in artificial intelligence suggest that vehicle navigation will be possible by autonomous agents [5].

In this regard, a special problem domain of RobustMAS has been defined making use of the traffic problem as an application scenario for RobustMAS. This domain, which is called "RobustMAS Traffic", deals with intersections of autonomous vehicles in order to solve the traffic problem.

It is known that human driver errors represent the main cause of road traffic accidents. These human errors have been the reason of a high proportion of the automobile accidents on roads. Recent research in this domain indicates that human driver errors contribute to a very large part of all roadway crashes. Therefore, transportation would be able to gain safety and efficiency by using fully autonomous vehicles. Additionally, by eliminating such human driver errors, some estimates suggest as much as 96% of all automobile accidents can be avoided [16]. Autonomous vehicles would bring about an overall improvement in safety, even if each automobile accident were worse [6]. This means that fewer than 5% of all automobile accidents are caused by other reasons. Therefore, fully autonomous vehicles could avoid about 96% of automobile accidents. In addition to that, the autonomous vehicles and the environment, an intersection without traffic lights, should be observed. This observation aims to detect deviations from plan (trajectories of vehicles) or disturbances (accidents) that may occur. Consequently, replanning and corrective intervention will be directed, if necessary, toward replanning (trajectories replanning) so that the system remains demonstrating safety and robustness. In this case, the system can deliver a bigger degree of safety. In short, using fully autonomous vehicles will reduce road traffic accidents, because of eliminating the major cause of road accidents (human driver errors).

Figure 2-1 illustrates the form of the traffic intersection without traffic lights that has to be implemented in this thesis and consequently to be used by the evaluation of the RobustMAS concept. Here, the intersection was modelled as a grid-based layout. Vehicles that are controlled by agents, try to move through the intersection as quickly as possible.

Figure 2-1: The intersection without traffic lights "RobustMAS Traffic"

Vehicles behave differently regarding their locations, outside or inside the centre of the intersection (shared environment). Vehicles, which are outside the shared environment, attempt to move forward avoiding collisions (act in a fully autonomous way). However, vehicles get collision-free trajectories from the central controller of the intersection. These planned trajectories are provided to vehicles as a recommendation, so that every vehicle has its best possible (desired from controller) path inside the centre of the intersection. Therefore, autonomous vehicles either move faster than their planned trajectories causing deviations from the planned behaviour, or they follow them if deviations are not possible. Here, it is worth mentioning the assumption that the wishes for turning of vehicles are known.

In this application scenario, RobustMAS aims to develop a robust traffic intersection, in the presence of accidents (disturbances) in the intersection, and unplanned autonomous behaviour of vehicles (deviations from planned trajectories). In this regard, the robustness measurement is based on the size of the accident (disturbance strength). Therefore, the simulation has been carried out in the cases that the size of the accident is 1, 2, and 4 (the accident occupies an area of size 1, 2 and 4 cells inside the intersection).

More details about the used scenario can be found in section 6.1 (Experimental setup and the simulation environment).

In the context of the scenario used in this thesis, shared spaces are of particular interest. Shared space is an approach, developed by Hans Monderman, which aims to minimise demarcations between vehicles and pedestrians in busier roads. This means that streets will be without traffic signs, without signals and lane markings, without sidewalks and bike paths. Here, the goal is the freedom of the shared space, as well as all road users having equal rights. So, the shared space approach is an urban design, which is used usually in the more narrow streets of residential areas. An example for applying the shared space approach is the Exhibition Road in Kensington in London. It is important to distinguish that the shared space approach depends on uncertainty about who has the right of way. Therefore, all road users should decrease their speed aiming to reduce risks and damages [130].

For generalisation of the RobustMAS concept, the current scenario used in this thesis, intersections without traffic lights, can be replaced also with the more general scenario, shared spaces. This generalisation may be possible due to the similarities between the working circumstances and the environments presented in both systems. In this regard, both systems can be considered as unregulated traffic space, where vehicles move in a fully autonomous way without traffic lights.

2.2 Required technology

The implementation of autonomous cars requires a variety of technologies. In the context of this thesis, these technologies are assumed to have been created and merged completely and consequently they are not subject of this work.

Autonomous vehicles require a variety of capabilities in order to function properly and safely on road networks. The most important capability is the communication or the cooperation with other vehicles or traffic lanes. Car-to-Car (C2C) or Vehicle-to-Vehicle (V2V) communication in addition to Car-to-X communication are promising technologies for autonomous vehicles. They enable the interaction between vehicles and infrastructures of roads aiming to enhance the safety of traffic (for details see section 3.7 Autonomous driving and autonomous cars).

Autonomous vehicles have to capture their environment using available techniques like laser, radar, lidar, GPS and computer vision [131] (see section 3.7). Additionally, autonomous vehicles should keep safe distances from other vehicles, e.g., by means of adaptive cruise control (ACC) that adjusts the vehicle's speed in compliance with the surrounding traffic (see section 3.7). Furthermore, autonomous vehicles have to follow their lane, e.g., using a Lane Departure Warning System (LDWS) (see section 3.7).

On the other hand, on the intersection level, Intersection Collision Avoidance (ICA) can be used to warn the vehicle while entering the intersection unsafely. Also, Cooperative Intersection Collision Avoidance (CICA) aims to prevent collisions in the intersection by means of the cooperation of intersections with vehicles (for details see section 3.7.1 Intersections for autonomous cars).

In this context, Intelligent Transportation Systems (ITS) were proposed as an active research field to optimise the use of traffic infrastructure. ITS is able to observe and consequently to adapt traffic dynamics achieving transport safety and transport efficiency (for details see the section 3.4 Intelligent Transportation Systems). Furthermore, agent technologies and MAS technologies are used to design and build traffic and transportation systems where safety and efficiency are key features (for details see the section 3.5 Agents in Traffic and Transportation).

The next chapter gives an overview of existing related work aiming to highlight the need of a novel approach to cover the gap recognised in the previous chapter.

3 State of the art

Keeping a system at a desired performance level in presence of disturbances or deviations from plan has been investigated by researchers for years. Consequently, many approaches or architectures were introduced towards building robust systems. Therefore, this chapter attempts to present an overview of existing related work and to draw attention to the requirement of a novel system to fill the gap, building robust hybrid organic systems, considered in chapter 1.

Since Organic Computing (OC) represents the theoretical basis of this thesis, section 3.1 presents the generic observer/controller architecture proposed on the way to develop organic systems. Afterwards, several architectures for technical systems will be introduced in section 3.2 using various methodologies. Subsequently, many research areas investigating the robustness of systems will be considered in section 3.3 containing the following subsections: robustness in general, robustness of OC systems, robustness in MAS and measures for robustness. Accordingly, different definitions of robustness will be discussed according to the context in which they are considered. The remaining sections of this chapter, section 3.4 - 3.7, point out the current state-of-the-art as described in the publications most closely related to the scenario "traffic intersection without traffic lights". This contains relevant research areas and related research projects including: Intelligent Transportation Systems (ITS), Agents in Traffic and Transportation (ATT), Adaptive traffic control systems, autonomous driving and autonomous cars and intersections of autonomous cars respectively. Finally, section 3.8 compares the RobustMAS concept introduced in this thesis with the most closely related work.

3.1 Organic Computing (Observer/Controller architecture)

As described above in section 1.2.2, Organic Computing (OC) is based on various distribution possibilities of the generic observer/controller (O/C) architecture. The O/C architecture is required, because self-organising systems are provided with some degrees of autonomy that may lead in turn to unwanted behaviours [146].

A generic observer/controller architecture was proposed as depicted in Figure 3-1. This architecture aims to establish the controlled self-organisation in technical systems. Concerning this goal, each organic system should be able to keep working even when the observer and the controller can not continue to work for any reason.

The concept based on the O/C architecture contains three main components forming the generic Observer/Controller design pattern. This design pattern provides a regulatory feedback loop that is able to observe and control the organic system using various mechanisms of observing, analysing, predicting, feedback, and deciding. The O/C architecture has a set of sensors and actuators to measure system variables and influence the system.

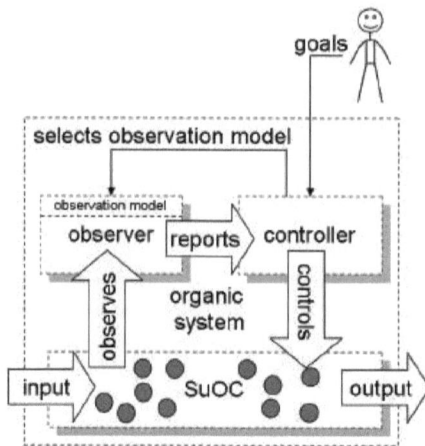

Figure 3-1: Concept of the Observer/Controller architecture [13]

As depicted in Figure 3-1, the three main components are: the observer, the controller, and the system under observation and control (SuOC). The observer has to monitor the system state and its dynamics. It measures, quantifies, and predicts emergent behaviour using metrics and collecting information about the SuOC [13]. After that, the observer aggregates its observations as a vector of situation parameters, which will be sent to the controller. These situation parameters describe the current state of the SuOC. The controller has to evaluate these situation parameters so that appropriate actions can be taken to influence the SuOC concerning the goals given by the user. The system under observation and control (SuOC) is the lowest layer of the O/C architecture. It represents the productive part of the organic system and consists of a (possibly) large number of interacting sub-systems. Further details on the generic observer/controller architecture can be seen in [146].

It should be pointed out that this generic O/C architecture can be applied to diverse application scenarios. In particular, centralised as well as distributed variants are possible. Thus, according to the used scenario, the system designer chooses the most appropriate distribution possibility of the O/C architecture (see section 4.4.1).

Shortly, it can be inferred that the observer and the controller of the O/C architecture have the function of surveillance and feedback. Therefore, sensors and actuators will be required so that the O/C architecture can observe and control the SuOC's behaviour and its environment [13].

3.2 Architectures for technical systems

In the literature, diverse architectures were suggested in order to be applied to various technical systems. Architectures for technical systems are depending on specific requirements using design principles and methodologies in order to achieve desired goals, to solve specific problems, to create behaviour patterns of the technical system applied to.

Chapter 3. State of the art

The Adaptive Agent Architecture (AAA) introduced in [63] [64] is a multi-agent system architecture that was developed on the basis of the research in fault-tolerance and agent communication languages. This architecture works closely with the Open Agent Architecture. It was employed in multi-agent systems like Quickset [64]. Additionally, it depends on the teamwork-based approach, which is a decentralised approach. Due to the fault-tolerant trait of AAA-architecture, a robust multi-agent system can be designed by means of this architecture. For details see section 3.3.1.14 Fault-tolerance to design robust multi-agent systems.

The AAA architecture is not useful for RobustMAS, because of its approach, which assumes that agents work as teams. This approach does not comply with the RobustMAS concept, which supposes that the agents are self-interested.

Other work relating to the architectures proposed in order to solve collaborative or coordinate problems in multi-agent systems can be summarised as follows:

- An application of the generic O/C architecture was presented in [146]. This application was applied to swarm robot scenarios, where the observer determines the unwanted clustering behaviour of robots. Based on this, the controller decides how the environment will be changed so that the system can be influenced indirectly in order to avoid this clustering behaviour. However, this application addresses only clustering behaviour, while RobustMAS deals with disturbances and deviations from plan (desired behaviour).

- A computational framework for the coordination of large robot teams (at least 100 robots) was developed and implemented in the CentiBOTS project [149]. The robots are mobile and resource limited. The robot teams have exploration tasks in dynamic environments, which have to be done collaboratively with least possible monitoring effort. The project introduces a collaborative, distributed, multi-level control architecture in order to create a proposed collaborative behaviour. This architecture is adaptive to new tasks and team organisations. Additionally, it is fault-tolerant and scalable to very big robot teams so that it is appropriate for large-scale robot swarms. As a result, the CentiBOTS project does not deal with turbulent environment (disturbances).

- A novel modelling methodology for distributed and collectively intelligent systems was proposed in [147]. This methodology was developed by the Swarm-Intelligent Systems Group (SWIS) of the EPFL (Swiss Federal Institute of Technology). They presented distributed control algorithm (architecture) using some swarm intelligence methods in order to inspect the overall collective behaviour of the swarm. The resultant methodology does not consider the system robustness against disturbances.

- The Centre for Robot-Assisted Search and Rescue at the University of South Florida has extended the Sensor Fusion Effects (SFX) architecture that serves as the base for the cognitive model of a team of robots. The aim of this extension was to insert a distributed layer so that the concept of a person from psychology can be mimicked. This architecture is called the Distributed Field Robot Architecture (DFRA) [151]. DFRA is a distributed, decentralised implementation of the SFX-architecture. The DFRA architecture allows for dynamic discovery and acquisition of robot resources and the integration of humans and artificial agents in a team of robots [151]. So, it is a control architecture that manages the resources in robot teams, where Jini-services are used for the access to the capabilities of a team of robots. One application of the DFRA architecture was a simulated demining task, where a heterogeneous team of ground and aerial robots was used [151]. However, DFRA architecture does not take into account the influence of disturbances on system functionality, while RobustMAS tries to reduce the effect of disturbances on system performance.

- A behavioural architecture for swarm robots was suggested in [148]. This architecture is very effective for self-assembling tasks (swarm of self-assembling robots). It was developed in the Swarm-bots project that is sponsored by the Future and Emerging Technologies program of the European Commission. This project investigates novel methodologies to the design and implementation of self-assembling and self-organising artefacts. The authors have proposed a control architecture that allows the definition of robot behaviours. Consequently, a group of robots is able to create the desired pattern through their interactions so that a collaboration between the robots is achieved in order to carry out a required task. In this architecture, the key role is played by the interactions among agents, which are responsible for the formation of the needed pattern. On the contrary, RobustMAS uses a central component that performs the desired behaviour (collision-free trajectories), where this planned behaviour is given to agents only as a recommendation.

- The Autonomic Nano-Technology Swarm (ANTS) is a generic mission architecture introduced by NASA. The goal of NASA is to utilise approaches of multi-agent systems in space missions. The ANTS architecture is a mission/system architecture that can be applied to robust, scalable, highly distributed systems [150]. This architecture consists of autonomous and reconfigurable components (structures). It relies on social insect colonies in order to achieve the 'swarm' behaviour by means of utilising the success of such colonies. In this regard, task specialisation for the individual agents (elements) of the system is the main responsibility of ANTS architecture, where every agent performs its specific mission optimally. Consequently, cooperation between system agents is needed to accomplish mission goals. Shortly, it is using for human/robotic mission for the Human Exploration and Development of Space (HEDS) by NASA [150]. However, ANTS architecture has no consideration for the system robustness when disturbances occur in the environment.

- Different distribution possibilities of the generic O/C architecture were investigated in [3]. The study aims to create collaboration patterns in multi-agent systems using the O/C architecture and to apply it to a traffic scenario. The authors have implemented a fully central and a fully distributed O/C architecture in order to compare them, where these both O/C architectures represent extreme possibilities (a multi-level O/C architecture is located between these two extremes). The results show that the design optimum should be somewhere between these two extremes (the central and distributed approaches) [3]. Therefore, it is recommended preferably to use an adaptive architecture that is able to utilise the advantages of these both O/C architectures (the centralised and distributed architectures). The proposed adaptive architecture is capable to switch between the centralised and distributed O/C architecture according to the recent complexity domain (the degree of collaboration between the system agents) [3].

Chapter 3. State of the art 15

Briefly, it can be seen that most system architectures discussed above are focused on specific problems aiming to solve them (collaborative or coordinate problems) in context of multi-agent systems. However, the generic O/C architecture presented in [146] introduces generic methodologies and approaches, where the observation and control of such systems will supply the desired results avoiding unwanted behaviour of agents. In this regard, RobustMAS uses an O/C architecture to observe autonomous agents within a shared environment in order to detect deviations (unplanned autonomous behaviours) from desired behaviour. Additionally, RobustMAS intervenes when it is necessary, so that the system maintains a desired level of system performance in spite of disturbances in the environment. Consequently, RobustMAS focuses on the robustness of hybrid central/self-organising multi-agent systems.

3.3 Robustness of systems

This section deals with the large research field investigating robust systems. First, section 3.3.1 introduces robustness in general aiming to give different definitions of the robustness, which are referenced in the literature. There are many robustness definitions regarding the context. Second, section 3.3.2 presents the robustness of Organic Computing (OC) systems. Third, section 3.3.3 highlights key characteristics of robustness discussed in multi-agent systems (MAS). Forth, section 3.3.4 deals with efforts that are related to measure robustness in different research projects.

3.3.1 Robustness in general

What is robustness? Initially, it is important to mention that the definition of robustness differs in several points according to the context in which the robustness is considered. Therefore, this section will give a wide overview of existing related work discussing robustness in various relevant research fields.

3.3.1.1 Robust API

As a simple definition, robustness means the system should not break at the slightest disturbance [22]. Robustness requirements with examples were introduced in [22]. Five example requirements for robust API's were discussed there. Figure 3-2 illustrates these requirements.

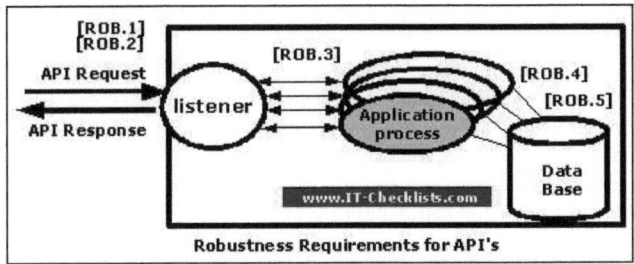

Figure 3-2: Robustness requirements for API's [22]

These five requirements can be summarised as follows:

- [ROB.1] The listener shall be robust against invalid API-requests. It rejects any invalid API-requests and shall not terminate.
- [ROB.2] The listener shall be robust against unexpected flood of requests (e.g., by an intentional attack).
- [ROB.3] The listener shall never produce many application processes (e.g., to prevent the server to run out of memory).
- [ROB.4] The application process shall be robust if it could not connect to the database. It shall terminate with an error message (no a zombie process).
- [ROB.5] The database shall be robust against reaching the session limit (due to unexpected number of database connections).

Based on this, robust API's provide the flexibility of programming and guarantee that applications are suitably designed with better maintainability. Therefore, a monitoring system, which can reliably detect the failed component or identify abnormalities, is required. Consequently, a robust application design can be achieved by integrating this monitoring capability.

3.3.1.2 Robustness of structural systems

The term structural system is used in structural engineering. It refers to load-resisting of a structure. The structural system is composed of interconnected structural components that carry the load. For an example, structures are buildings, bridges, roads, etc.

In the context of structural systems, an effort in [25] is made to offer a practical overview of the main elements of robustness. Here, engineers are working in the field of structural robustness and structural reliability dealing with some typical circumstances and also establishing a guideline on robust structural design. They aim to enhance survival, or to mitigate the consequences of unforeseen events to structural systems. So, the robustness of a structural system is the property of the system that facilitates them to survive unforeseen or unusual circumstances [26]. Survival is a key concept for the robustness of a structural system. In this context, survival denotes the survival of function. This means that the robustness of the structural system enables it making the function available permanently independent of circumstances [25]. A review of the elements of robustness can be found in [25]. The review contains elements of robustness and also strategies and considerations for the establishment of robustness at the design phase of a structural system.

Another related work in this context has the goal to achieve robust design of bridges [27]. This work presents the developed strategies and methods that can be used to quantify robustness in structures aiming to achieve improvements in the robustness. Methods for quantification of robustness were classified in [28]. These methods were compared and distinguished into two main categories: approaches based on structural behaviour and approaches based on structural attributes of systems.

In short, the robustness of structural systems shows the importance of considering robustness not only of technical systems (or computer systems), but also of other systems that are not mainly related to computer systems.

3.3.1.3 Typical definitions of robustness in various domains

Robustness definitions vary significantly containing definitions from engineering, scheduling, statistics, self-organising systems, multi-agent systems, etc. However, it can be typically defined as follows (selection of proposed definitions, among others):

- "The ability of a system to maintain function even with changes in internal structure or external environment" [70].
- "The degree to which a system is insensitive to effects that are not considered in the design" [71].
- "A robust solution in an optimization problem is one that has the best performance under its worst case (max-min rule)" [72].

In the following, robustness definitions in engineering, computing and scheduling systems will be presented.

Robustness in engineering design is a design principle in order to achieve stability. This means that the system should continue working without failure under different circumstances. In this context, manufacturing tolerances have to be considered showing their impact on the performance as well as their role in the design optimisation phase [73].

Robustness in computing systems is mainly related to fault tolerance as described in section 3.3.1.12 Robustness and fault-tolerance.

Robustness in scheduling is a necessary requirement for obtaining acceptable outcomes of a schedule (a plan) in changing and unexpected conditions. Thus, robustness should be provided for the schedule (the plan) during the schedule design process. A robust schedule has to generate solutions facing probable disturbances. A robust schedule was defined as follows: "A solution for a scheduling problem is robust if it has the ability of reacting to external events maintaining the solution as stable as possible" [74].

3.3.1.4 Robustness, flexibility, adaptivity and reliability

The term Robustness is often linked to several other terms, e.g., flexibility, adaptivity, reliability, etc. These terms play a role to clarify requirements or attributes that must be owned by any system in order to consider it as a robust system.

The notions robustness and flexibility were defined in [23]. These two notions depend on the adaptivity of the system. From both definitions, it can be concluded that every robust system, regardless of the degree of the robustness, is also adaptive. That means an adaptive system should not break even if the control mechanism of the system has temporarily lost the ability to work and consequently the system performs its function but likely with a reduced performance. Robustness is the capability to maintain an acceptable behaviour or a required functionality despite limited variations of system's parameters. On the other side, flexibility is the need to modify the behaviour of the system's elements when parameter values change [23].

According to Waldschmidt et al. ([24]), two system features are significant when the robustness of the system is defined: reliability and adaptivity, which should be considered. Consequently, a robust system must be certainly reliable. Additionally, the availability of adaptivity is a crucial requirement for robustness [24].

3.3.1.5 Robustness and trust in Organic Computing (OC Trust)

Trust-based mechanisms and algorithms taking advantage of the organic properties of Organic Computing (OC) were used in the OC Trust project [30] and other research communities. The OC-Trust project deals with trust of complex and highly dynamic technical systems. One of the goals is the robustness of a trust-adaptive agent approach. The project investigates the robustness and the efficiency of a trusted desktop grid using trusted communities in [29]. The authors have shown that trust can improve the robustness of self-organising complex systems (e.g., desktop grid systems) regarding malicious nodes. The robustness there was a concern according to disturbances where the malicious agents try to exploit the system. In this approach, trust-enhancement with agent adaptivity was used trying to improve the robustness and the efficiency of the desktop grid system. So, each node of the system was extended with an agent component where the relations between these agents were modelled with a trust mechanism. The experiments have confirmed that trust-adaptive agents are strongly robust against disturbances. Additionally, the system needs a recovery phase in order to return to its old state as it was before the disturbance occurred.

3.3.1.6 Robustness in Trust and Reputation Systems (TRS)

Similar to the robustness introduced in the OC Trust project, it is relevant to mention an interesting study given in [31] focusing on the robustness of Trust and Reputation Systems (TRS) [32]. The design and implementation of robust trust and reputation systems is a grave challenge. Trust and reputation systems shall be sufficiently robust in the face of attacks or strategic manipulation in order to achieve their goal (e.g., high quality services). According to the importance of the robustness in a system, robustness requirements are determined [31]. Achieving robustness in trust and reputation systems is one of the concerns that are inherent in the engineering of trustworthy self-organising systems [33].

3.3.1.7 General approaches for achieving robustness in unpredictable environments

In order to deal successfully with unpredictable environments, complex systems try to unify the terms: adaptation, anticipation, and robustness using self-organisation [34]. As consequence of that, a system should exhibit sufficient robustness so that it can adapt and anticipate in an effective way [35]. A robust system has to be able to counteract disturbances or perturbations. Otherwise, a fragile system may break easily at the slightest disturbance or perturbation that may hinder the proper operation of the system. In this context, a robust system will continue to work in spite of disturbances or other environmental perturbations [36]. In this case, there are several approaches to perform the robustness of such systems. Among others, the following approaches, according to [34], can be mentioned: modularity [37], degeneracy [38] [41], distributed robustness [39] [42] or redundancy [40].

- Modularity is a general systems concept where system's components can be separated and recombined. One of the more important features of modules is "autonomy" [44]. That means, modules are independent of other modules. Therefore, modules (modularity in design of systems) are able to guarantee the robustness of a system by avoiding any spreading of injury in the whole system.

- Degeneracy lets elements or objects change their nature from one case to another so that the final state may be probably simpler than its original state [45]. In an analogous manner, degeneracy as a design principle is used to obtain the robustness of a system by allowing other elements in absence of an element to carry out the same task even though they have different structures.

- Distributed robustness is used to define a network free from any single point of failure [43]. There are at least two alternative paths between any two points on the network. Here, if any one component is removed then the network will remain in function as before. That means, distributed robustness is against the loss of individual components. Consequently, the main advantage of the distributed robustness is the ability to use resources more efficiently, whether in computation or biology [43].

- Redundancy is the additional presence of functionally identical or comparable resources (components, elements, nodes, etc) of a technical system, if they are not needed for a failure-free operation under normal conditions [46]. Redundancy aims to increase the reliability of a system (fail-safe) so that every component has a back-up to take its role by occurrence of failure.

3.3.1.8 Robustness and self-organisation in complex systems

Complex systems are characterised by nonlinear dynamics, a high-dimensional degree of order, self-organisation and emergent behaviour. These systems are limited in their predictability. What is a self-organising system?

"A system described as self-organizing is one in which elements interact in order to achieve dynamically a global function or behavior" [47].

In engineering, a self-organising system generally has elements, which are designed so that a certain problem can be solved or a defined function can be accomplished at the system level [47]. This should be made dynamically and autonomously. The main point here is that elements of the system are self-organising where each element has to make its decision about its next action. This decision is based only on local information according to its actual state.

Self-organisation can be used to design and control complex systems where the unpredictability of their environment can be solved by means of combining several approaches: adaptation, anticipation, and robustness [34]. Therefore, design and control of self-organising systems have become recently the most important research fields aiming to develop complex systems. Adaptation lets a system react and adapt (changes or modifies itself) better in a changing environment. Robustness lets a system continue to work in spite of disturbances or perturbations. Anticipation lets a system predict changes in advance and hereby adapt to these predicted changes [34].

In this regard, the modelling of a self-organising system has to apply a control mechanism based on the required goals of this system. It guarantees the integrity of the system in the face of potential internal or external disturbances, i.e., it should be robust. However, a control mechanism should not extremely control a self-organising system and its elements, because self-organising systems and their elements are autonomous and hereby have their own goals. Consequently, a control mechanism of a self-organising system should be adaptive in order to be able to cope with its changing environment [34].

3.3.1.9 Robustness and trust in Autonomic Systems

Autonomic Computing (AC) is characterised by systems with self-managing characteristics of their distributed resources. AC is an IBM initiative [153] [154] to cope with increasing complexity of technical systems. It uses the adaptation capability so as to allow systems to adapt to their unpredictable environments. So, autonomic systems consist of several individual autonomic elements (components or subsystems), which are able to change (adapt) itself to their changing environment achieving the self-management property. In this regard, trust in autonomic systems (predominantly meant technical, not social) is needed, because the emphasis here is on developing trustworthy autonomic (i.e., trustworthy self-managing systems). These trusted systems try to prohibit unwanted behaviour and of course reward the desired behaviour (i.e., controlled self-organisation). It is important to mention that trust in autonomic systems or in organic systems is comprised of the following facets [48] [49], where robustness, the main focus of this thesis, is of course one of these facets:

- Functional correctness: Whether the system works truly as it is planned (with respect to its functional specifications).
- Safety: Whether there will be undesired effects (Whether there will be states or outputs, which could cause any injury).
- Security: Whether the system is able to prevent any unauthorised process (announce private information or modify data without authorisation).
- Robustness / reliability: Whether the system is able to guarantee the availability, i.e., it offers one of its services as soon as a service is required. In other words, whether the system (or its services) remains available even though disturbances (or partial failure) occur in the system or in its environment.
- Credibility: Whether the system has the ability to interact with a user (or subsystems interact with each other).
- Usability: Whether the system provides easy user interfaces so that the user can use it efficiently and effectively.

Consequently, the definition of robustness in autonomic systems corresponds to the suggested robustness definition given in [50] in the context of complex systems: "Robustness is the invariance of [a property] of [a system] to [a set of perturbations]". This means that a robust system has to preserve a certain property for a certain set of perturbations. However, it may be fragile for another property or other perturbations. Autonomic systems are self-managing systems which provide robustness in face of changes or partial failures, where self-healing properties provide recovery capabilities and thus an autonomic system can repair itself. In this regard, the degree of robustness that an autonomic system demonstrates is the main point. This degree plays a major role w.r.t. trust in such systems, which provide their services even under various perturbations, disturbances or partial failures [48].

3.3.1.10 Robustness in real-time complex systems

A brief summary of the struggle between complexity and robustness was discussed in [53], where they considered struggle in both evolution and human design. In this regard, several mechanisms are required in order to increase the robustness of fragile systems and therefore the desired system will be more complex. Consequently, the extra complexity may lead to unforeseen malfunction so that new mechanisms are required to maintain the system robustness. So, the desired system will be even more complex and a trade-off between complexity and robustness has to be made [53]. The problem in this context raises the questions: "Could complex system behaviour really be modelled?" and "How to model complex system behaviour?".

A new concept was introduced in [52] based on the continuing struggle between complexity and robustness. This concept presented the idea: avoiding, accepting and influencing complex system behaviour. It is important that a Systems Engineer should take these three notions into account. First, Avoid complexity following the "KISS" design principle. It is the principle of simplicity (KISS principle: Keep It Simple, Stupid) and it aims to avoid unnecessary complexity. Second, Accept complex system behaviour using the "Live with it" or "Normal Accidents" principle. The "Normal Accidents" principle is an "unanticipated interaction of multiple failures" in a complex system [54]. Third, Influence complex system behaviour. This can be made possible by attempting to predict and hereby to avoid outlier behaviour [52].

3.3.1.11 Robustness in Software Engineering

According to the Food and Drug Administration (FDA), the definition of robustness can be summed up in the next statement: "Robustness is the degree to which a software system or component can function correctly in the presence of invalid inputs or stressful environmental conditions" [55].

It is very important, by a testing-based approach for performing robustness testing, to establish the robustness of input validation mechanisms and error-handling mechanisms. For an example, destructive testing tries to cause failure of the tested software aiming to measure its robustness and to prove that requirements of this software are met.

In this context, poor robustness indicates that the modules of the tested software can not recover in the case of run-time errors. In order to improve robustness of such systems, better exception handling has to be added. Additionally, the use of test models should be intensively brought into focus [56].

3.3.1.12 Robustness and fault-tolerance

In computing systems, robustness is mainly related to fault tolerance. Also, when a system exhibits fault-tolerant behaviour, it can tolerate deviations (faults, disturbances) and therefore it does not fail to deliver the expected service at the appropriate quality that will ensure the robustness of such system.

In this context, a definition which indicates the relationship between robustness and fault tolerance was presented in [58]. A reformulation of this definition, in order to make it clearer, was introduced in [65] as follows: "Robustness is the ability of a system to tolerate inputs that deviate from what is specified as correct input". More details of fault tolerance can be found in this thesis in section 3.3.5 Faults and fault tolerance.

3.3.1.13 An architectural process for achieving robustness

Robust programming has become increasingly important in software engineering. This issue raises the question: How complex will be a simple program if the robustness of software has to be taken into account?.

The related work in [66] deals with this problem and describes how architecture can be handled in relation to robustness demonstrating the significance and complexity of robustness. It gives a survey of several works which concentrate on the current software development industry from viewpoint of robustness. The survey aims to find a common way to define robustness of software application, to determine the characterisations of a robust application and to improve robustness in the development phase. The author has tried to define a process in order to perform analysis and design of software architecture from the viewpoint of robustness. So, the author's goal was to obtain robustness using a special architectural process in software solution.

There are various definitions of software robustness in the industry of software development. Therefore, the definition of robustness was proposed in [66] regarding the interview results that were conducted with various companies about their view of robustness and consequently the required means to obtain it (the interviews deal with the theme robustness and architecture). Additionally, an evaluation of the current related methods in the literature was used. The interviewees that work with software architecture introduced the robustness as a broad concept that is related to other existing concepts. As a consequence of this, the proposed definition of robustness comprises several concepts as depicted in Figure 3-3.

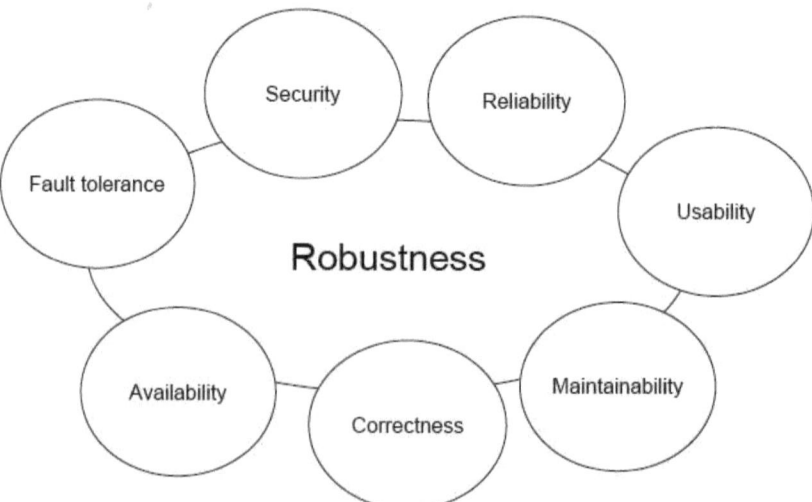

Figure 3-3: Robustness with relation to other concepts [66]

Chapter 3. State of the art   23

It is noteworthy that the proposed definition of robustness in [66] is very similar to that suggested in [58], which defines dependability as a collection of attributes: availability, reliability, safety, confidentiality, integrity and maintainability. So, the significance of the used attributes is based on requirements of the software product and the selection of a technical platform [66].

Figure 3-4 illustrates the wide definition of robustness proposed in [66] including the interviewees' concepts as well as the concepts noted in Figure 3-3.

> Robustness can be defined as the ability to:
> - have a high degree of correctness, and gracefully handle any remaining faults, errors and failures
> - have predictable behaviour under specified conditions, and fail gracefully if outside these conditions
> - provide means to easily detect and remove faults
> - accept modifications in modules in such a way that it does not affect other modules
> - handle all input from users, components, and other systems in a safe and predictable way
> - keep a required level of security despite a changing environment and variations in input
> - not be vulnerable to security related faults

Figure 3-4: The wide definition of robustness of software architecture according to [66]

Moreover, the central focus was on process measures, architectural solutions (software architecture) and implementation. Also, the architecture plays a role in achieving a robust software solution. In this context, a variety of analysis and design methods were then evaluated aiming to find an optimal method to design or analyse for robustness. As a consequence of this evaluation a design and analysis method was suggested. This method is based on two methods which were already evaluated (TRIAD: Trustworthy Refinement through Intrusion-Aware Design and ATAM: Architecture Tradeoff Analysis Method). The main point of this method is that it is composed of two parts. First, a design process that contributes to supporting the design of robust software architectures. Second, an evaluation process that contributes to supporting the analysis of the architecture for robustness concerns. Additionally, this method is applicable over the entire architectural design step.

3.3.1.14 Fault-tolerance to design robust multi-agent systems

An approach to combine issues from multi-agent systems and primitive fault-tolerance techniques was presented in [63]. This approach addresses the problem of fault-tolerance in a multi-agent system. It is based on the theory of teamwork: A multi-agent system that is based on a teamwork-based approach is characterised by the fact that the agents, which work as teams, make the multi-agent system more robust than self-interested agents. The goal of this approach is to design a robust multi-agent system by means of a fault-tolerant architecture. The authors showed that they have designed a robust brokered architecture which has the ability to recover a multi-agent system from broker failures. The important feature here is that this architecture does not require excessive overheads. It uses a recovery scheme, which is based on teamwork. This scheme avoids the use of redundant brokers (overhead) that should be used to achieve the fault-tolerance. That means, this teamwork-based recovery scheme was proposed in order to utilise the redundancy of middle agents, instead of utilising traditional techniques, which are clearly based on redundancy. Additionally, it possesses the ability of scalability, i.e., it can accommodate a large number of brokers (assure a defined amount of them) in a complex multi-agent system. Furthermore, the agent autonomy assures an adequate quality of service and also contributes to make a multi-agent system more robust. The authors introduced the Adaptive Agent Architecture (AAA) in order to achieve experimental evidence for their approach. This multi-agent system architecture is based on a fault-tolerant middle agent (fault handling, detection and recovery from faults). Particularly interesting here is that the teamwork-based approach used here is considerably a decentralised approach. Moreover, no specific fault-tolerance techniques, which are specially designed for multi-agent systems, are required. So, basic fault-tolerance techniques were used on the basis of common concepts from multi-agent systems. Accordingly, the more appropriate traditional techniques aiming to recover a multi-agent system from broker failure are: warm and hot backups, object group replication with virtual synchrony [64]. As a result, the brokers which are already parts of the system and work as a team can deliver results akin to those from traditional fault-tolerance techniques (e.g., warm backups techniques, or object groups with virtual synchrony techniques). That can be made using the reasoning and planning capabilities which are already present in agents [63].

3.3.1.15 Robustness in Systems on Chip (SOC) design

Embedded systems are typical applications of Systems on Chip (SOC), where an embedded system is designed as integrated circuit (IC), which contains entire components of an electronic system in a single chip. However, heterogeneity and complexity pose a challenge in SOC designs due to various hardware and software components.

The work in [24] addresses this challenge by dealing with the design methodology aiming to achieve robust system design. It discusses formal measures and metrics to obtain this robustness. Additionally, it deals with modelling and designing of adaptive computing systems (ACS), where the focus is on the reliability, adaptivity and robustness. That is because, when the robustness of a system is defined, two other system features, reliability (a robust system should be reliable) and adaptivity (to support robustness by adaptivity) should be considered.

The authors introduced a new design methodology for robust adaptive system. Their methodology withstands changes of the environment as well as internal system deviations using the top-down design principle. The used methodology was characterised by the so-called ABC philosophy that provides metrics for robust design. This ABC philosophy is a design paradigm with the ability to produce robust systems. In this context, the SystemC-AMS framework can be employed in order to describe robust systems (structure and behaviour) using the ABC philosophy, where the support of robustness and adaptivity should be incorporated into this framework [24].

Figure 3-5 shows the ABC design methodology that includes three phases. ABC is an abbreviation for the words: Avoid, Build and Correct.

Chapter 3. State of the art 25

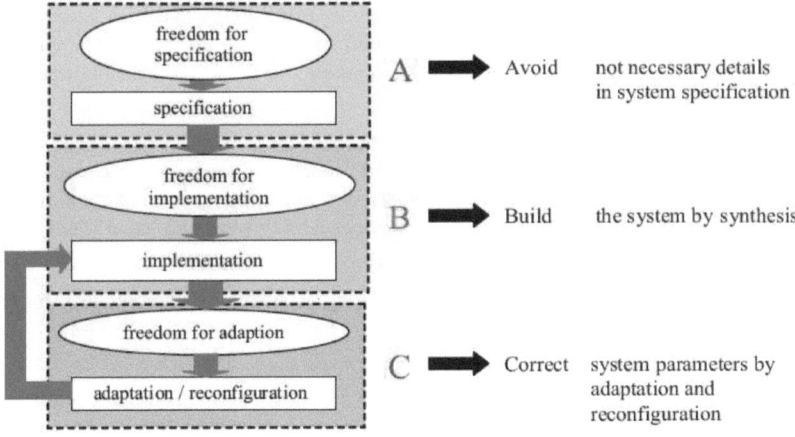

Figure 3-5: The ABC design methodology [24]

A. In design phase A, unnecessary specification has to be avoided keeping sufficient freedom for adaptivity and robustness specification, since in this phase degrees of specification freedom can be expressed. Thus, an adaptation to internal and external changes will be guaranteed by means of intervals of freedom for system specification.
B. In design phase B, the implementation will be carried out (the process of synthesis and refinement of the specification). Here, the specified intervals of freedom have to be considered.
C. Design phase C concentrates on the adaptation of the system to the environment. However, this adaptation should not exceed the limits of degrees of freedom that were defined in phase A. The specified interval of freedom can be implemented by reconfiguration. In summary, it is necessary to provide the ABC philosophy with the ability to control the automated design process. This can be achieved using measures and metrics of the intervals of freedom [24].

Furthermore, the authors in [24] have analysed two quantitative approaches, presented in [67] and in [69], towards a generalised robustness metric, where they discussed the ability to apply them in embedded systems designed as Systems on Chip (SOC). Details of this analysis can be found in section 3.3.4 (Metrics for robustness) in this thesis.

3.3.1.16 Robustness and dependability of self-organising systems

The analysis of robustness and dependability in the context of self-organising systems was introduced in [51]. It is based on the identification of perturbations (changes or faults) and subsequently showing the arising influence on invariants, robustness and dependability properties. The author compared the notions robustness and dependability. The robustness notion was defined as follows: "A computing system can be said to be robust if it retains its ability to deliver service in conditions which are beyond its normal domain of operation" [57]; whereas the dependability notion is: "Dependability is the ability to deliver a service that can justifiably be trusted" (as qualitative definition) or "The dependability of a system is the ability to avoid service failures that are more frequent and more severe than is acceptable" (as quantitative definition) [58].

Dependability was introduced as a generic and integrating concept in [58] [59]. This concept encompasses the attributes: availability, reliability, safety, confidentiality, integrity, maintainability. Additionally, dependability faces threats (faults, errors, failures). According to these threats, several means to attain the dependability were originated (fault prevention, fault tolerance, fault removal, fault forecasting).

Figure 3-6 shows the tree of the complete taxonomy of dependability (dependable computing) as described above.

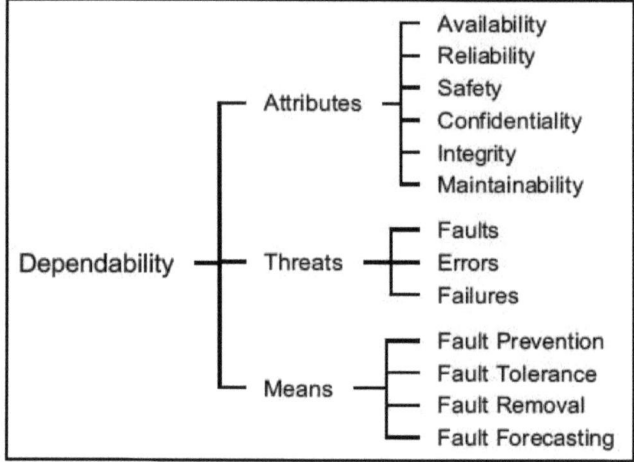

Figure 3-6: The dependability tree [59]

The authors there discussed also the relationship of dependability with several other notions: security, survivability and trustworthiness.

Attributes of dependability:

- Availability: Guarantee for correct service.
- Reliability: Guarantee for permanence of correct service.
- Safety: Prohibition of dangerous impacts on the environment or on the users.
- Confidentiality: Prohibition of any unauthorised revelation of information (actually, confidentiality is a further required attribute of security)

- Integrity: Prohibition of unacceptable system modifications.
- Maintainability: Capability to overcome changes and repairs.

Threats of dependability:
- Failures: A service failure takes place if the delivered service deviates from correct service.
- Errors: An error is the occurred deviation from correct service.
- Faults: A fault is the cause of an error (the cause of a deviation).

Means of dependability:
- Fault prevention: in order to prevent the occurrence of faults.
- Fault tolerance: in order to avoid service failures when faults occur.
- Fault removal: in order to minimise the number and gravity of faults.
- Fault forecasting: in order to assess the current state of faults and their expected impacts.

The author in [51] discussed those four means to achieve dependability in the case of self-organising systems as specific case.

According to [59], robustness can be defined as a secondary attribute that specialises the primary attributes of dependability. That means, robustness of a system is the dependability of this system with regard to external faults (e.g., deviating input values) where the system reaction is characterised by a particular category of faults. Thus, the robustness is a combination of a specialisation of all primary attributes of dependability.

Designers of self-organising systems need to identify the limits of the natural robustness. This means that the properties and the set of disturbances, which cause a system to be fragile, have to be recognised. This procedure for the design of self-organising systems is similar to that by safety engineers, where the technique (failure mode and effects analysis) is used by designing the system in order to discover all faults which may arise [51].

In this context, a definition of resilience is required because self-organising systems always encounter changes to the design condition. Thus, resilience can be defined with relation to the notion "dependability" as the persistence of dependability in the case that a system encounters changes [51].

The author listed types of faults that occur in self-organising systems. These faults may occur from each of the elements of a self-organising system (environment, agents, self-organising mechanism or artefacts).

Figure 3-7 illustrates the characterisation of such types.

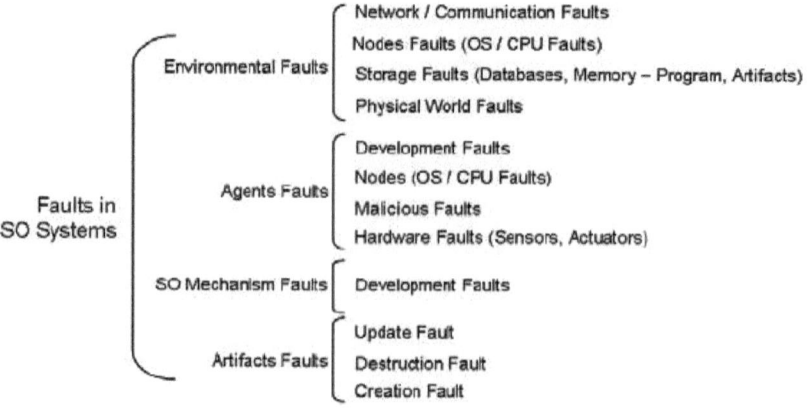

Figure 3-7: Types of Faults in self-organising Systems [51]

Considering the types of faults described above, the following properties of self-organising systems can be specified: (invariants, self-organising systems robustness attributes and dependability attributes).

Figure 3-8 shows the specified properties of self-organising systems.

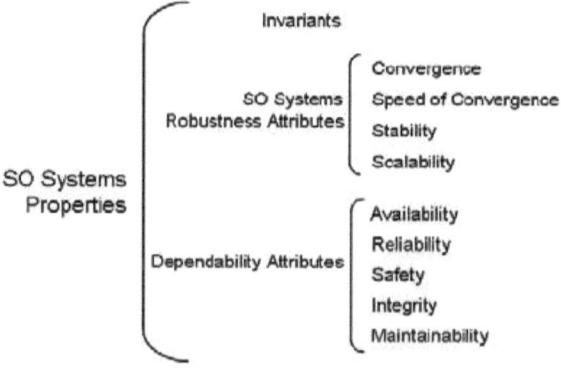

Figure 3-8: Properties of self-organising systems [51]

Of particular interest for this thesis are the robustness attributes of self-organising systems, which are listed as follow:

- Convergence: This property refers to the degree, to which the system converges to the desired target.

- Speed of convergence: The rate (speed) at which the system approaches its desired target.
- Stability: This property indicates whether the system can keep (to be preserved) its target after obtaining it.
- Scalability: The ability of the system to deal with increasing amounts of agents and artefacts.

According to an investigated example (Ant-Based System) as a self-organising system, the author in [51] has concluded some remarks concerning the robustness and dependability attributes. First, the robustness attribute "convergence" is a critical factor that is required by a self-organising system in order to designate the dependability limits. Second, extra resilience (extra resilience techniques) will be required by a self-organising system when the robustness attribute "convergence" cannot be obtained or when the robustness attribute "Speed of convergence" to rational expectations is very slow (not good enough). This additional resilience contributes to sustain the self-organising mechanism. Otherwise, a self-organising system can tackle obviously disturbances in any specified conditions when this system always converges towards its desired target in spite of these disturbances.

Summary: Robustness in general

Many research fields investigate the robustness of systems in general. Therefore, very different definitions of robustness were introduced in the literature according to the context, in which the system is used. Consequently, a wide overview of existing related work was given in this section discussing robustness in various relevant research projects.

One of the most appropriate definitions of robustness discussed above in relation to the RobustMAS concept would be the definition given in [70]:

Definition: "Robustness is the ability of a system to maintain function even with changes in internal structure or external environment".

In this regard, RobustMAS considers a system to be robust if its performance degradation is kept below an acceptable level (at a minimum). Consequently, a robust system will continue working (at a desired performance level) in spite of the presence of deviations from desired behaviour (e.g., unplanned autonomous behaviour) and disturbances in the system environment.

As a result, not one of these projects discussed above has focused on the robustness of hybrid central/self-organising multi-agent systems.

3.3.2 Robustness of OC systems

As mentioned above in section 1.2.1, the robustness of distributed self-organising systems, i.e. OC systems, was investigated in the project Organic Computing in [23]. Robustness is a critical property of OC systems that deal with dynamic and uncertain environments. In this project, robustness is a concept which is related to other concepts like flexibility and adaptivity. The emphasis was that robustness and flexibility depend on the adaptivity of the system, where definitions of these three concepts were presented. Robustness in OC systems was defined as follows:

"Robustness is the capability to maintain a required behaviour or functionality in spite of a certain range of parameter variations" [23].

This means that robustness is a key property of a system. This property reflects the ability of this system in order to keep its function or an acceptable behaviour even though abnormal environment changes and failures might occur.

More accurately, the notion of robustness (as well as of flexibility) was defined based on a state space model. State spaces are used to model the system behaviour as illustrated in Figure 3-9. Based on this, a system will be more robust when it has a big amount of states, which do not cause unwanted behaviour or decreased, even deteriorated, performance.

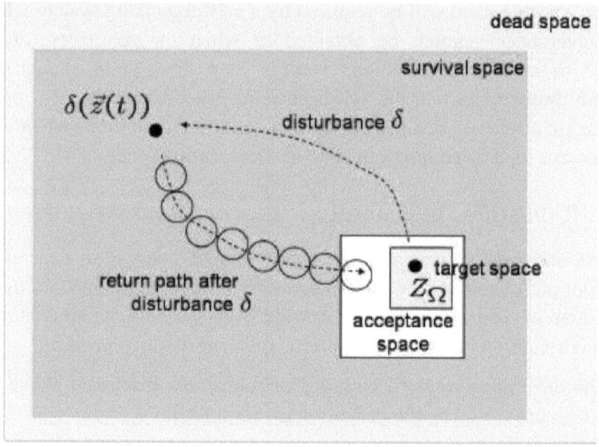

Figure 3-9: System state spaces model [23]

Figure 3-9 shows that the system has to attempt permanently to reach either the target space (optimal performance) or at least the acceptance space (acceptable but not optimal performance) without any explicit external control. However, a potential disturbance can move the system state from $\vec{z}$(t) to ($\vec{z}$(t)), where the new state may lie outside of its acceptance space, for example in its survival space (minimal performance). In this case, a corrective intervention should be performed by means of the internal control mechanism aiming to move the system back to its acceptance space or may be to its target space. This intervention can be done by reconfiguration of the system. Finally, if a disturbance moves the system outside its survival space, the system will reach its dead space (permanently damaged), where the internal control mechanism is unable to move the system back to its acceptance space [23].

The authors categorised a system according to its degree of robustness into strongly robust, weakly robust and non-robust. First, a strongly robust system will keep an optimal performance (an ideal behaviour), where ideal states are mapped into ideal states (the target space is mapped into itself). Second, a weakly robust system exhibits an acceptable but not optimal performance (an acceptable behaviour but not an ideal behaviour), where ideal states are mapped into acceptable states (the target space is mapped into the acceptance space). Finally, a non-robust system can not maintain an acceptable behaviour in the face of disturbances [23].

In other related work, the robustness of OC systems is defined as a property of the system, where the system should not leave a defined state space [1]. As result, the robustness demonstrates how a system reacts sensitively to changes in the environment or improper use. That means, it characterises the system reaction to a specific class of faults.

Summary: Robustness of OC systems

The project "Observation and Control of Collaborative Systems" (OCCS) [144] [145] has focused on Robustness of OC systems. However, OCCS defines robustness in such a way that it should comply with a state space model. The critique of this method is that it does not comply with the RobustMAS concept introduced in this thesis to characterise robustness.

This non-compliance can be traced back to the fact that OCCS deals only with disturbances in the system environment. However, RobustMAS addresses deviations from desired behaviour (e.g., unplanned autonomous behaviour) as well as disturbances in the system environment. Consequently, on one hand, RobustMAS observes autonomous agents within a shared environment in order to detect deviations from desired (planned) behaviour. Moreover, on the other hand, RobustMAS intervenes if necessary, so that the system keeps at a nominal performance level in spite of disturbances in the system environment. Therefore, the focus of RobustMAS is on the robustness of hybrid central/self-organising multi-agent systems. Additionally, RobustMAS defines a new metric for the quantitative determination of the robustness.

3.3.3 Robustness in multi-agent systems (MAS)

Nowadays, robustness is one of several concepts that have to be considered when designing multi-agent systems. Thus, achieving robustness in multi-agent systems is of central importance. In the literature, a lot of research projects have been concerned with robustness of a multi-agent system in different research areas. However, there is a clear lack of study of robustness, to the best of our knowledge, in developing robust multi-agent systems in technical systems. In this context, various goals can be defined such as:

- Addressing robustness issues (robustness considerations).
- Providing a language for robustness.
- Supporting agent system robustness.
- Embedding a robustness-service into MAS.
- Guaranteeing a robust MAS behaviour.
- Supporting robustness mechanisms in agents to build robust agents (robust agent behaviour and robust agent architecture).
- Building more robust MAS (increasing or improving robustness of an agent system).
- Building robust teams of agents.

- Guaranteeing the robust execution of agent tasks.
- Addressing robustness guaranteeing mechanisms.
- Measuring robustness of MAS.

The development of robust multi-agent systems can address the robustness in the face of various kinds of factors (i.e., in the sense of turbulences) such as unreliable agents, faulty agents, malicious attacks, system uncertainty, common disruptions, failing elements or components, unreliable components, variable (turbulent) environments, environmental catastrophes, unexpected situations and exceptional conditions. In short, the goal is to develop a robust multi-agent system despite disturbances and deviations occurred in the system (intern) or in the environment (extern).

In the following, several research projects and approaches will be presented that are of interest in the context of this thesis. They deal in some way with robustness of multi-agent systems in various research fields.

- The work in [75] tried to build robust multi-agent systems against unreliable agents and infrastructures using a domain-independent exception handling approach. The authors have proved that their approach has the ability to achieve the robustness of multi-agent systems. They have implemented their proposed approach for multi-agent systems that accomplish resource allocation using double auctions to handle communication exceptions.

- Similar to the work in [75], the so-called "citizen" approach, was presented in [76]. The "citizen" approach tries to improve the robustness of multi-agent systems by off-loading exception handling from problem solving agents to distinct domain-independent services. It facilitates robust open multi-agent systems. This approach observes a multi-agent system in order to detect problems (exceptions) and consequently to intervene if needed. The case study of this approach was handling the agent death exception in the contract net protocol. According to the "citizen" approach, citizens embrace optimistic rules of behaviour but a whole host of social institutions will be used so as most exceptions can be handled (institutions deals with exceptions more efficiently than individual citizens). The main factor which leads to applying the citizen approach efficiently to the development of multi-agent systems is that widely reusable, domain independent exception handling expertise can be separated from the knowledge that agents in MAS can act upon to perform their usual jobs [76].

- Another approach to support robustness of multi-agent systems was introduced in [77]. This approach is based on logging aiming to build more robust multi-agent systems. It tries to deal with problems occurring in multi-agent systems and consequently to recover from them. It uses an execution logging in order to build robust agents. The execution logging (execution history) has to be ensured at the architectural level. This means that agents in MAS should possess architectural-level support for logging and recovery methods when the robustness of MAS is considered. The authors presented also how an infrastructure-level logging approach can sustain agents so that run-time problems in BDI agents can be recovered [77]. Additionally, the authors have defined a special programming language, called APLR (Agent Programming Language for Robustness). This language is a developer-level language

Chapter 3. State of the art 33

and defined especially for BDI agent programming. It aims to encode agent problem-handling knowledge so that a specification of problem-handling information will be supported as well as the developer can be insulated and constrained from the infrastructure-level reasoning [77].

- In production planning and control (PPC), an approach in [78] has addressed the robustness of such systems that were designed as multi-agent systems. In this context, flexibility and robustness are especially looked for in the case of production environments that are subject to continual, substantial and rapid changes in conditions (disturbances or turbulences). The authors have applied database technologies on the basis of transactions in order to achieve the robustness of multi-agent systems. They assumed that robustness and reliability, which are common characteristics of current database systems, will solve the detected lack of reliability and robustness in the industrial deployment whether database technologies are applied. The database technologies will allow agents to perform their tasks robustly via providing robustness services, since robustness services are widespread in database techniques. Additionally, it is assumed that MAS can handle this problem more effectively than conventional centralised approaches on account of their flexible and robust behaviour. The authors have modelled a multi-agent system and then compared it to an Operations Research Job-Shop algorithm. The comparison was made using a simulation-based benchmarking scenario. According to this approach, robustness on the shop floor will be assured by using MAS and rescheduling algorithms. As a result, robustness of a production system against disturbances can be supported not only by scheduling algorithms but also by a proper MAS architecture [79]. On the other hand, a simulation-based benchmarking platform was developed at the University of Karlsruhe in Germany. This platform was part of the Karlsruhe Robust Agent SHell (KRASH) project that is based on a real world production scenario (shop floor scenario). The goal of the benchmarking platform was to discover whether MAS can improve the planning quality in the shop floor scenario. In short, due to the fact that robustness is a significant aspect of a manufacturing system, this approach presented a transaction-based robustness service using database technology so that disturbances (e.g., machine failures) can be handled [78].

- Closely related to the work in [78], an approach was developed in [80] aiming to increase the robustness of multi-agent systems. This approach is called transactional conversation. It applies transaction-based robustness mechanisms, which are common in database management systems (DBMS). These mechanisms were integrated in a robust FIPA-compliant MAS development framework. More accurately, agent conversations will be handled as distributed transactions. The authors have defined the robustness of MAS as following: "Robustness for Multi-Agent Systems means their ability to show predefined qualitative behavior in the presence of unaccounted types of events and technical disturbances". According to this definition, the problems arising from disturbances during the agent interaction should be resolved so that the operation of MAS will be more robust. This approach was applied to applications of production planning and control (PPC). The authors have presented an agent implementation architecture that was used as a framework to argue about the various aspects of robustness as well as to categorise the heterogeneous approaches in this area to increase the robustness of MAS. This architecture is a structured overview that organises the development tasks in ascending order based on abstraction levels that lead in turn to several layers (layered architecture) as depicted in Figure 3-10. In this regard, diverse issues were taken into account from the point of view of developers through the development process in order to build that agent architecture [80].

(7)	user layer
(6)	mechanism layer
(5)	agent architecture
(4)	ontology layer
(3)	conversation layer
(2)	MAS infrastructure layer
(1)	communication layer

Figure 3-10: Layered agent implementation architecture [80]

Obviously in this work, the concentration of robustness considerations has to be on the third layer, the conversation layer, where the agent cooperation is controlled, because this layer is the most critical layer for ensuring the general robustness of MAS. On the other hand, agent communication describes the meaning of a communication and is arranged in various conversations (interaction of the involved agents) which should comply with predetermined conversation protocol such as the contract net protocol (CNP) [80].

- Similar to the works in [78] [80], a promising approach was developed in [81] demonstrating a first step towards achieving robust multi-agent systems. This approach aims to increase the robustness of a multi-agent system that is applied in the distributed Information Systems (IS) field of study by means of an underlying middleware. This middleware has to guarantee the robustness of the MAS. The main point in this interdisciplinary approach is to discuss the relation between the technologies of both agents and databases, where agents need to share data asynchronously. Thus, the author claims that the agents of a MAS share a world model in which the present situations can be reflected in a common database. The author has defined the robustness as follows: "We define the robustness provided by the middleware in terms of guarantees given on a technical basis, which is guaranteeing the correctness in normal operation and recoverability of the system in case of disturbances." [81]. The key idea of this work is to develop an extended transaction model encompassing agent plans and their emergency behaviour (emergency behaviour in the case of disturbances in order to react to them). Additionally, an execution agent has to be involved in order to execute this transaction model. This execution agent ensures the robustness of execution of agent actions. At the same time, the execution agent characterises the interactions with different elements of a generic MAS architecture [81]. Figure 3-11 shows the proposed robust MAS architecture.

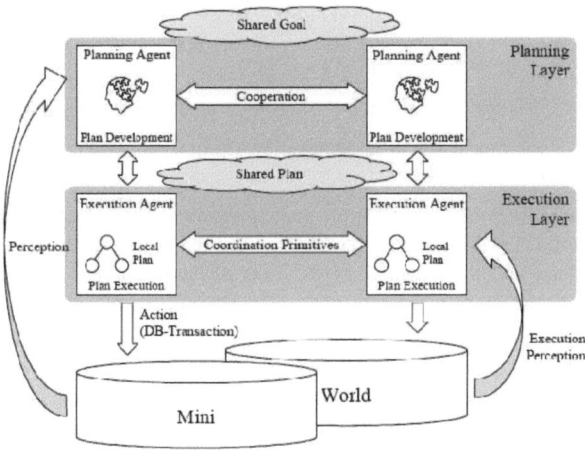

Figure 3-11: Proposed robust MAS architecture [82]

Here, the environment (the world) of the MAS is represented by databases. Every agent perceives its environment (reading from databases) and possibly changes it by producing certain actions (writing to databases). It is noteworthy that every agent is divided in two entities; a planning agent (located in the planning layer) and an execution agent (located in the execution layer) [82]. A planning agent has to cooperate with other planning agents to create the common shared plan, where each planning agent has its common goal and creates its local part of the shared plan and then hands it over to a peer execution agent. Every execution agent executes its received local plan, where coordination protocols will be used to coordinate the execution with other execution agents. In this context, local plans are represented by transaction trees, so that each single-agent action will be encapsulated in an ACID transaction (atomicity, consistency, isolation and durability). ACID transactions are utilities that can be used to guarantee the robust execution of agent actions, where it is known that the most commercial DBMS provide the ACID transactions [81].

- In the context of market-style open multi-agent systems, a study was introduced in [83] in order to define robustness quantitatively in such systems. This study assumes that robustness of MAS is more than redundancy, because problems caused by malicious agents in open systems can not be solved using redundancy. Therefore, it defines robustness of MAS with respect to performance measures and consequently a robust MAS keeps safety responsibilities despite events which cause disturbances. Thus, a MAS system will be robust if it preserves a certain level of performance. The authors presented quantitative definition of robustness, using an electronic market, as follows: "the expected drop of the performance measure in four perturbation scenarios (i) increase of population size, (ii) change of task profile over time, (iii) malicious agent intrusion, and (iv) drop-outs of agents." [83]. According to this definition, robustness of the MAS presents the amount of performance decrease measured in a perturbation scenario (e.g., in case of double population size). The contribution of this study lies in social agents, organisation of agent societies and robustness of social systems. In short, the authors suppose that the four properties (scalability, flexibility, resistance, and drop-out safety), which are required to cope with the perturbation scenarios, will be accomplished using [83]:

1) Two types of operation (task delegation and social delegation).
2) Four mechanisms for delegation (voting, authority, economic exchange and social exchange).

It is important to pay attention that delegation is a complex concept that is very significant in the context of MAS. The delegation concept facilitates attaining robustness and flexibility of MAS. Task delegation is based on delegating tasks to other agents, which leads in turn to agents specialising in certain tasks [83].

- Another related work to attain robustness of multi-agent systems using the delegation concept was introduced in [84]. This work is based on simulation of social systems using the "social order" concept in the social sciences, because social order bears similarity to robustness in this context. Additionally, it illustrates the properties that agents should have in order to develop them in complex social systems. In this regard, the concept of flexible holons was used. This concept depends on arrangement of agents in groups (task delegation and social delegation) to model institutions in MAS and consequently to utilise their facility of achieving robustness of MAS. Thus, the authors have analysed the delegation between agents and applied it to holonic systems. Holons (holonic agents) are a useful method for purposes of modelling institutions in MAS [84]. This method is inspired from the notion of "recursive" or "self-similar" structures in the field of biological systems. The authors have stated that a holon (a holonic agent) consists of parts, which in turn are agents (and maybe holonic agents themselves). As a result, a holonic agent is part of a whole and consequently it assists to attain the aims of this superior whole. Additionally, modelling of institutions will make MAS robust, since institutions reduce complexity. A dynamic electronic market, which is able to manage transportation orders, has served as scenario for this work, where agents were created for this purpose [84].

- One additional study in this field was performed in [85], which proposed a new sociological concept. It studied self-organisation in multi-agent systems. Of particular interest in this study is the developed Framework for Self-Organization and Robustness in Multi-agent systems (FORM). The reason for that is that robustness (within the meaning of scalability) is closely related to self-organisation in some application scenarios. The authors have illustrated this framework with respect to the sociological features of organisations. FORM characterises organisational forms and relationships by means of the delegation concept in MAS. However, the study of MAS was limited to those developed for task-assignment. In short, the FORM-framework is used to model (and hereby to accomplish) self-organisation of MAS organisations [85].

- Most closely related to the work in [85], a new concept was introduced in [86] investigating organisational forms of MAS. This concept aims to build robust MAS utilising genetic algorithms that can be used as a search heuristic, since genetic algorithms are effective mechanisms to deal with enormous search spaces. Based on this, the implemented genetic algorithm searches this space for superior forms of organisation. The authors have defined robustness with respect to a performance measure as follows: "Robustness is considered as graceful degradation of a system's performance under perturbation." [86]. Therefore, in order to evaluate the performance of the recent discovered forms (will be formed by recombination of mechanisms) of organisation under various circumstances, diverse robustness criteria were defined according to sociological theory (for details see [86]). That means, the evaluation of those forms of organisation was based on their involvement (beneficial effects) in the performance and robustness of the MAS in order to search for optimal combinations of the mechanisms. On the other hand, organisational forms (structures) are characterised by the specific applied mechanisms. This means that the behaviour of each organisational form will develop via the different possible mechanisms used by the organisations to satisfy their particular attributes. Here, the numbers within the gene stand for the used mechanism. For example, the first gene characterises the mechanism used for task delegation, where three specific mechanisms were implemented (economic exchange, economic exchange combined with gift exchange or authority). Based on this, the search process delivers organisational forms that have the ability to conform and act in a certain way, so that they demonstrate the best possible performance [86].

Summary: Robustness in MAS

Many research projects in the area of multi-agent systems focus on robustness. These works investigate the robustness in various research fields, such as distributed Information Systems (IS), database technologies, social systems and organisation of agent societies. However, there is a clear lack of study of robustness in building multi-agent systems in technical systems.

3.3.4 Metrics for robustness

In order to have the ability to design robust multi-agent systems, robustness metrics are required. These metrics play the role to mitigate the expected degradation of the system performance when any disturbances occur. Many research projects deal with system robustness. Their objective is to measure robustness and to find an appropriate metric for it.

To the best of our knowledge, there is a clear lack of study of these metrics in designing robust multi-agent systems. This thesis raises the question how the robustness can be guaranteed and measured in technical systems.

In literature, there are diverse potential measures of system robustness proposed. Every robustness measure is based and designed according to the definition of the robustness concept in a specific context. The most common robustness measure uses the robustness definition related to the definition of a performance measure. Some robustness measures estimate the system performance using the average performance and its standard deviation, the signal-to-noise ratio, or the worst-case performance. Other robustness measures take into account the probability of failure of a system as well as the maximum deviation from a benchmark where the system has still the ability to deal with failures [23].

Generalised robustness metric

Viable quantitative approaches in order to measure robustness are required. Some approaches were introduced, among others, in [67] [69] [24]. Among those, both the FePIA procedure in [67] and the statistical approach in [69] are general approaches and consequently can be adapted to specific purposes (arbitrary environment). In both approaches, diverse general metrics were used to quantify robustness. These metrics estimate specific system features in the case of disturbances (perturbations) in components or in the environment of the system. Additionally, these metrics were mathematically described. Both approaches are applicable in embedded systems design [24] where embedded systems are designed as Systems on Chip (SoC).

In the following, the FePIA procedure and the statistical approach will be explained.

3.3.4.1 FePIA procedure

The FePIA procedure is presented in [67] in order to derive a robustness metric so that it can be used for an arbitrary system. The authors there discussed the robustness of resource allocations in parallel and distributed computing systems. Consequently, a derived metric from the FePIA procedure was designed for a certain allocation of independent applications in a heterogeneous distributed system demonstrating the utility of the robustness metric. Here, the goal was to maximise the robustness of the produced resource allocations. Moreover, the authors have defined the robustness (indeed, a resource allocation is to be robust) as a restricted degradation of the system performance against uncertainties (perturbations) in specified system parameters.

FePIA stands for Features Perturbation Impact Analysis. The FePIA procedure defines a schema that presents a robustness-radius for the system based on a tolerance region. This procedure identifies four general steps [67] [24]:

1. The important system performance features f_i that may cause degradation of the system performance. They are combined into a feature vector Φ: $\Phi = \{\varphi_1, ..., \varphi_n\}$.

2. The perturbation parameters: $\pi = \{\pi_1, ..., \pi_m\}$.

3. The impact of perturbation parameters on system performance features. This is modelled with individual functions $f_{ij} : \pi_i \rightarrow \varphi_j$, selecting a tolerance region (β_j^{min}, β_j^{max}) for each φ_j (see Figure 3-12).

4. The analysis (it analyses the values of π_i) to determine the degree of robustness.

The main point here is to produce a mathematical relationship between the system performance features and the perturbation parameters (in the sense of the impact). After that, a variation in the perturbation parameters, which lead to a performance degradation exceeding the allowable performance limits (tolerance region), can be detected. This variation represents the robustness radius (optimisation problem) [69].

So, $r(\varphi_j, \pi_i)$ represents the robustness-radius of the system according to the system performance feature φ_j and the perturbation parameter π_i. Accordingly, in order to calculate the robustness of the whole system in the case of a certain perturbation parameter, the minimum across all features of system performance has to be found. Figure 3-12 illustrates the FePIA procedure.

Chapter 3. State of the art

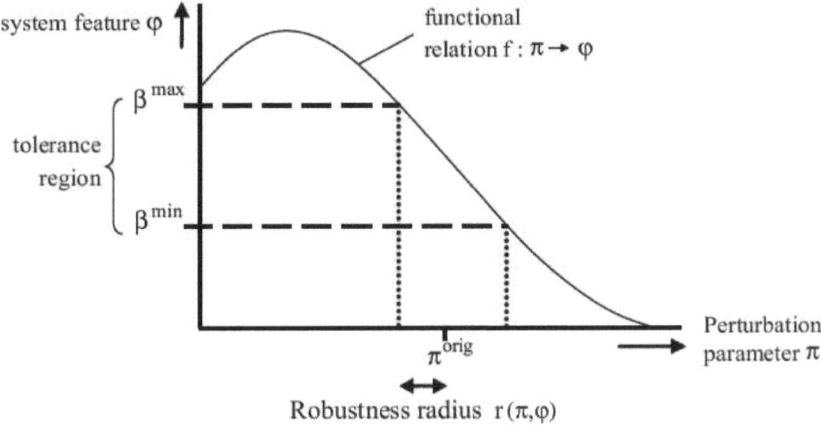

Figure 3-12: The general FePIA procedure [24]

Here, a tolerance region is defined by a lower boundary (β^{min}) and an upper boundary (β^{max}), which can be expressed as in the next formulas:

$$\beta^{min} = \min \left\{ f\left(\pi^{orig} - r\right), f\left(\pi^{orig} + r\right) \right\} \tag{3.1}$$

$$\beta^{max} = \max \left\{ f\left(\pi^{orig} - r\right), f\left(\pi^{orig} + r\right) \right\} \tag{3.2}$$

A robustness definition for analog and mixed signal systems was derived in [24] using the FePIA procedure. The author has evaluated the proposed robustness formula applying affine arithmetic (modelling the deviations by affine expressions as in [68]) with a semi-symbolic simulation. The symbolic representation used in semi-symbolic simulations makes designers aware of the contribution of uncertainty to the deviation at the output of the simulated system. Also, the outcomes of the simulation are affine expressions, which semi-symbolically represent possible deviations [68].

As a result, a robustness definition for analog and mixed signal systems was derived that is based on the estimation of precision versus the robustness radius using the FePIA procedure as described in the next formula:

$$robustness(\varphi, \pi) := \frac{r(\varphi, \pi)}{rad(\pi)} \tag{3.3}$$

Where $rad(\pi)$ characterises the confidence interval of deviations from π [24].

According to this formula, which can be used in the design phase, three cases can be considered.

- First, the robustness is less than 1 and hence the system is not robust and it may fail.
- Second, the robustness is equal to 1 and therefore the system is robust to some extent and it fulfils the minimum requirements.

- Third, the robustness is greater than 1 and hence the system is robust against additional deviations [24].

The drawback of the FePIA procedure is that the tolerance regions (the limits of the performance features) are arbitrarily selected. Thus, the FePIA procedure is applicable for systems where the system performance and the tolerable deviations can be well-defined [24].

3.3.4.2 Statistical approach

The statistical approach has been introduced by England et al. in [69] to obtain a type of robustness metric, which can be used for an arbitrary system. The authors there present a methodology aiming to characterise and measure the robustness of a system (using a quantitative metric) in the face of a specific disturbance (perturbation).

The authors define robustness as follows: "Robustness is the persistence of certain specified system features despite the presence of perturbations in the system's environment." [69].

Similar to the FePIA procedure, system performance features in the statistical approach will be taken into consideration versus the perturbation size (disturbance size). Therefore, the intention of the authors was to measure the amount of degradation of the system performance relative to the perturbation size [24] [69]. For this purpose, the cumulative distribution function (CDF) of a system performance feature is used. CDF is the proportion of observations less than or equal to a specified value (x) when a set of performance observations (X) is given [69]. The robustness can be determined according to the difference between functions F and F*. The function F is the CDF of a performance feature in the case of normal operating conditions; whereas the function F* is the CDF of a performance feature in the case of perturbations.

The maximum distance between F and F* represents the amount of performance degradation. This distance ( ) was computed by means of the Kolmogorov-Smirnov (K-S) statistic (sup is the supremum):

$$\delta = \sup_{-\infty < x < \infty} \left(F(x) - F^*(x) \right) \tag{3.4}$$

Moreover, the distance ( ) has to be weighted with a weighting function $\Psi(x)$ (to compensate for the underestimation of) producing the adjusted K-S statistic ($_w$):

$$\delta_w = \sup_{-\infty < x < \infty} \left(F(x) - F^*(x) \right) \Psi(x) \tag{3.5}$$

The advantage of this method is that it considers the complete distribution of system performance (performance observations); whereas other methods consider only average measurements. In this context, it can be inferred that the system is robust against the applied perturbation when the distance between F and F* (the amount of performance degradation) is very small. Therefore, the smaller the distance is, the more robust the system becomes. Figure 3-13 illustrates the statistical approach (the adjusted K-S statistic) [69].

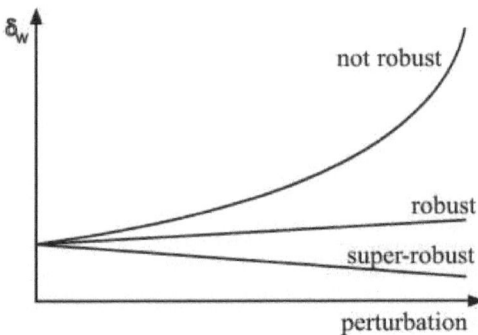

Figure 3-13: Characterising the robustness of a system according to the statistical approach [24]

In Figure 3-13, the robustness of a system is characterised by the measurement of δ_w as a function of the applied perturbation size (in other words, by the gradient of δ_w relative to the amount of perturbation experienced [24]). This means that this system can withstand different levels of perturbation. Here, three cases can be recognised. First, the robust system, wherein δ_w exhibits a slight increase with increasing the perturbation size. Second, non-robust system, wherein δ_w shows a great (probably non-linear) increase with increasing the perturbation size. Third, the super-robust system, wherein δ_w exhibits a slight decrease with increasing the perturbation size. The perturbation in the last case is a profitable perturbation (see [69] for an example).

According to [24], the proposed robustness metric based on the statistical approach is appropriate to use in the design process, where it acts as absolute robustness indicator for profiling targets. In this case, specifications must be executable, so that simulations can be carried out to supply an adequate amount of statistical data.

Comparing with the FePIA procedure, this methodology is generally applicable to various classes of computing systems. Also, it is easier to determine the robustness. That means, the statistical approach has avoided the drawback of the FePIA procedure, so that a tolerance region needs not to be formed. Additionally, they employed their methodology in three applications of job scheduling: backfilling jobs on supercomputers (parallel machines), overload control in a streaming video server, and routing requests in a distributed network service. The third application shows the role of robustness to obtain improvements in system design. Additionally, as mentioned above, this robustness metric would have the advantage of the consideration of the complete distribution of system performance.

Summary: Measures for robustness

Several research projects propose diverse measures of system robustness. These projects measure robustness according to their definition of the robustness in different application areas. In this context, some quantitative approaches were used, such as the FePIA procedure in [67] and the statistical approach in [69]. However, there is a clear lack of study of the robustness metrics in designing robust multi-agent systems in technical systems. Therefore, there still is the question how the robustness can be guaranteed and measured in technical systems. As a result, both approaches discussed above do not comply with the RobustMAS concept introduced in this thesis to characterise robustness.

This non-compliance can be traced back to the fact that RobustMAS focuses on the robustness of hybrid central/self-organising multi-agent systems. For this purpose, RobustMAS proposes the concept of relative robustness for measuring the ability to maintain a specific minimum level of system performance (a desired performance level) in the presence of deviations from desired behaviour (e.g., unplanned autonomous behaviour) and disturbances in the system environment. Based on this, according to the RobustMAS concept, robustness is the ability of the system, with minimal central planning intervention, to return after disturbances (internal and external changes) to the normal state.

3.3.5 Faults and fault tolerance

Faults, errors and failures are threats which can be faced when the dependability and robustness of a system are addressed. These three threats are defined as follows [59]:

"An error has been defined as the part of a system's total state that may lead to a failure — a failure occurs when the error causes the delivered service to deviate from correct service. The cause of the error has been called a fault".

Consequently, ways or means have to be used so that the robustness and dependability of a system can be guaranteed in face of such threats. Fault prevention, fault tolerance, fault removal and fault forecasting are some of the ways that were developed to achieve this goal [59].

Robust systems should be fault-tolerant in order to deal (tolerate) with deviations (faults) and to continue working effectively and fulfilling their major tasks. When a system can not tolerate faults in the behaviour of its elements, then that may lead to a bad performance or even cause a system failure. In this context, a fault is the cause of an error (the cause of a deviation from correct behaviour) which may cause a failure.

Many systems use different mechanisms (using specific architectures or algorithms) to detect faults (deviations) and to intervene if necessary. This means that such designed systems remain demonstrating fault-tolerant operation against a set of faults. Fault tolerance avoids system failures in the presence of faults. Systems therefore will exhibit a safe behaviour in spite of faults.

However, attention may be paid to related concepts of fault tolerance. For an example, the repair concept is related to fault tolerance. Repairs and modifications, which occur during the use phase, are included under the notion "maintenance". That means, repair is one form of maintenance and can be seen as part of fault removal. Additionally, repair situations should be taken into account by fault forecasting [58].

3.3.5.1 The taxonomy of faults

Various faults, as mentioned in [59], may have an effect of a system during its development and use. These faults can be grouped in accordance with eight major classification criteria.

Figure 3-14 shows these fault classes (elementary faults).

Chapter 3. State of the art   43

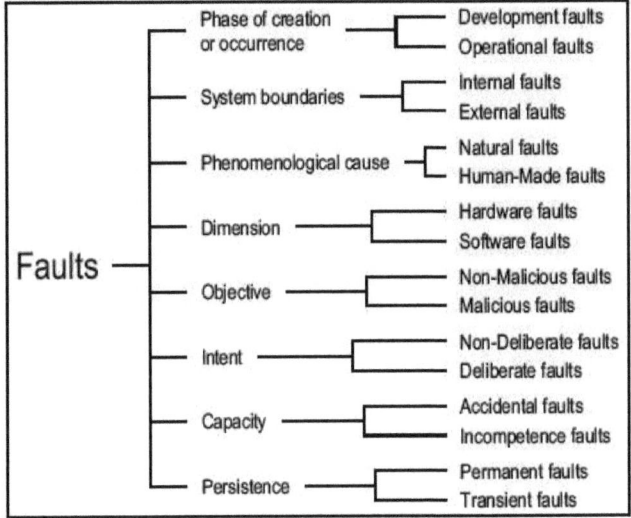

Figure 3-14: The elementary fault classes [59]

It is possible that combinations of these fault classes can be created. The classes of combined faults and their matrix and tree representation were introduced in [59].

3.3.5.2 The taxonomy of failures

Failures of a system can be grouped in accordance with four viewpoints [58]. Figure 3-15 shows these failures aspects, whereas every failure mode describes incorrect service with respect to one viewpoint. For complementary information about every viewpoint, the reader can refer to [58].

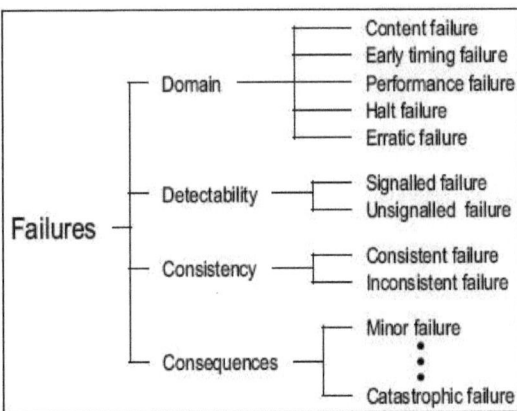

Figure 3-15: Failure modes [58]

In this regard, two types of systems can be found in the literature according to their modes of failure: fail-uncontrolled and fail-controlled systems. The fail-controlled systems do not own mechanisms to detect errors and therefore they may behave arbitrarily and maliciously [60]. However, the fail-controlled systems were designed so that they fail certainly in dedicated modes of failure.

In the literature, approaches to fault-tolerance can be found in two domains:

- Multi-agent systems
- Traditional distributed and database systems.

3.3.5.3 Fault-tolerance in multi-agent systems

A (multi-agent) system is fragile because failures may bring down the whole system. Therefore, a multi-agent system has to possess the ability to avoid such failures. Fault-tolerance is one of the more common concepts (means) that can be used to design robust multi-agent systems. In order to do that, several approaches were developed using algorithms or specific architectures. Two major approaches were suggested for fault-tolerance in multi-agent systems. The first approach is based on exception handling and recovery (healing approach) [60]. The second approach is based on redundancy, i.e., replication (prevention approach), which is commonly used in data bases. A brief study by [62] on multi-agent systems and fault-tolerance demonstrated both approaches. The authors showed that the redundancy approach achieves fault-tolerance by means of tolerating faults of the components in the MAS so as it avoids happening of problems. However, the exception handling approach claims that the system programmer has to handle the occurrence of exceptions through the use of additional code. Since the system programmer may neglect potential exceptions, it would be better to detect any abnormal behaviour autonomously whenever the tolerance range is exceeded.

The authors of [63] propose two categories of fault tolerance in multi-agent systems. Both have to identify failures and try recovering from them. The first category uses guards (sentinels) that are located external to the agents. These guards observe all inter-agent communications. The second category uses self-monitoring (introspection) observing the agent's behaviour at run time. Regarding the first category, several approaches from the literature to fault tolerance in multi-agent systems are also pointed out by [63]:

- Use of external sentinel agents: The sentinel agents have the tasks of monitoring all communications, detecting agent crashes, and taking corrective actions.
- Use of exception-handling service: The exception-handling service is a centralised approach to monitor the overall progress of the system aiming to detect, diagnose faults, and take corrective measures.
- Use of a social diagnosis: The social diagnosis approach enables agents with similar social behaviour to compare their individual state with the state of other agents in order to detect possible failures.
- Use of caching.

The last approach of this category is very interesting for the study of robustness. The caching approach has been studied in [156] in the context of a multi-agent system, which uses matchmakers in order to improve the system robustness against matchmaker failures. This

Chapter 3. State of the art 45

approach uses caching of the matchmaking knowledge by individual agents (locally) of the multi-agent system. Consequently, the use of matchmaking information cached locally will decrease the load on a matchmaker [156]. This approach compliments the work in [64] [63] and may be deployed with techniques that are based on teamwork (see the section 3.3.1.14 "Fault-tolerance to design robust multi-agent systems" that presented an approach to combine issues from multi-agent systems and primitive fault-tolerance techniques).

3.3.5.4 Traditional Fault-Tolerance Techniques (Fault-tolerance in traditional distributed and database systems)

In general, the traditional fault-tolerance techniques are considered to be appropriate for particular cases and consequently for particular failures. Therefore extra support, such as infrastructures, equipment, mechanisms ...etc is needed [63]. There are various techniques for fault-tolerance that have been developed in traditional distributed and database systems. These techniques address the occurred failures using recovery strategies. A brief review in [63] showed that the most essential fault-tolerance techniques used in traditional distributed and database systems use redundancy as main principle. Here are some examples of these techniques:

- Object group replication.
- Virtual synchrony.
- N-version voting.
- Warm and hot backups.

The first three techniques require particular mechanisms, wherein the replicas can communicate and synchronise among them. Several of these traditional techniques, which are categorised in three groups (techniques for database recovery, techniques for application recovery, and techniques for recovery of distributed systems) are illustrated in Figure 3-16.

Database Recovery:
Redo-undo Logs, Fuzzy and Basic Checkpointing, Database Replication

TP Monitors, Application Servers, Resource Managers:
Recoverable Queues, Pseudo-conversations, Fault-tolerant Input Logging, Checkpointing based Recovery, Transaction based Recovery, Stateless Servers, Warm Backups and Hot Backups, Regenerative Processes

Fault-Tolerant Distributed Systems:
Object Group Replication + Virtual Synchrony, Message Logging, N-Version Voting

Figure 3-16: Traditional Fault-Tolerance Techniques [63]

It is noteworthy that most of these recovery techniques largely concentrate on replication in order to achieve more robustness. Replication techniques have the advantage of duplicating all important system data and services that may fail. That means, the needed replication is for the purpose of fault-tolerance, but this leads in turn to overheads (due to replicas).

Summary: Faults and fault tolerance

Robustness in computing systems is mainly related to fault tolerance. Fault-tolerance is one of the more common concepts used to design robust multi-agent systems. Additionally, fault tolerance is one of the means to attain dependability, since fault tolerance is generally used to avoid service failures when faults occur.

Robust systems should be fault-tolerant with the aim of making them capable of dealing (tolerating) with deviations (faults, disturbances) so that they continue working. On the contrary, systems that are not fault-tolerant, regarding the faults identified in behaviours of their individual components, may fail or their performance may deteriorate considerably leading to inacceptable situations. Consequently, the fault-tolerant trait of a multi-agent system architecture can play a main role in designing a robust multi-agent system. Based on this, the performance of such multi-agent systems has to remain acceptable in the face of faults (deviations) or disturbances.

RobustMAS uses the fault-tolerance (deviation-tolerance) capabilities. It makes a decision whether the detected deviations (faults) from the desired (planned) behaviour can be tolerated. That means, it determines if replanning is necessary according to the tolerable deviation limit, where a tolerance region should be formed. RobustMAS defines a safety distance (free positions) around the agents in their shared environment. Accordingly, it tolerates a deviation from planned behaviour unless the limit of the safety distance is exceeded.

Similar to the authors of [63], RobustMAS uses two categories of fault tolerance in multi-agent systems. These categories will detect deviations (faults) or disturbances and try recovering from them. The first category uses an O/C architecture. This architecture observes behaviours of agents and detects if the agents are not respecting their commitments (central plan, where the planned behaviour is given to agents only as a recommendation). The second category uses self-organising behaviour, because the agents in RobustMAS are autonomous (decentral, self-organised) and thus deviations from the planned behaviour are possible. Here, autonomous agents may behave in a fully autonomous way using only their local rules (in the sense of self-monitoring supported by the limited local capabilities) causing deviations. Both categories form the hybrid central/self-organising approach of RobustMAS.

3.4 Intelligent Transportation Systems

In general, the notion "Intelligent Transportation Systems (ITS)" is nowadays used by many researchers who deal with the problems of transport systems in order to improve them, taking into account many aspects, such as: transport safety, transport efficiency. ITS is based on communication and information technologies that can be applied to vehicles and to the available infrastructure of transport systems [87]. Additionally, it contains the applications of both informatics and telecommunications in traffic and automotive engineering [88]. ITS's goals can be summarised as follows [88]: increase of traffic safety, improvement of efficiency of road traffic, reduce of environmental pollution and increase of travel comfort. For many years, diverse research projects were engaged in vehicular traffic aiming to achieve one or more of these goals.

In this context, several notions became well-known such as: intelligent cars (vehicles), intelligent intersections, autonomous cars (vehicles), floating car data, autonomous driving, Car-to-Car (Vehicle-to-Vehicle) communications, Car-to-X communications, telematics systems, and cooperative traffic management (e.g., cooperative traffic signal system).

The work in [89] deals with Vehicle-to-Vehicle communications demonstrating the problem of vehicular ad hoc network (VANET) where the robustness of message exchange between vehicles by means of radio communication is considered. The authors have provided an appropriate model of communication in VANETs (packet reception model).

In the context of ITS, several intelligent transport applications were developed such as [87]: emergency vehicle notification systems (via in-vehicle eCall devices that make an emergency call automatically after an accident), automatic road enforcement (e.g., a traffic enforcement camera system, to identify vehicles that violate the speed limit), variable speed limits (with respect to the road congestion, e.g., on Britain's M25 motorway), collision avoidance systems (e.g., sensors on highways in Japan), cordon zones with congestion pricing (e.g., in Singapore, London and Stockholm to collect a congestion fee from vehicles in a city centre) and dynamic traffic light sequence (via intelligent RFID traffic control).

Intelligent transport applications utilise one or more of various technologies such as [87]: wireless communications (e.g., UHF and VHF frequencies, WAVE (IEEE 802.11) and WiMAX (IEEE 802.16) protocols, GSM, or 3G), computational technologies (microcontroller, microprocessor, embedded system platforms, artificial intelligence, and ubiquitous computing), floating car data/floating cellular data (in order to collect raw data for vehicles using one of the following methods: triangulation method, vehicle re-identification, or GPS-based methods), sensing technologies (e.g., RFID, intelligent beacon, infrastructure sensors such as in-road reflectors, vehicle-sensing systems to deploy the infrastructure-to-vehicle and vehicle-to-infrastructure electronic beacons), inductive loop detection (inductive loops in a roadbed are used to detect vehicles via loop's magnetic field in order to count the number of vehicles, as well as to measure the speed, length, and weight of vehicles and the distance between them), and video vehicle detection (e.g., automatic incident detection or automatic number plate recognition).

ITS is of particular interest to this thesis, since it is related to the application scenario used. Traffic control is a special application domain of RobustMAS, particularly the application scenario "a traffic intersection without traffic lights". This scenario uses autonomous vehicles aiming to solve a traffic problem. In this context, ITS has numerous applications in traffic and automotive engineering, where intelligent vehicles and intelligent intersections are used. Additionally, ITS tries to achieve transport safety and transport efficiency.

3.5 Agents in Traffic and Transportation

Diverse research projects use agent technologies and MAS technologies to develop modern and efficient traffic and transportation systems. Safety and efficiency of traffic and transportation systems was, for a long time, and still is a great challenge for researchers and engineers of traffic and transportation systems. Thus, traffic engineering (transportation engineering) becomes more and more important in line with the tremendous development in modern technology. In this context, complex traffic and transportation scenarios can be modelled using MAS techniques and agent techniques and then simulated. With respect to the purpose of the selected transportation scenario, appropriate control strategies will be selected (e.g., single intersection control, traffic restrictions in roads, and synchronization of traffic lights) [90]. Furthermore, Cooperative Adaptive Cruise Control (CACC) system is a part of ITS. CACC introduces solutions to problems of automotive transportation (e.g., security, efficiency and passenger comfort) [91].

Agents in Traffic and Transportation (ATT) is one of the most active research areas closely related to the application scenario "traffic intersection without traffic lights". In this scenario, vehicles are modelled as agents. In the context of ATT, a lot of research projects are carried out. This section will explain initially some Non-MAS traffic control systems focusing on the centralised solution in urban traffic systems. After that, MAS in traditional traffic control systems will be discussed. Finally, related work that mainly uses agent technologies to support the self-organisation of autonomous cars will be described.

Non-MAS traffic control systems

There are several approaches that deal with traditional traffic systems (traditional traffic lights) trying to optimise traffic light phases. SCOOT [157] and SCAT [158] are two well-known traditional traffic control systems (not MAS), which use a centralised approach in order to solve control tasks in urban traffic systems. However, these centralised approaches have the drawback that they are not scalable and they need long response times. Therefore, the focus was shifted towards the investigation of self-organised or locally organised solutions to traffic control. In this regard, there are many approaches that attempt to improve the traditional traffic control systems, which are based on traffic lights, using agent technologies and MAS technologies.

MAS in traditional traffic control systems

An agent-oriented approach combining MAS and evolutionary game theory has been developed by Bazzan in [159]. The approach represents a new method for decentralised traffic control. In this approach, each intersection is modelled as an individually-motivated agent. Therefore, the system contains multiple intersection managers (multiple agents). These agents have two types of goals. First, local goals are to enable vehicles to cross the intersection. Second, global goals are to minimise travel times of vehicles across the intersection. Consequently, intersection managers (agents) form a distributed traffic signal system, which should be coordinated in an efficient and decentralised manner. Compared to the RobustMAS concept, Bazzan's system focuses on the coordination of multiple intersection managers, while RobustMAS concentrates on the coordination of agents (vehicles) at one intersection.

Another approach has been presented by Roozemond in [160]. The author tries to provide vast amounts of reliable traffic data so that the drawbacks of the SCOOT approach (the lack of traffic data) can be solved. The approach aims to enable traffic intersections to act autonomously w.r.t. sharing the data they collect. After that, the gathered information will be utilised by the intersections in order to predict the traffic flow in short- and long-term using an urban traffic network model. Consequently, multiple intersections are able to share information so that each intersection can be kept informed about the recent traffic situations. Compared to the RobustMAS concept, Roozemond's system focuses on the cooperation of multiple intersections to gather more traffic data, while RobustMAS concentrates on the coordination of vehicles at one intersection.

In contrast to the system targeted by this thesis, both Bazzan's system and Roozemond's system consider traditional traffic control systems and consequently human drivers (human-controlled vehicles). However, RobustMAS considers virtual traffic lights and autonomous vehicles.

In the context of the fairness approach of vehicles in traffic systems, Balan et al. [161] presented an approach that represents a history-based traffic control. The approach aims to maximise fairness of vehicles so that all vehicles may encounter similar delays. It is a multi-intersection approach, where traditional traffic lights are used at each intersection. Additionally, credits for vehicles will be allocated according to the delays (shorter or longer) of these vehicles earlier in their journey (historically) so that vehicle A will take a higher credit than vehicle B if vehicle A has a longer delay than vehicle B. Consequently, vehicle A will take a higher priority (expected to encounter shorter delays) than vehicle B at following intersections. Compared to the RobustMAS concept, Balan's system is a multi-intersection approach considering traditional traffic control (traffic lights), while RobustMAS is an intersection approach using virtual traffic lights to coordinate autonomous vehicles.

Related work regarding the control of the individual vehicles is also carried out. In contrast to a multi-intersection system, such related work is known as a multi-vehicle system. However, much of this work focuses on the concept of vehicle platoons. This concept enables vehicles to create platoons of vehicles, where these platoons are groups of vehicles (like the train). The foremost vehicle makes decisions for the whole platoon so that the effect of stop-and-go driving will be minimised. A MAS approach has been presented by Halle et al. [162]. Here, every vehicle is controlled by an agent. The approach forms platoons, which represent groups of vehicles with different degrees of autonomy aiming to create a proposed collaborative behaviour of multiple vehicles. Compared to the RobustMAS concept, Halle's system exploits traditional traffic lights at an intersection to provide automated control of vehicles, while RobustMAS coordinates autonomous vehicles in an intersection without traffic lights (autonomous vehicles are free from the control of traffic lights).

MAS in traffic intersections of autonomous cars

In the context of using MAS in traffic intersections of autonomous cars, several research projects are carried out. Such works are considered as artificial examples, since most of them are not applicable presently to realistic environments. Moreover, they demand further additional car features, as well as intersections infrastructure. Works more related to this topic are: Multiagent Traffic Management [5], OCCS [3], SKY [136], various ICA- and CICA projects focusing on Intersection Collision Avoidance (ICA) and Cooperative Intersection Collision Avoidance (CICA) [142]. These works will be explained and discussed in section 3.7.1 (Intersections for autonomous cars).

As a result, not one of these research projects discussed above focuses on the robustness of traffic systems use agent technologies. Additionally, the idea of applying a hybrid solution (central/self-organising) to control traffic systems using MAS technologies has not been addressed.

3.6 Adaptive traffic control systems

Traffic control is a multi-disciplinary and a very active area of research. It deals generally with traffic congestion and the management of traffic flows by using certain means which observe the traffic status in order to detect abnormal and emergency situations and to change its control strategy accordingly. Static traffic control systems typically have a static timer controller that manages the traffic lights; whereas adaptive traffic control systems have the ability to adapt their control strategy aiming to increase the system performance or to avoid the traffic congestion.

Several related works, which deal with such systems, have developed adaptive and self-configuring traffic systems (self-configuration or self-control indicates adaptivity). Two related works will be presented in this section.

The first work, Organic Traffic Control (OTC) [92] [93], is a novel approach to control traffic lights at urban traffic intersections. It proposes an architecture for an adaptive learning node controller that enables the dynamic reconfiguration of the traffic parameters [96]. This architecture is based on the Observer/Controller concept of the Organic Computing community (OC), where OC systems can reconfigure themselves at runtime according to internal or external changes [98]. OTC is based on traffic-responsive control in order to realise a decentralised control of road traffic [97]. Based on this OTC approach, another approach, Organic Traffic Control Collaborative (OTCC) [94] [95], was presented. It tries to enable an OTC system to control and optimise traffic signals in urban road networks. Therefore, the OTC architecture was extended to facilitate the collaboration among the node controllers [98]. Furthermore, this approach represents a decentralised solution (hierarchically organised) to achieve self-improvement at runtime [99] [100]. After that, the (OTC^3) project was coordinated in order to realise an OTC system extending the presented system with route guidance as well as a driver information component [101]. According to the current and expected state of the urban road networks, route recommendations will be conducted so that travel times of drivers can be minimised and traffic congestions can be avoided. A novel DRG (Dynamic Route Guidance) approach for road networks was presented in [102] based on the OTC system.

The second work, Adaptive Self-Configuring Traffic Control Systems [103], is a completely adaptive and self-configuring traffic light controller. It aims to decrease the waiting times (mean and variance of them), which are measured by using fixed cycle or fixed time interval algorithms. The traffic light controller presented in this approach integrates a feedback loop based on the sensed traffic rate. Hereby, the collected information will be used to optimise the mean waiting time at the traffic lights. It is an embedded controller that adapts its strategy in order to improve the traffic flows by adjusting the intervals of the traffic lights [103] . The authors have attempted to design the traffic control system as general as possible in order to be able to test different models. The system model has three components: an intersection module, a simulator module and lane modules, where the lane module includes traffic rate, state, and car arrival times. Briefly, this proposed adaptive control approach demonstrates better performance than a static control system (fixed-cycle controller) in various different scenarios. Additionally, it is a general approach to optimise the traffic flows; thereby it can be applied to any environment (traffic intersection) [103].

3.7 Autonomous driving and autonomous cars

In the near future, it is expected that vehicle driving will be an opportunity for human (drivers) to utilise driving time in a positive way. Over decades, new driver assistant devices were integrated into modern cars aiming to reduce the driver's responsibility of driving and to make the driving more safe and comfortable. In this context, two categories of autonomous cars can be recognised; partially autonomous cars and fully autonomous cars (an autonomous car is also known as robotic, driverless or vehicle).

Several research projects aim to construct a fully autonomous car, where autonomous driving in dynamic environments is a big challenge. Autonomous driving aims to replace ordinary cars (manual cars) that are controlled completely by humans with autonomous (self-driving) cars that can drive themselves. Some advantages of fully autonomous cars can be stated as follows: human safety (less car accidents), convenience (as personal chauffeur, simple or automated parking, save the time of all family members) and beneficial side effects to the environment (avoid wasting gas due to their optimised driving) [104]. An autonomous car has the ability to capture the environment and sense the world by means of several available techniques like laser, radar, lidar, GPS and computer vision [131].

RADAR (Radio Detection and Ranging) is a sensor that detects objects using electromagnetic waves (especially metal) allowing to avoid collisions or to coordinate car's speed. Similar to RADAR, LIDAR (Light Detection and Ranging) sensor is an enhancement of RADAR sensor using pulses of light instead of electromagnetic waves and consequently it can be easily manipulated. In the case of a LIDAR sensor on the front of the car, this car is able to recognise objects and their distance, which are located directly in front of the vehicle to perform an emergency stop if necessary. In the case of a LIDAR sensor on the roof of the car, the sensor unit consists of two LIDAR sensors orientated at 90 degrees to each other. By the rotation of this unit and the entanglement of both LIDAR sensors, a 3D image of the current environment can be produced [132]. Moreover, GPS (Global Positioning System) / IMU (Inertial measurement unit) is a receiver used for global positioning of the car and for three-dimensional positioning in space. Furthermore, cameras can be used in order to take pictures of the current environment and then evaluated in terms of their information content [132]. Additionally, infrared sensors are also employed in modern cars where a thermographic camera (sensor) or infrared camera (sensor) can be utilised to generate an image using infrared radiation. Infrared sensors will support the driver especially during a night drive to highlight objects, mostly creatures, from the environment making them widely visible [132].

The autonomous automobile "RAVON" (Robust Autonomous Vehicle for Off-road Navigation) is a realistic example of an autonomous car where different types of sensors are combined. This car was developed at the University of Kaiserslautern for use in its surrounding area [133]. Other research projects carried out in the context of autonomous cars are:

- The projects "CAR EcoSystem" and "SMART@CAR" of the "Center for Automotive Research" at the Ohio State University (OSU) [106].
- The project "DARPA Grand Challenge", earlier known as "DARPA Urban Challenge" [107].

- Autonomous Outdoor Robot RTS-HANNA, at the Institute for Systems Engineering (ISE), Real Time Systems Group (RTS) of the Leibniz University Hannover [108]. The RTS Group is active in several research fields. Of particular interest is the field of autonomous and mobile robots. An interesting study of self-organisation and task distribution in autonomous mobile robotic systems is done by Smolorz and Wagner [111].
- The "Autonome 2030 concept" that is a transport system designed for the future [109] [110].
- The project "Stadtpilot" at the "Technical University Braunschweig (TU Braunschweig)" in Germany, including the CarOLO team and two cars: "Henry" and "Leonie" [112] [113].
- The project "AutoNOMOS" at the "Free University Berlin (FU Berlin)" in Germany [114], including the autonomous cars: "Spirit of Berlin" [115], "Dodge Grand Caravan" [116], and "MadeInGermany" [117].
- The project "Google Driverless Car" has modified the car "Toyota Prius" so that it can operate as a Google self-driving car [119].
- The issue of "driving 3.0" at the Karlsruhe Institute of Technology (KIT) in Germany [121].
- The "Halo Interceptor" concept by the UK designer Philip Pauley [122] [123]. This concept presents a multi functional vehicle that would serve as car, boat, plane and helicopter.

Other projects do not aim to construct a fully autonomous car, but aim to provide technologies or components for future autonomous cars. Therefore, these components, which can be considered supporting partially autonomous features, were included in modern cars such as traction control and electronic stability control systems in order to increase driver's safety [104]. These partial autonomous features are called "driver-assistance" in other literature and can be categorised in various groups: sensorial-informative, actuation-corrective and systemic [131].

- First, sensorial-informative: This group of mechanisms can notify the driver of events that may be ignored by him like; Lane Departure Warning System (LDWS), rear-view alarm, visibility aids, blind spots, night vision, etc [131].
- Second, actuation-corrective: This group of mechanisms can perform the instructions of the driver more effectively than he does. Examples are: Anti-lock Braking System (ABS) also known as Emergency Braking Assistance (EBA), Traction Control system (TCS), Four Wheel Drive (AWD), Electronic Stability Control (ESC) also known as Electronic Stability Program (ESP), Dynamic Steering Response (DSR), traction control, airbag systems and Intelligent Speed Adaptation (ISA) [131] [132].
- Third, systemic: This group provides several mechanisms such as; automatic parking, following another car on a motorway – "Enhanced" or "Adaptive" Cruise Control (ACC) [105], Cooperative Adaptive Cruise Control (CACC) [135], distance control assist, dead man's switch [131].

Chapter 3. State of the art 53

However, the communication with other vehicles or with the intersections is a prerequisite for implementing such systems. Here, Car-to-Car (C2C) in addition to Car-to-X are communication technologies used by autonomous vehicles.

Car-to-Car (C2C) communication

Car-to-Car (C2C) or Vehicle-to-Vehicle (V2V) communication is a promising technology aiming to improve road safety and comfort as well as to decrease the risk of accidents and congestion in traffic systems. Since the implementation of modern WLAN technologies is achieved fast for C2C communication, modern cars utilise widely available WLAN technologies. Here, WLAN 802.11p was used to enable a Wireless Access for Vehicular Environments (WAVE) such as ambulances and traveller cars [124]. In this regard, many project researches in the area of Car-to-Car communication are managed such as: FleetNet [127], Invent [128], NOW (Network On Wheels) [129].

Car-to-X communication

Another budding technology in this context is Car-to-X communication. This technology is based on using wireless communication between vehicles (V2V), or cars (C2C), on one side and between vehicles and infrastructure on the other side. Car-to-X communication means that any road user can involve in this communication system. It was employed in diverse applications so that safety measures can be improved. In this context, Car-to-X communication can be regarded as main application of mobile ad hoc networks that enable various communication network users to exchange the information needed about the traffic system like safety and traffic data [125]. This data can be used by warning and assistance systems in order to hand out warnings about any upcoming danger. One of the most important researches in the area of Car-to-X communication is the "simTD" project in Germany [126].

Summary: Autonomous cars

Many research projects have been carried out in the context of autonomous cars. Here, the more important communication technologies needed are Car-to-Car (C2C) and Car-to-X communications. Moreover, a variety of technologies are required for the effective implementation of autonomous cars. These technologies are presumed to have been developed entirely and consequently they are not subject of this thesis. Likewise, RobustMAS assumes that (for details see section 2.2 Required technology):

- An autonomous car is able to capture its environment sensing the world around it using techniques like laser, radar, lidar, GPS and computer vision.
- Some partial autonomous features are available like Lane Departure Warning System (LDWS), Anti-lock Braking System (ABS), and Adaptive Cruise Control (ACC).
- Car-to-Car (C2C) and Car-to-X communications are existing technologies that are responsible for the interaction between vehicles and infrastructures of roads.

3.7.1 Intersections for autonomous cars

As mentioned in section 3.7, many research projects were carried out towards building autonomous cars that navigate through roads and drive themselves. This section presents the idea that deals with the problem of coordination and management of autonomous cars at traffic intersections without traffic lights. Such intersections will be available and possible in the near future according to the recent advances in autonomous cars that will be controlled without direct human involvement, as well as the recent advances in Car-to-X communication technology. In this regard, the coordination of movements of autonomous cars can be considered as a path planning problem which was studied in several works such as in [11] [2] [5]. Thus, a plan for multiple agents (autonomous cars, robots, etc.) to move in a common environment was required so that they can travel reliably in their environment.

Most closely related work to this idea was proposed in the project "Multiagent Traffic Management" by the University of Texas at Austin [5]. In this project, autonomous cars are modelled as agents that depend on a central plan developed by the intersection manager. Every car uses (obeys) this plan to cross the intersection without traffic lights safely so that the movements of all cars can be coordinated. Moreover, several strategies were defined to coordinate the autonomous cars, but all strategies are based completely on central planning where all cars must comply with the plan. The car agents work according to a reservation-based concept so that traffic congestion can be avoided. The intersection manager agent can grant time slots as reservation for the cars in the intersection, which is divided into a grid of tiles of reservation. The work defines a traffic system called a managed intersection control mechanism (a traffic light system that guides an intersection is also a managed mechanism, where the traffic light acts as the coordinator agent), because an intersection manager by every intersection operates as the coordinator agent of the intersection that has to coordinate traffic [143].

According to the high costs of the managed intersection control that involves specialised infrastructure, the project "Multiagent Traffic Management" has suggested an unmanaged intersection control mechanism, particularly at low-traffic intersections. The unmanaged intersection control is based on vehicle-to-vehicle "V2V" technology (peer-to-peer) so that no specialised infrastructure at the intersection is required. This means that no coordinator agent will be needed to manage the traffic in the intersection (a stop sign system that guides an intersection is also an unmanaged mechanism, where the stop sign acts as the coordinator agent) [143]. The unmanaged intersection control is useful in the case that the managed intersection control is not feasible (too costly and even not required or efficient for small intersections). It should be pointed out that the behaviour of the developed driver agent encompasses three steps: lurking (with respect to lurk distance in order to communicate with other agents), creation of a reservation and intersection crossing [143]. Additionally, the vehicle safety can be assured only if the driver agent's behaviour will abide predetermined rules in the intersection. The authors have compared the three competing systems: unmanaged V2V system, unmanaged four-way stop signs system, and managed traffic-lights system. The simulation was based on a 4-way intersection so that each direction has only one lane for traffic. The results have showed that the unmanaged V2V system performs better than other systems in terms of performance, but only in the case of intersections with low traffic volumes [143]. On the contrary, in the case of high traffic volume intersections, the managed traffic-lights system will have enormous advantages in terms of performance and thereby it is more appropriate. Consequently, the authors in [143] have concluded that the best test case of unmanaged intersection control will be attained by using a 4-way intersection that has a single lane in each direction.

A study of the impact of a multi-agent intersection control protocol for fully autonomous vehicles on driver safety is presented in [6] in the project "Multiagent Traffic Management".

The safety mechanisms in the intersection were explained to cope with catastrophic mechanical failures. In this study the simulations deal only with collisions. It assumes that the colliding vehicle sends a signal and the intersection manager becomes aware of the situation immediately. Thus, the goal of the work is to mitigate any catastrophic failure that may be encountered in intersections of autonomous vehicles.

Other related work to cope with the coordination problem of autonomous cars at intersection was introduced in [3]. The work proposed a priority-based algorithm that produces a collaborative behaviour between cars of an intersection without traffic lights. The priority allocation mechanism was applied on diverse distribution levels of the generic O/C (observer/controller) architecture. Consequently, the priority allocation occurs on diverse abstraction levels (a macro or a micro level) with respect to the implemented O/C architecture [3]. In this context, priorities for cars will be allocated according to the waiting times of these cars in the intersection so that car A will take a higher priority than car B if car A has a higher waiting time than car B. So, the controller of the O/C architecture has to determine these priorities of the cars and thereby it will send the appropriate command to the corresponding cars (drive or stop). The advantage of this concept is that the dynamic priority allocation algorithm enables the O/C architecture to adapt itself to changes in traffic flows of the intersection without traffic lights [3].

A detailed comparison of RobustMAS with these works can be found in section 3.8 (Comparison of the RobustMAS concept with related work), or a brief comparison in (Summary: Intersections for autonomous cars). The comparison shows one of the more distinguishing features of RobustMAS. The advantage of this feature is that the intersection size can be arbitrary and thus RobustMAS can handle a large amount of cars. Moreover, the comparison illustrates that the OCCS project is the start point of RobustMAS.

Intersection Collision Avoidance (ICA)

In the context of intersections of autonomous cars, focus can be placed on Intersection Collision Avoidance (ICA) that is able to warn a human driver in the case of entering the intersection perilously. In the future, it may even enable autonomous cars to carry out safety measures by such unsafely or riskily entering. Therefore, a Field Operational Test (FOT) is required to conceive the efficiency and usefulness of ICA in order to avoid: crossing collision, stop-sign violation, red signal violation and rear-end collision by red signal queue [136].

There are several projects that deal with the concept of Intersection Collision Avoidance. The SKY Project is one of these projects. It is a national project in Japan with 6 partners; the project management is by NISSAN MOTOR CO.,LTD. The project has started in 2004 in Yokohama city in Japan as a field operational test of applications of real traffic systems. Some of SKY the project ideas are: intelligent speed advisory, intersection collision avoidance using Vehicle-to-Intersection (V2I) communication, small children traffic safety using RFID, pedestrian traffic safety using GPS cell phone, hazard warning on winter road and real time probe car data collection [136]. The goals of this project are to mitigate traffic congestion utilising ITS as well as to decrease traffic accidents. For this purpose measures should be taken such as: collaboration with infrastructure, technology in vehicles, and also taking advantage of information about the state of vehicles in the neighbourhood and the immediate traffic environment [136].

Another ICA work was the project by the Mechatronics Laboratory and Department of Computer Science at the University of Paderborn, in addition to C-LAB at the University of Paderborn and Siemens Nixdorf Informationssysteme AG. The goal of this project was to develop a decentralised solution to the problem of intersection collision avoidance aiming to manage autonomous vehicles at intersections. The proposed decentralised intersection management can be achieved without the need to any additional infrastructure at the intersection with the intent to enhance safety as well as to avoid congestion [139]. So, semaphore-based (permissions-based) algorithms were used in order to guarantee collision avoidance, where all intersecting points of vehicle's trajectories are considered as potential points of collision [137]. Such algorithms ensure that only one vehicle can stay in a critical section of the intersection. The idea is similar to the token-ring concept used in computer networking. In this regard, computers in the network (vehicles in the intersection) try to attain a token to send out data (vehicles try to reserve all required tiles in the intersection to traverse across it); whereas other computers can only receive data (other vehicles can not traverse across the same tiles simultaneously) [138]. After that, the current computer has to pass the token to the next computer (the next vehicle will get the opportunity to reserve its required tiles). The collision avoidance algorithm was verified by simulations using a Petri net analysis demonstrating its security and correctness [137].

Another idea related to the concept of Intersection Collision Avoidance (ICA) using autonomous cars is "Steering behaviours for autonomous characters" introduced in [140]. Autonomous characters are a kind of autonomous agents used in computer animation as well as in interactive media like video games and virtual reality [140]. This work has shown the capability to steer autonomous characters (to navigate finding the way) in the neighbourhood. The applied mechanism (autonomous steering) enables autonomous cars in intersections to avoid collisions. The important highlight of this work was that no special agent or particular infrastructure at the intersection is needed. Additionally, autonomous steering mechanisms will run at arbitrary intersections in the case that cars are supplied with such mechanisms [141]. However, the disadvantage of this mechanism is that it is inappropriate to apply in real traffic systems, because cars have only to avoid collisions, but not to consider safety features [141].

Cooperative Intersection Collision Avoidance (CICA)

CICA is known also as Cooperative Intersection Collision Avoidance Systems (CICAS). A CICA system is an ICA system where the intersection contributes cooperatively with cars (cars have internal ICA systems) to avoid collisions in the intersection. CICA systems will be required when the driver can not see that another driver commits a traffic violation. This can be situations where vision is restricted by buildings or other road users that leads in turn to the need for a cooperative system (e.g., using cameras that are able to detect cars which have overrun a red light). CICA is an application of a cooperative vehicular highway system (CVHS) that attempts to achieve improvements in road traffic. CICA has to warn drivers against any probable violation of traffic (traffic control devices). Additionally, it can facilitate crossing over the intersection through manoeuvres in addition to notify other concerned drivers of upcoming violations. Furthermore, it can recognise cyclists and pedestrians that are currently present inside the intersection [142].

A CICA system is composed of three components: car-based technologies, infrastructure-based technologies and communications systems-dedicated short-range communications

Chapter 3. State of the art 57

(DSRC) where the last component is responsible for the communication between the infrastructure and cars (warnings or data) [142]. It is noteworthy that various ICA- and CICA projects are sponsored by U.S. Department of Transportation (U.S. DOT.). In this context, Infrastructure Consortium was a research program founded in cooperation with the Intelligent Vehicle Initiative (IVI) aiming to accomplish intersection decision support systems that concentrates on two types of ICA systems (infrastructure-based and cooperative-based systems) [142].

Summary: Intersections for autonomous cars

In contrast to the system targeted by this thesis, not one of these research projects discussed above concentrates on the robustness of the traffic intersections, while RobustMAS focuses on the robustness of intersections. RobustMAS develops a robust traffic intersection, in the presence of unplanned autonomous behaviour of vehicles (deviations from desired behaviour of agents) and accidents (disturbances) in the intersection. Additionally, no projects use a hybrid central/self-organising approach to control traffic intersections. On the contrary, RobustMAS applies a hybrid solution (central/self-organising), where collision-free trajectories for vehicles (the desired behaviour) are calculated by a central component and then given to vehicles only as a recommendation. Consequently, autonomous vehicles either obey their planned trajectories or deviate from them. Moreover, in contrast to the related work in the context of intersections of autonomous cars discussed above, RobustMAS deals with a large amount of cars. Accordingly, a distinguishing feature of RobustMAS is that the intersection size can be arbitrary and consequently it concerns also the issue of shared spaces in intersections (environments).

3.8 Comparison of the RobustMAS concept with related work

In this thesis, we focus the discussion of related work on:

- Agent-based approaches used for fully autonomous vehicles within an intersection without traffic lights. Additionally, the related work that combines
- Hybrid forms of a central/self-organising solutions aiming to resolve the coordination problem for multi-agent systems was at the centre of attention. Finally, most closely related work that places emphasis on
- Building robust multi-agent systems was considered.

The main results of the comparison can be roughly listed as follows:

I. The project "Multiagent Traffic Management" introduced in [5] is based on centralised control (central plan). The autonomous cars modelled as agents interact directly with the intersection manager agent, which is alone responsible for planning the path reservation for all cars. The autonomous cars have to obey this plan so that they can traverse the intersection without traffic lights safely (for details see section 3.7.1).

- RobustMAS is based on a hybrid form of central/self-organising control for a multi-agent system, where the fully autonomous agents (autonomous cars) are allowed to deviate from the central plan. Therefore, RobustMAS recognises the autonomy of the agents as a deviation from the plan of the central planning algorithm. Consequently, RobustMAS solves the conflict between a central planning algorithm and the autonomy of the agents (decentral, self-organised) so that agents that behave in a fully autonomous way can be tolerated.

II. The project "Multiagent Traffic Management" has dealt with driver's safety in a study [6] explaining the impact of the control protocol for fully autonomous cars at an intersection without traffic lights on driver's safety. In this study, the simulations deal only with collisions (i.e., with catastrophic mechanical failures) in intersections of autonomous vehicles. This means that the study deals only with the problem after an accident has already happened aiming to minimise the losses and to mitigate catastrophic events. However, it can be noted that the study has not considered the robustness of the intersection system (for details see section 3.7.1).

- RobustMAS focuses on the robustness and safety of multi-agent systems in intersections without traffic lights. It deals not only with collisions (accidents) but also with deviations from the plan. That means, it deals with the deviation from plan before an accident has occurred aiming to avoid accidents, as well as it is able to handle the situation caused by accidents. Therefore, the observer in RobustMAS observes the autonomous cars within an intersection without traffic lights in order to detect any deviations from the plan (several deviation classes are presented). Consequently, the controller intervenes when it is necessary so that the system remains demonstrating robustness and safety.

III. The project "Multiagent Traffic Management" works as managed or unmanaged system. The managed intersection control mechanism depends on an intersection manager at every intersection, like the work in [5]. On the other hand, the unmanaged intersection control mechanism is based on vehicle-to-vehicle (V2V) technology, like the work in [143]. This means that a managed system is centralised (like a traffic-light system); whereas an unmanaged system is decentralised (like a stop sign system). It should be pointed out that the unmanaged system by the project "Multiagent Traffic Management" operates satisfactorily, only under special conditions where traffic flows are low and the intersection is small (4-way intersection that has one lane in each direction) (for details see section 3.7.1).

- RobustMAS is a hybrid system that is able to operate with both systems, managed and unmanaged. Path planning of RobustMAS indicates that RobustMAS is a managed system, because path planning is performed centrally (central planning). However, deviations from plan are possible due to the fully autonomous behaviour of vehicles (decentralise). Therefore, an autonomous vehicle may cause deviations from its plan when it decides to move faster than its planned trajectory or when it attempts to avoid an accident (disturbance), which could occur in the intersection. The shortcoming of low traffic volumes by the unmanaged system of the project "Multiagent Traffic Management" was overcome mainly by means of the hybrid trait (a hybrid central/self-organising architecture) of RobustMAS. Here, despite the autonomous behaviour of vehicles, they always get the best possible (desired) trajectories from the central unit of the intersection.

Chapter 3. State of the art   59

        Consequently, RobustMAS can work under different conditions; low and high traffic flows and as well at small and large intersections.

IV. The project "Observation and Control of Collaborative Systems" (OCCS) [144] [145] investigates different types of the generic observer/controller architecture: central, decentral and multi-level architecture (for details see section 4.4.1). It concentrates on the design of distributed observer/controller O/C architectures for Organic Computing systems. Additionally, it considers the robustness of self-organising technical systems that are based on distributed O/C architectures. In this regard, the robustness has to comply with the state space model that represents the system behaviour. Shortly, it deals with robustness of distributed self-organising systems.

- RobustMAS is based on a hybrid form of O/C architectures. This form contains both central and self-organising systems. Consequently, it concentrates on the investigation of robustness of such hybrid central/self-organising systems, especially in disturbed environments (for details see section 4.4.2.). So, RobustMAS deals with robustness as a key property of OC systems.

V. Another point of comparison lies in the results of the project "Observation and Control of Collaborative Systems" (OCCS) presented in [3]. The study compares a fully central and a fully distributed O/C architecture using a traffic scenario. The authors have shown that the central O/C architecture is better than the distributed one when the traffic load is low (low-complexity scenario). Otherwise, when the traffic load is high, the distributed O/C architecture is better than the central one. Therefore, the more complex the scenario is, the better will be the results of the distributed architecture compared to the central one. Accordingly, the design optimum can be possibly achieved by using an adaptive architecture, which switches between the central and distributed O/C architecture as needed [3].

- Regarding the results of the OCCS project presented in [3], it can be considered that the OCCS project is the starting point for the RobustMAS concept. RobustMAS has been made in response to the urgent need to develop hybrid organic systems. These systems use both central and distributed approaches, so that the benefits of both approaches can be combined. Thus, RobustMAS aims to keep the system as decentralised as possible, i.e., agents (vehicles) are designed to be as autonomous as possible. Furthermore, RobustMAS plans to take a centralised intervention as little as possible, especially needed in cases of conflicts and disturbances (accidents). Accordingly, the hybrid approach used by RobustMAS exhibits the central/self-organising trait simultaneously.

VI. Various works related to robust multi-agent systems investigate the robustness in different research domains, such as database technologies, organisation of agent societies and social systems. As an example, the approach of transaction agents introduced in [81] applied database technologies on the basis of transactions aiming to increase the robustness of multi-agent systems. This approach aims to assess the applicability of MAS in the information systems (IS) applications, where robustness is an essential factor.

- RobustMAS is a methodology to design robust technical systems using the Organic Computing (OC) concept. Thus, it provides technical systems with some life-like properties (self-organising) to avoid deterioration of system performance in case of arising disturbances or strong deviations in the system behaviour from the desired one. Accordingly, RobustMAS focuses on the applicability of robust MAS in technical systems (e.g., traffic systems).

In general, RobustMAS contributes to build a robust hybrid central/self-organising architecture for multi-agent systems. Furthermore, in the context of intersections of autonomous vehicles, RobustMAS has the feature that the intersection size can be arbitrary.

The next section 3.9 will summarise the comparison of RobustMAS concept with this closely related work.

3.9 Summary

The analysis of the state-of-the-art confirms that none of the addressed approaches or projects has filled the recognised gap, building robust hybrid organic systems (robust hybrid central/self-organising systems). That means, there is no approach that is able to achieve such needed systems satisfactorily.

There are enormous works concerning safety properties of usual traffic intersections that concerns only human-operated vehicles. Additionally, there are some works in connection with safety measures of autonomous vehicles within an intersection. In this regard, according to our knowledge, there are no projects that focus on the robustness of autonomous vehicles within an intersection without traffic lights, where disturbances occur.

There are a variety of works in relation to the study of multi-agent systems as centralised or decentralised systems, but there is a clear lack of study of the hybrid form of multi-agent systems (e.g., the central/self-organising form), particularly in technical systems. In the literature, diverse architectures were presented in order to be applied to various technical systems, where the most distribution possibilities of system architectures are either centralised or decentralised. However, hybrid central/self-organising architectures, which support a hybrid coordination (central and decentral), are not thoroughly investigated, where the conflict between a central algorithm and the autonomy of agents has to be solved.

Although there are numerous research projects made towards building robust multi-agent systems in diverse fields, a study of robustness of technical systems, which are modelled as multi-agent systems, does not exist yet (at least it is extremely rare, e.g., an attempt by the Organic Computing Initiative [152]).

To the best of our knowledge, this thesis (RobustMAS concept) represents the first study towards building robust hybrid central/self-organising multi-agent systems in intersections without traffic lights using the organic computing concept.

The following Table 3-1 summarises the discussed results demonstrating the RobustMAS concept's similarities and differences with selected related work (OCCS: Observation and Control of Collaborative Systems, MTM: Multiagent Traffic Management, TA: Transaction Agents). This serves as an overview of closely related work and the abilities they lack in comparison to the RobustMAS concept developed in this thesis.

Chapter 3. State of the art

	OCCS	MTM	TA	RobustMAS
Robustness (Robust multi-agent system)	limited	no	yes	yes
Hybrid (Central/self-organising)	no	no	no	yes
Technical system	yes	yes	no (database and information system)	yes
Resource sharing problem (Resource allocation conflict)	no	no	no	yes
Measuring robustness (quantitatively)	limited	no	limited	yes (new metric)
Traffic system	limited	yes	no	yes
Autonomous vehicles	no	yes	no	yes
Organic Computing (O/C architecture)	yes	no	no	yes
Fault-tolerance	no	no	no	yes (deviation-tolerance)
Turbulent environments	yes	limited	limited	yes (deviations + disturbances)
Path planning	no	yes	no	yes (adapted A*-algorithm)

Table 3-1: RobustMAS in comparison with selected related work

The next chapter introduces in detail the general problem domain of RobustMAS, the resource sharing problem in addition to the proposed solution to cope with it. Subsequently, it presents the traffic problem as a special problem domain (RobustMAS Traffic).

4 Design and architecture for robust multi-agent systems

The concept and objectives of RobustMAS will be presented in the next sections. Additionally, the problem domain, the components, the agent classes and the proposed system architecture of RobustMAS will be clarified highlighting the hybrid central/self-organising architecture as the key concept of RobustMAS. Subsequently, the approach of RobustMAS in a special problem domain, RobustMAS Traffic, will be described accordingly. The measurement of robustness and gain of a multi-agent system according to the RobustMAS concept will be presented in term of definition and proposition of a new appropriate method for their measurement.

4.1 Robust system with disturbance

The RobustMAS concept introduces a robust hybrid central/self-organising multi-agent system (hybrid coordination) solving the conflict between a central planning algorithm and the autonomy of the agents (decentral, self-organised). Here, the autonomy of the agents is recognised as a deviation from the plan of the central algorithm, if the agents are not respecting this plan.

The application scenario used in this work is an intersection without traffic lights, where vehicles are modelled as autonomous (semi-autonomous) agents (Driver Agents) with limited local capabilities. The vehicles are trying as quickly as possible to cross the intersection without traffic lights. In the meantime, an interaction between decentralised mechanisms (autonomous vehicles) and centralised interventions arises. Here, the goal is to build a robust intersection without traffic lights when disturbances (e.g., accidents) and deviations (e.g., unplanned autonomous behaviour) occur.

Moreover, RobustMAS addresses a further problem that occurs in the system wherever multiple agents (e.g., robots, vehicles, etc.) move in a common environment. This problem is called resource sharing conflict (Resource Allocation Problem). This problem raises the question: "How can agents of a system move reliably in their environment?". RobustMAS uses coordination mechanisms (a manager is responsible for coordinating tasks) to solve the resource sharing conflict. These coordination mechanisms are based on the idea of path planning, which must be performed taking into consideration other agents (vehicles) and the geometry of the environment (intersection). The path planning is performed in a 3-dimensional space with two geometrical dimensions (x, y) representing the intersection and time t.

For the path planning, RobustMAS uses an adapted A*- algorithm to calculate collision-free trajectories (central planning) for all agents (vehicles) in a shared environment (the centre of the intersection) enabling them to avoid collisions. This path planning (collision-free trajectories) is given to agents (vehicles) as a recommendation.

Since the agents (vehicles) are autonomous (decentral, self-organised) and thus deviations from the plan (trajectories) in principle are possible, RobustMAS performs an observation of compliance with these trajectories (e.g., by an observer).

RobustMAS aims to make the system capable to return to its normal state with minimal central planning intervention after disturbances occur (e.g., by a controller).

Furthermore, RobustMAS has the capability to support real time systems (discussed in the evaluation chapter by means of the metric "response time"). It makes the system (intersection without traffic lights as traffic system) capable of operating under real time conditions, where a short response time is required in such systems.

A generic O/C (Observer/Controller) architecture has been proposed in [13]. RobustMAS shows how to use an O/C architecture to observe autonomous agents (vehicles) within an environment (an intersection without traffic lights) in order to detect deviations and to intervene when it is necessary, so that the system remains demonstrating robust, safe and fault-tolerant operation. The controller is informed by the observer about the detected deviations from the plan, so that it can intervene in time. The controller selects the best corrective action that corresponds to the current situation so that the target performance of the system is maintained.

Robust systems should be fault-tolerant in order to deal with faults, deviations or disturbances and to continue working effectively and fulfilling their major tasks. In the context of this thesis, fault tolerance avoids system failures in the presence of deviations and disturbances that occur in the system allowing the agents (vehicles) of the system to move reliably in their environment (intersection without traffic lights).

In order to conceive the fundamental idea of RobustMAS, three cases of the system operation will be considered:

1. Operation without disturbance.
2. Operation with disturbance without intervention.
3. Operation with disturbance with intelligent intervention.

Figure 4-1 illustrates the main idea of this thesis in establishing a robust system that tolerates faults, disturbances and deviations which could be occurred in the system.

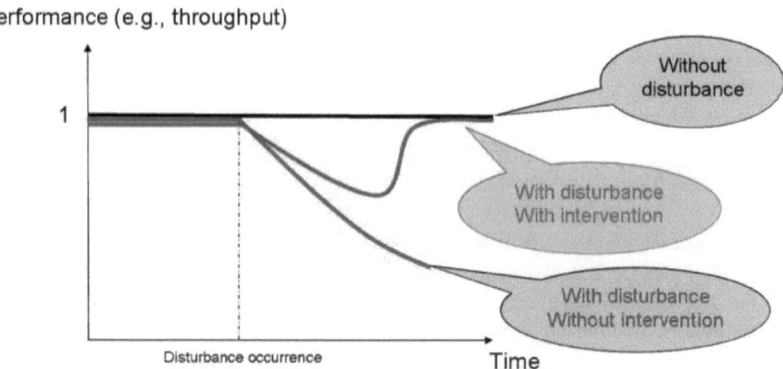

Figure 4-1: Robust system with disturbance occurrence

Chapter 4. Design and architecture for robust multi-agent systems   65

As depicted in Figure 4-1, the performance (e.g., throughput) of the system is at its best (i.e., equal to 1) when no disturbances occur. When a disturbance occurs, the system performance would begin to fall and probably it would become worse (deteriorate) over time, if no corrective intervention is taken in due time. In contrast, if the corrective intervention is intelligent and fast enough, the system performance should improve in the course of time when a disturbance occurs. This means that the system performance remains acceptable despite the occurrence of disturbance.

4.2 Goals (contributions) of RobustMAS

The main contribution of this thesis is the integration of concepts from different research areas into a practically applicable methodology. Figure 4-2 summarises the methodologies integrated within RobustMAS.

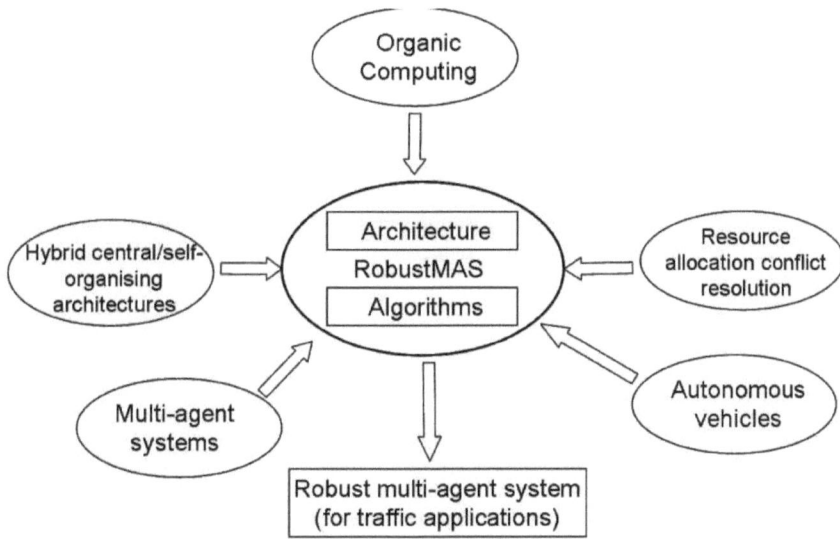

Figure 4-2: The methodologies integrated within (RobustMAS)

The main goal of the new concept (RobustMAS) is to solve the conflict between a central planning algorithm and the autonomy of the agents using a hybrid form of a central/self-organising solution of the coordination problem for multi-agent systems. This approach:

- Keeps a multi-agent system at a desired performance level when disturbances and deviations occur.
- Coordinates autonomous/semi-autonomous agents.
- Recognises the autonomy of the agents as a deviation from the plan.
- Tolerates that some agents behave in a fully autonomous way.

Chapter 4. Design and architecture for robust multi-agent systems   66

- Tolerates that some autonomous agents leave the control of the fully central architecture.
- Forms a hybrid central/self-organising architecture for a multi-agent system, which is a special form of the fully central architecture.
- Deals with turbulent environment (disturbances).
- Has the goal to develop a robust multi-agent system despite disturbances and deviations in the system (internal) or in the environment (external).

A key point in the work is the coordination of autonomous vehicles. This is the central component of the application example, a traffic intersection without traffic lights, which will be used for the evaluation.

Furthermore, RobustMAS establishes a robust traffic intersection without traffic lights. Here, the deviations will be first detected by the observer, so that the controller could intervene in time, if needed, in order to guarantee the robustness of the intersection. A disturbance is, for example, an accident in the intersection; and a deviation is, for example, an unplanned autonomous behaviour of a vehicle.

In addition, RobustMAS solves a coordination problem by a central algorithm (a central-planning algorithm), using an adapted A*- algorithm that was used for path planning. Here, the path planning is considered as a resource allocation problem (resource sharing problem) where multiple agents move in a shared environment and need to avoid collisions. For evaluation, it is necessary to determine the degree of the system robustness using a suitable metric, which quantifies this robustness.

4.3 Objectives of RobustMAS

Overall, RobustMAS provides contributions to:

(1) The system architecture.

(2) The system property (robustness), and

(3) The specific problem domain (traffic).

First, the system architecture is a hybrid form of a central/decentral (a combination of a central controller and self-organising autonomous agents) solution of the coordination problem for multi-agent systems. RobustMAS deals with the conflict between a central controller (i.e., a central planning algorithm) and the autonomy of the agents, leaching to a hybrid coordination of a multi-agent system (central and decentral).

Second, as a desired system property, RobustMAS focuses on the robustness of multi-agent systems against disturbances and deviations from the plan. Furthermore, RobustMAS provides a new method to measure the robustness of such hybrid multi-agent systems.

Third, the general problem domain of RobustMAS is the resource allocation problem (resource sharing problem). RobustMAS enables agents to move reliably in their common environment. In addition, RobustMAS gives a solution for the special problem domain, the traffic scenario.

Chapter 4. Design and architecture for robust multi-agent systems

4.4 Concept and architecture

The main idea and goals of RobustMAS have been defined in sections 4.1 and 4.2. This section describes the approach and the proposed architecture of RobustMAS demonstrating the distribution possibilities of system architecture, which are varying from fully central to fully distributed architectures.

4.4.1 Distribution possibilities

Organic Computing investigates basic mechanisms of an O/C architecture in order to observe and control the behaviour of organic systems. The behaviour of the technical system should be observed to intervene in time when it is necessary. For the purpose of this thesis, the generic O/C architecture has to be customised to the traffic application scenario.

The distribution possibilities of the proposed O/C architecture are varying from a fully central to fully distributed architecture [17]. The three main options to realise the generic architecture as depicted in Figure 4-3 are:

(a) Central: One O/C for the whole system.

(b) Decentral: One O/C for each subsystem.

(c) Multi-level: One O/C for each subsystem as well as one (or more) for the whole system.

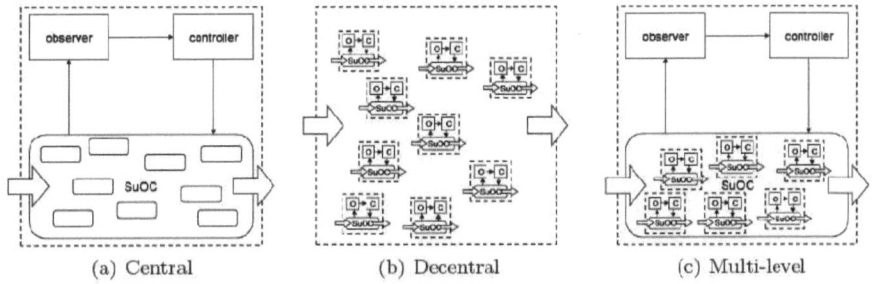

(a) Central   (b) Decentral   (c) Multi-level

(This graphic is for illustration only, the text is therefore unrecognizable)
Figure 4-3: Distribution possibilities of the generic observer/controller architecture [17]

Organic Computing proposes concepts to achieve controlled self-organisation as a new design paradigm, which requires coping with degrees of freedom as a necessity of the self-organisation [18]. The developer has to select an adequate version of the O/C architecture in the design phase in order to realise the specific O/C architecture.

4.4.2 Hybrid central/self-organising concept for multi-agent systems

In this thesis, the term "hybrid central/self-organising multi-agent system" is introduced. It is a new possibility of the distribution of the proposed architecture.

Figure 4-4 shows the main idea of this hybrid central/self-organising concept derived from the fully central architecture.

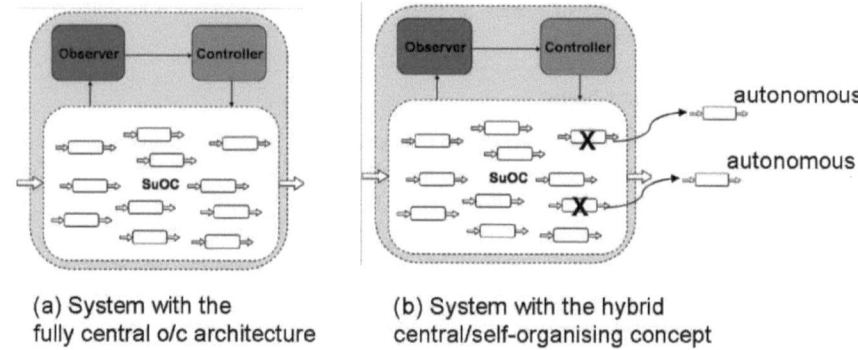

(a) System with the fully central o/c architecture

(b) System with the hybrid central/self-organising concept

Figure 4-4: The hybrid central/self-organising concept

(a) Fully central architecture: One O/C for the whole system under observation and control.

(b) Hybrid central/self-organising concept: One O/C for the whole system under observation and control, but the autonomous agents can leave the control of the fully central architecture to behave in a fully autonomous way (but still under observation).

In this work, the hybrid central/self-organising concept aims to increase the autonomy of agents compared to the central architecture. This means, the hybrid concept tolerates that some agents behave autonomously. It solves the conflict between a central planning algorithm (a component in the controller) and the autonomy of the agents (the entities of the system under observation and control). The autonomy of the agents is recognised as a deviation from the plan of the central algorithm, if the agents are not respecting this plan.

Figure 4-5 shows the general flow plan proposed by RobustMAS to solve the conflict between a central planning algorithm and the autonomy of the agents. A central planning algorithm generates a plan for every agent in the system. Since the agents are autonomous and they behave in a completely autonomous way, they may not obey this central plan. If they comply with the central plan then the system works effectively as planned (no deviations from plan). However, if they do not comply with the central plan then RobustMAS detects this deviations from the plan (e.g., by an observer) in order to arrange an appropriate corrective intervention (e.g., by a controller). It makes also replanning, if necessary, with respect to the new situation.

Chapter 4. Design and architecture for robust multi-agent systems 69

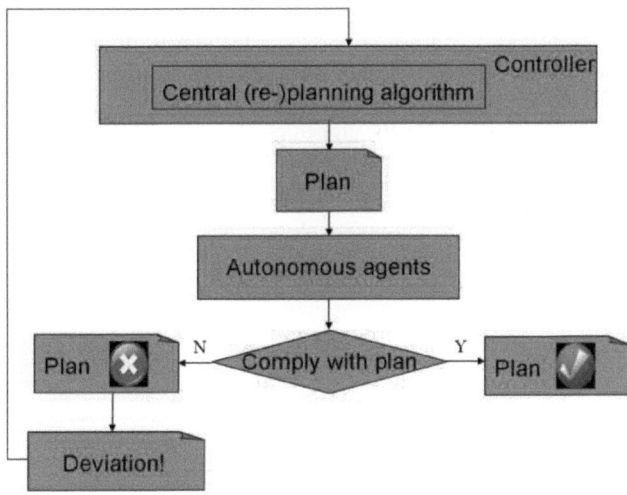

Figure 4-5: The conflict between a central planning algorithm and the autonomy of the agents (The general flow plan proposed by RobustMAS solving the conflict)

Consequently, RobustMAS comprises the use of a central O/C architecture, autonomous agents and deviations from a central plan in order to solve coordination problems in multi-agent systems. Additionally, it keeps the system at a desired performance level (via replanning and corrective intervention of the controller) when deviations and disturbances occur in the system behaviour, so that the agents of a system can move reliably in their environment.

4.4.3 Approach of RobustMAS

The key issue of RobustMAS, hybrid central/self-organising concept, has been clarified in sections 4.4.2. This section describes the approach of RobustMAS. It deals with the life cycle, the problem domain, the components, the agent classes and the proposed system architecture of RobustMAS.

4.4.3.1 Life cycle of RobustMAS

As mentioned in section 4.2 and 4.3, the general problem domain of RobustMAS is the resource allocation problem (resource sharing problem) which occurs in the system wherever multiple agents move in a common environment. This section presents the proposed solution to cope with this problem.

RobustMAS uses coordination mechanisms to solve the resource sharing problem. These coordination mechanisms are based on the idea of path planning, which must be performed taking into consideration other agents and the geometry of the shared environment in the configuration space-time (x, y, t). Here, the path planning is considered as a resource allocation problem (resource sharing problem).

Since the goal of RobustMAS is to keep a multi-agent system at a desired performance level when disturbances and deviations occur in the system behaviour, agents have to be observed (through the observer) within the shared environment. This will be made to intervene (through the controller) in time when it is necessary so that the system remains demonstrating robustness and safety properties. The paradigm of the proposed solution consisting in an Observer/Controller architecture can be seen in Figure 4-6.

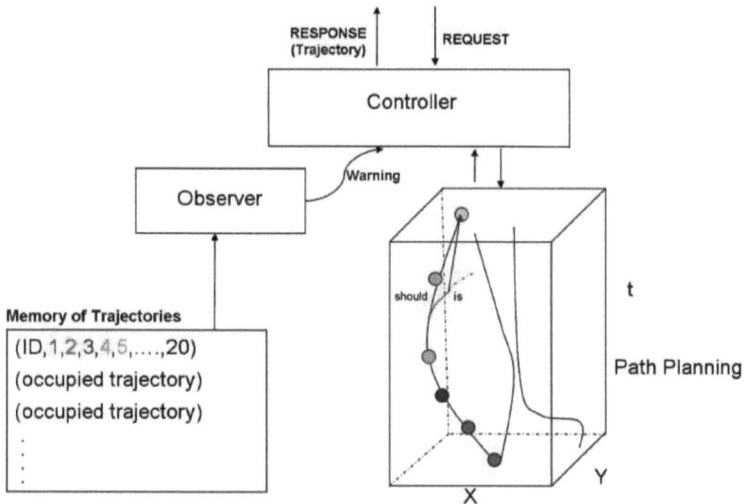

Figure 4-6: The paradigm of the proposed solution consisting in an Observer/Controller architecture

This Figure depicts a hybrid coordination scheme of a multi-agent system. It takes place in three steps:

1. Path planning: The agents send requests to the controller, which computes collision-free trajectories and arranges the participants. This means that the first step is a central planning of the trajectories without deviations of the agents. The agents get their planned trajectories only as recommendation from the controller. Autonomous behaviour of the agents means that they either obey the plan or deviate from it or the agents are completely outside of the plan.

2. Observation: The observation of actual trajectories of agents in the shared environment is done by an observer component in order to identify eventual deviations from the plan, using the memory of all planned trajectories. The observer informs the controller about its observation.

3. Controlling: The controller carries out a replanning for the trajectories of the affected agents, if needed, in order to accomplish an appropriate corrective intervention. The

Chapter 4. Design and architecture for robust multi-agent systems   71

controller uses a decision mechanism to take a decision how it could intervene most suitably.

4.4.3.2 Problem domain of RobustMAS

As mentioned in section 4.2 and 4.3, the general problem domain of RobustMAS is the resource allocation problem (resource sharing problem). This section presents the general problem domain of RobustMAS and the proposed solution to cope with it.

There are different works proposed in the literature, which present solutions to cope with the resource sharing conflict occurring in the system wherever multiple agents (e.g., robots, cars, etc.) move in a common environment. In [3], a priority-based algorithm, in [7], traffic rules, and in [14], a communication architecture have been used in order to solve this problem.

Compared to the RobustMAS concept, all of these approaches lack the ability to consider virtual obstacles by planning of resource allocation (resource allocation is considered as a path planning by RobustMAS, where multiple agents act in a common shared environment). In RobustMAS, virtual obstacles are used to model blocked surfaces, restricted areas (prohibited allocations of resources). Often, these obstacles are produced due to the reservation results or other barriers. Additionally, these approaches do not consider potential deviations from the desired resource allocations, while RobustMAS takes into account all possible deviations from the resource allocation plan.

The resource allocation problem considered in RobustMAS occurs in a multi-agent system wherever multiple agents move in a shared environment. That means, agents compete for the shared environment (a shared resource) in order to move over it quickly, and coordination of these agents in its common environment has to be achieved.

In order to avoid a potential resource sharing conflict in such multi-agent systems, RobustMAS introduces a coordination mechanism. This coordination mechanism is based on the idea of path planning (planning of resource allocation over a certain period of time), which must be performed taking into consideration other agents and the geometry of the shared environment in the configuration space-time (x, y, t).

The central controller of the O/C architecture performs the resource allocation, i.e., the path planning (by a controller component). This means that the resource allocation used by RobustMAS is done by a central planning algorithm, while the agents consume these resources.

Since the goal of this work is to keep a multi-agent system at a desired performance level when deviations occur in the system behaviour and when disturbances occur in the environment, autonomous agents have to be observed (through the observer) within a shared environment to detect deviations and to intervene (through the controller) when necessary. Furthermore, autonomous behaviour of agents with low delays is desired in this work. In order to achieve this, a generic proposed system architecture, an O/C architecture, has been designed as depicted in Figure 4-7.

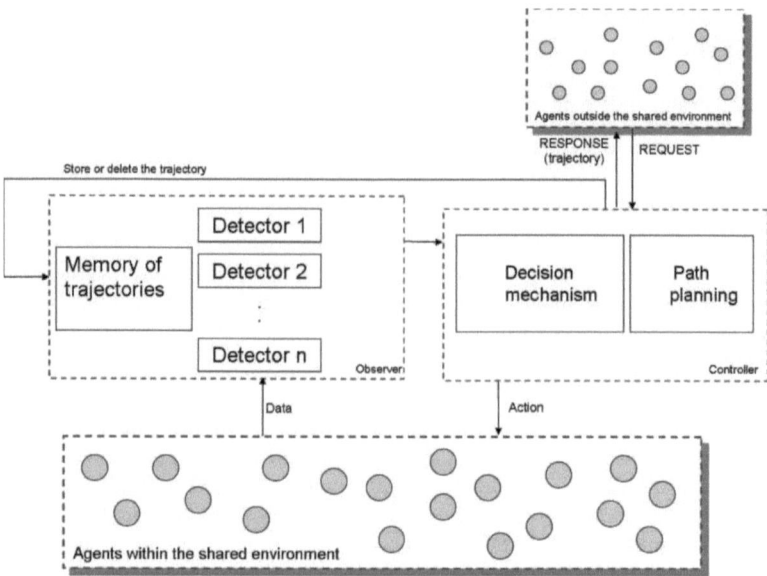

Figure 4-7: System architecture

However, the resource allocation in RobustMAS is characterised by "Spatial-dependent resource assignment". Spatial-dependent resource assignment is a plan-based resource allocation in the 3-dimensional configuration space-time (x, y, t), so that the next requested resource at the next time-step is nearby (successive time-steps). That means if the space (x_1, y_1) is the allocated resource at the time-step (t_1) for an agent, then the planning algorithm must take into account that the next potential resource, the space (x_2, y_2), at the next time-step (t_2) for this agent has to be close (1-neighbourhood, see section 5.2.2.1) to the previous allocated resource. In the same way the next space (x_3, y_3), at the next time-step (t_3) for this agent has to be close to the former allocated resource, etc.

Figure 4-8 shows the simplification of a shared environment in the 3-dimensional configuration space-time. It illustrates the resulting trajectories (planned resource allocations). For simplification, only one planned trajectory is shown.

Chapter 4. Design and architecture for robust multi-agent systems   73

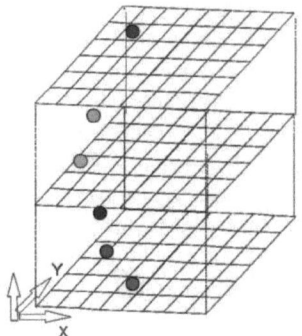

Trajectory = { 1,2,3,4,5,6}

Trajectory = { ((x_1,y_1,t_1) , (x_2,y_2,t_2) , (x_3,y_3,t_3) , (x_4,y_4,t_4) , (x_5,y_5,t_5) , (x_6,y_6,t_6)) }

Figure 4-8: Simplification of a shared environment, example for planning of trajectories
(resulting resource allocations)

In this example, the planned trajectory consists of six points, where every point has its (x, y, t). Consequently, this trajectory can be modelled as a vector of six space-time points as follows:

$$\text{Trajectory} = \{ (x_1,y_1,t_1) , (x_2,y_2,t_2) , (x_3,y_3,t_3) , (x_4,y_4,t_4) , (x_5,y_5,t_5) , (x_6,y_6,t_6) \} \quad (4.1)$$

In this context, it is noteworthy that the shared environment (intersection in the traffic scenario) is divided into a grid of n×n cells (tiles or resources), where n represents the granularity of the resource allocations (reservation) system. Figure 4-9 shows an example for a shared environment, which are divided into a 12 x 12 grid of reservation tiles. So, each tile that has its coordinates (x_i, y_i) can be reserved by one agent A_i at time t_i.

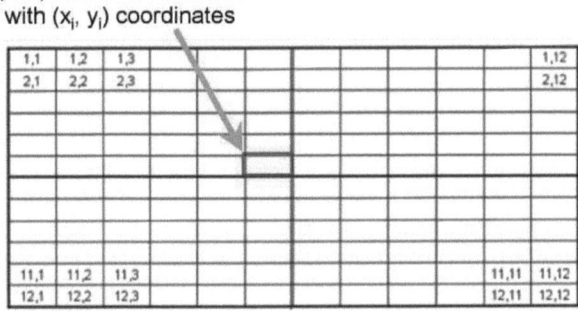

Figure 4-9: A shared environment as a 12 x 12 grid of reservation cells (tiles)

If the shared environment is divided into a 1x1 grid of reservation tiles (i.e., 1-tile granularity or 1-tile reservation), only one agent is allowed to occupy the shared environment at time t_i. Similarly, when the shared environment is a 2x2 grid of reservation tiles (i.e., 2-tiles granularity or 2-tiles reservation), then more than one agent can act in the shared environment at the same time t_i, but certainly not in the same quadrant [5].

Of course, a better performance level will be achieved by increasing the granularity of the shared environment (wider environments), but the computational complexity will be increased. The granularity of the intersection system, which is used later for the evaluation of RobustMAS concept, is 100 (10-tiles reservation), where the intersection is a 10x10 grid of reservation tiles.

4.4.3.3 System components

RobustMAS consists of two basic components: An Observer/Controller and the agents (the system under observation and control).

The O/C architecture consists of an observer and a controller. The main tasks of the observer are:

- Identification of deviations from planned resource allocation (via the deviation detector component in the observer).
- Identification of disturbances, which could occur in the environment (via the disturbance detector component in the observer).
- Storage of planned trajectories (via the trajectory memory unit), which will be used to detect any deviations from plan.

Since the proposed system architecture in Figure 4-7 is a generic architecture, the observer has n detectors. Therefore, the observer could apply a set of other detectors according to the used scenario. Furthermore, the controller has the following main tasks:

- Central planning of resource allocation (via the path planning component in the controller).
- Tolerance for some agents that behave in a completely autonomous way (via the decision maker component in the controller).
- Replanning (via the path planning component in the controller).
- Corrective intervention (via the decision maker component in the controller).

Other components are the system under observation and control (the agents). These agents consume the allocated resources. Since the agents are allowed to behave in a completely autonomous way, they may not obey the central plan. They agree to the allocation of resources (agree to the central plan) or they reject the allocation of resources (do not obey the central plan). In the case of agent's consent to the plan, the resource allocation is optimal (no deviations from plan), because the plan is performed by a central algorithm, which has a global view of all available resources that can be allocated to the system agents. In the case of an agent's rejection of the plan, a potential resource allocation conflict between the agents is recognised, because of the consumption of resources which are possibly reserved for other

Chapter 4. Design and architecture for robust multi-agent systems 75

agents. Based on this, it may be distinguished between two cases: there are no conflicts or conflicts occur.

1. If no resource allocation conflict arises (the consumption of other resources, which are not currently consumed by other agents but are reserved by other agents), the system will continue to work normally (no damage). However, a new resource allocation has to be performed trying to avoid any resource conflicts between the agents. Here, the system performance may go down depending on the available resources.

2. On the other hand, if a conflict arises (the attempt to consume other resources, which are currently consumed by other agents) the system will continue to work abnormally (damage). However, a new resource allocation has to be performed avoiding further resource conflicts between the agents. Here, the system performance probably goes down depending on the available resources.

4.4.3.4 Agent classes

In this section, the agent classes created in order to be used by RobustMAS will be described.

Each agent class represents a specialised role that can be performed by the agents of this class in run time. Each class has certain capabilities in order to interact with other agent classes, which should take into account the whole goal of the desired system.

RobustMAS implements agent classes allowing the agents to play their roles. Based on the type of their class that they belong to, the agents try to maximise:

- **Class 1:** Only their own fitness (e.g., their own utility), which can be achieved by travelling across the environment as quickly as possible, i.e., minimisation of their individual travel times of agents across the environment, or
- **Class 2:** Only the fitness of the whole system (the system throughput), or
- **Class 3:** Their own fitness and then the fitness of the whole system respectively in every step.

These agents are either Non-Autonomous Agents (NAA) or Autonomous Agents (AA).

$$A = \{NAA, AA\} \quad (4.2)$$

In turn, Autonomous Agents (AA) are either Autonomous and Rational Agents (ARA) or Autonomous and Non-Rational Agents (ANRA).

$$AA = \{ARA, ANRA\} \quad (4.3)$$

In this regard, "rational" means "reasonable autonomy", i.e., agents are aware of their capabilities to make a rational choice of an action that is reasonable to maximise their own utility. However, and simultaneously, these agents follow safety rules carefully, so that they do not cause resource sharing conflicts (efficiently aware of their environment).

As a result, these agents by RobustMAS are generally classified as follows:

- **Class 1: Autonomous and Non-Rational Agents (ANRA):** They deviate from the plan and cause disturbances. These agents are competitive. They try to maximise only their own fitness (e.g., their own utility) and they do not consider the fitness of the whole system (e.g., the system throughput). However, they do not agree to the allocated resources and they cause possibly a resource sharing conflicts with other agents, because of their non-rationality.

- **Class 2: Non-Autonomous Agents (NAA)**: They do not deviate from the plan and do not cause disturbances. These agents are cooperative. They try indirectly to maximise the fitness of the whole system (e.g., the system throughput) and they agree to the allocated resources. That means they do not cause resource sharing conflicts.

- **Class 3: Autonomous and Rational Agents (ARA)**: They deviate from the plan, but do not cause disturbances. These agents are cooperative and competitive at the same time. They try to maximise their own fitness (e.g., their own utility) and then the fitness of the whole system (e.g., the system throughput). However, they do not agree to the allocated resources, but they do not cause resource sharing conflicts, because of their rationality.

Consequently, RobustMAS has three classes of agents according to their behaviour:

- **Class 1: Competitive agents:** These agents are Autonomous and Non-Rational Agents (ANRA).
- **Class 2: Cooperative agents:** These agents are Non-Autonomous Agents (NAA).
- **Class 3: Cooperative & Competitive agents:** These agents are Autonomous and Rational Agents (ARA).

Class 3 agents, Autonomous and Rational Agents (ARA), are the desirable class. This is because RobustMAS aims to tolerate those agents to behave in a fully autonomous way and at the same time tries to keep the multi-agent system at a desired performance level even though deviations and disturbances occur. This class of agents (ARA) behaves as follows:

1. Avoid causing a resource sharing conflict with other agents.
2. Deviate from the allocated resources (the plan), if it is possible, trying to maximise its own fitness (e.g., its own utility).
3. Comply with the allocated resources (the plan), if it was not possible to deviate from the plan.

4.4.3.5 System architecture

This section gives an overview of the proposed system architecture and how to implement it on a highly relevant technical problem: the control of autonomous agents moving in a shared environment demonstrating a robust multi-agent system. Additionally, it describes the adaptation of this architecture to the traffic intersection without traffic lights.

Figure 4-10 shows the detailed internals of the RobustMAS architecture. The system under observation and control is considered as a set of elements possessing certain attributes in terms of multi-agent systems. This system under observation and control contains all agents that move within the shared environment avoiding collisions. The agents outside the shared environment send messages (requests) to the controller which replies with collision-free planned trajectories for all agents (path planning unit).

Chapter 4. Design and architecture for robust multi-agent systems 77

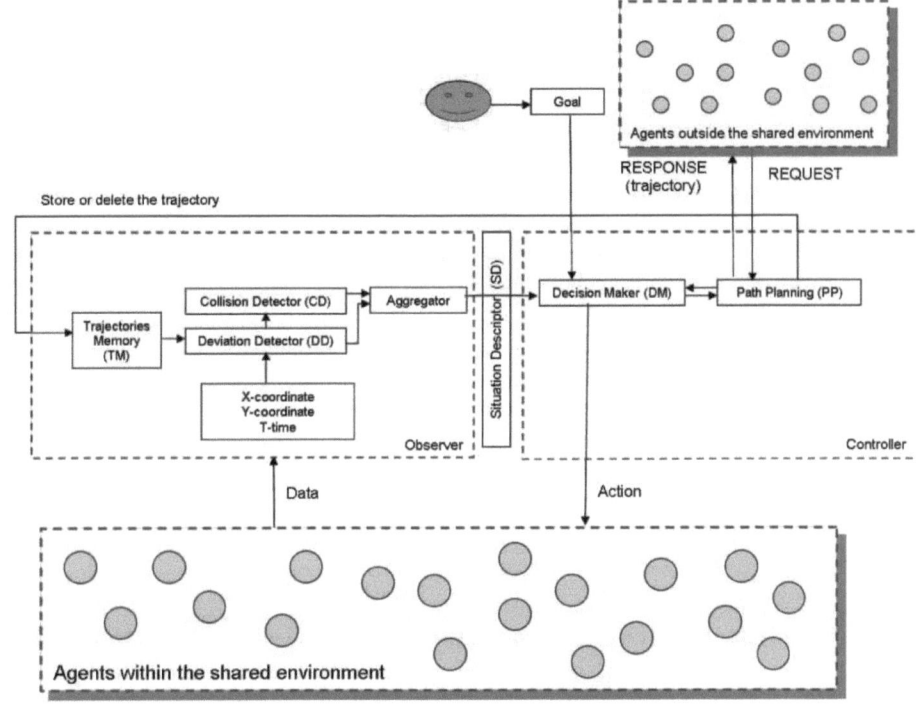

Figure 4-10: Detailed RobustMAS system architecture

Every agent by itself is assumed to be egoistic (class 1 and 3 agents), because it is autonomous and tries to quickly cross the shared environment so that it may not obey its planned trajectory. Therefore competition situations arise due to the egoistic behaviour (competition-based behaviour) of agents, which in turn leads to congestions, where agents with different moving directions block each other in the common environment. These congestions may cause a large cluster of blocked agents for a long time.

The observer reads the planned trajectory of an agent from the trajectory memory (memory of trajectories unit TM) only when this agent is located within the shared environment and compares it with the agent's actual travelled trajectory using the deviation detector (deviation detector unit DD) to identify all deviations from the planned trajectories. The observer uses also the collision detector (collision detector unit CD) to detect whether a deviation led to a collision and to detect the deviation class (see below). Afterwards, it aggregates (aggregator unit) its observations as a vector of situation parameters (situation descriptor unit SD). These parameters are then sent to the controller. The controller has to intervene on time if necessary (decision maker unit DM) and to select the best corrective action (it makes a decision whether a replanning is required and uses also the path planning unit PP if needed) that corresponds to the current situation so that the system performance remains acceptable and the target performance of the system is maintained. The intervention of the controller (the decision of the decision maker) will be done with respect to the goal given by the user.

4.4.3.6 Definition of deviation and disturbance in RobustMAS

Since the definition of deviation and disturbance varies according to the context condition, it is necessary to define both terms clearly in the context of this thesis.

According to the RobustMAS concept, the deviation and the disturbance can be defined as follows:

Definition 1: "A **deviation** is a different behaviour or path or plan from what was initially planned (desired or expected) for an agent. In other words, a deviation is an unplanned autonomous behaviour. Deviations from the plan of the central planning algorithm occur, if the agents are not respecting this plan".

Definition 2: "A **disturbance** is a permanent change in environmental conditions, which leads to an unwanted evident change in the target performance of the system. Moreover, disturbances are obstacles (blocked surfaces, restricted areas, or any additional difficulty) in the way of the agents. These obstacles block agents in the neighbourhood causing longer delays than planned".

Additionally, the disturbance strength can be defined according to the RobustMAS concept as follows:

Definition 3: "A **disturbance strength** is a positive constant defining the strength (size) of the disturbance".

4.4.4 Approach of RobustMAS in a special problem domain: "RobustMAS Traffic"

Section 4.4.3 discussed the general problem domain of RobustMAS and the proposed solution to cope with it. However, this section presents the approach of RobustMAS in a special problem domain, "RobustMAS Traffic", which deals with autonomous vehicles in order to solve a traffic problem.

4.4.4.1 Special problem domain "RobustMAS Traffic"

A special application domain of RobustMAS is the traffic, particularly the application scenario "a traffic intersection without traffic lights", where the resource allocation problem is considered as a shared space over time (the intersection area). Vehicles of the intersection are modelled as agents whereas an intersection manager (the controller of the O/C architecture) is responsible for coordinating tasks (trajectories planning for the vehicles) to solve the potential resource sharing conflict between the vehicles (to avoid collisions in the centre of the intersection). Here, "RobustMAS Traffic" tries to solve the question how vehicles move reliably in the intersection without traffic lights in order to cross over it as quickly as possible. That means, vehicles compete for the centre of the intersection (a shared resource) in order to cross over it quickly if possible and the coordination of those vehicles in the centre of the intersection has to be achieved. Consequently, a robust traffic intersection without traffic lights can be established despite deviations from the planned trajectories (due to the autonomous vehicles) and despite disturbances (e.g., an accident in the intersection).

4.4.4.2 System components of "RobustMAS Traffic"

Similar to the system components of RobustMAS discussed in section 4.4.3.3, the components of the special application domain, RobustMAS Traffic, can be utilised. For this purpose, the words agent, which is used in RobustMAS, and vehicle, which is used in RobustMAS Traffic, can be used interchangeably. Additionally, the term "shared environment" in RobustMAS is used interchangeably for "centre of the intersection" in RobustMAS Traffic.

For the special application domain, RobustMAS Traffic, the intersection area is a shared space over time. Therefore, the resource allocation problem is considered as a path planning in order to allocate appropriate trajectories for the autonomous vehicles in the intersection. Here, the O/C architecture represents the Intersection Manager which has the coordinating task of the autonomous vehicles in the intersection.

Compared to the RobustMAS, which plans the resource allocations, "RobustMAS Traffic" has to plan trajectories for all vehicles. Furthermore, "RobustMAS Traffic" should identify deviations from the planned trajectories, in addition to intervene in case of accidents (disturbances in RobustMAS).

The other components of the traffic intersection system are the vehicles (driver agents). These vehicles occupy tiles (cells) of the intersection area (the planned trajectories). Since the vehicles are allowed to behave in a completely autonomous way, they may not obey their planned trajectories. However, the existing intersection area is covered optimally by the vehicles, when vehicles follow the central plan. In this regard, two cases can be classified: accidents occur, and there are no accidents.

1. If a conflict arises (two vehicles or more occupy the same position in the intersection area at the same time), there will be deviations from the planned trajectories as well as an accident. Consequently, the traffic intersection may continue to work not normally (damage due to the accident). Nevertheless, the controller re-plans the trajectories trying to avoid further accidents.

2. There are deviations from the planned trajectories without an accident, if no conflict arose. In this case, every vehicle moves to another position only if this position is not occupied by another vehicle, and consequently there are no attempts to occupy cells of the intersection area, which are currently occupied by other vehicles. This means that the attempts here are to occupy cells of the intersection area, which are reserved for other vehicles. As a result, the traffic intersection keeps working normally even through deviations (no injury because no accident). Even so, a new trajectory planning is required to avoid accidents.

4.4.4.3 Vehicle classes

For "RobustMAS Traffic", the vehicles are modelled as agents (driver agents). Here, vehicles have their own utility to cross over the intersection as fast as possible.

In an analogous manner to the agent classes of RobustMAS discussed in section 4.4.3.4, the vehicle classes of "RobustMAS Traffic" can be classified. For this intention, the symbols "A", which corresponds to "Agent" in RobustMAS, and "V", which corresponds to "Vehicle" in RobustMAS Traffic, can be used synonymously. Consequently, vehicles are either Non-Autonomous Vehicles (NAV) or Autonomous Vehicles (AV).

$$V = \{NAV, AV\} \qquad (4.4)$$

On the other hand, Autonomous Vehicles (AV) are either Autonomous and Rational Vehicles (ARV) or Autonomous and Non-Rational Vehicles (ANRV), where the term "rational" denotes that vehicles do not cause accidents.

$$AV = \{ARV, ANRV\} \qquad (4.5)$$

Overall, vehicles by "RobustMAS Traffic" are categorised into three classes according to their behaviour in the intersection (for details see section 4.4.3.4):

- **Class 1:** Autonomous and Non-Rational Vehicles (ANRV).
- **Class 2:** Non-Autonomous Vehicles (NAV).
- **Class 3:** Autonomous and Rational Vehicles (ARV).

Accordingly, vehicles by "RobustMAS Traffic" can be also summarised as follows (for details see section 4.4.3.4):

- **Class 1:** Competitive vehicles (the ANRV vehicles)
- **Class 2:** Cooperative vehicles (the NAV vehicles).
- **Class 3:** Cooperative & Competitive vehicles (the ARV vehicles).

Class 3 vehicles, Autonomous and Rational Vehicles (ARV), are the desirable class, which behaves as follows:

1. Avoiding: Avoid causing an accident with other vehicles.
2. Speeding: Deviate from the planned trajectories, if it is possible, trying to move faster than their planned trajectories to maximise its own utility (crossing the intersection so quickly as possible).
3. Compliance: Comply with the planned trajectories, if it was not possible to deviate from their planned trajectories.

4.4.4.4 System architecture of "RobustMAS Traffic"

The system architecture of RobustMAS (see Figure 4-10) discussed in section 4.4.3.5 can be adapted to the traffic intersection without traffic lights. In this way, the agents are the vehicles and the intersection area (the centre of the intersection) is the shared environment. The system goal is the corrective intervention on time to guarantee the robustness of the intersection performance, so that the vehicles can move reliably in the intersection in order to cross it as soon as possible, while retaining their autonomy as far as possible. For more details see section 4.4.3.5 that discusses the generic proposed system architecture of RobustMAS.

4.4.4.5 Definition of deviation and disturbance in "RobustMAS Traffic"

Similar to the definition of deviation and disturbance introduced section 4.4.3.6, the definition of both terms can be defined, according to the "RobustMAS Traffic", as follows:

Chapter 4. Design and architecture for robust multi-agent systems 81

Definition 4: "A **deviation** is a different trajectory from what was initially planned (desired) for a vehicle. Deviations from the planned trajectories occur, if the vehicles are not respecting these trajectories".

Definition 5: "A **disturbance** is a permanent accident in the intersection".

Additionally, the disturbance strength can be defined according to the "RobustMAS Traffic" as follows:

Definition 6: "A **disturbance strength** is a simulation parameter that represents the size of the accident in the traffic intersection".

The disturbance strength is measured in terms of tiles (cells) occupied by an accident as depicted in Figure 4-14.

4.4.5 Measurement of robustness and gain

Since RobustMAS aims to keep a multi-agent system at a desired performance level even though disturbances and deviations occur in the system, a method to measure the robustness of a multi-agent system is required. The equivalent goal of RobustMAS by the application scenario, a traffic intersection without traffic lights, is to keep the traffic intersection at a desired performance level even though deviations from the planned trajectories and accidents occur in the intersection. Therefore, a new concept will be introduced in order to define the robustness of multi-agent systems. Additionally, the gain of RobustMAS will be defined and used to show the benefit of the hybrid central/self-organising concept.

The robustness of a multi-agent system can be defined as follows:

Definition 7: Robustness:

"A (multi-agent) system is considered robust against disturbances if its performance degradation is kept at a minimum".

Consequently, the RobustMAS concept assumes that a robust system keeps its performance acceptable after occurrence of disturbances and deviations from the plan.

Definition 8: Relative robustness:

"The relative robustness of a (multi-agent) system in the presence of a disturbance is the ratio of the performance degradation due to the disturbance divided by the undisturbed performance".

In order to measure the robustness of RobustMAS in the traffic intersection system, the throughput metric is used for determining the reduction of the performance (system throughput) of RobustMAS after disturbances (accidents) and deviations from the planned trajectories. That is because throughput is one of the most commonly used performance metrics. Therefore, the comparison of the throughput values is required in the three cases:

(1) Without disturbance.

(2) With disturbance with intervention.

(3) With disturbance without intervention.

Based on this, the robustness measurement of RobustMAS will be considered in two ways:

Chapter 4. Design and architecture for robust multi-agent systems   82

- Using cumulative system performance, i.e., cumulative throughput (# Agents), where the system is considered only until the time when the disturbance ends.
- Using system performance, i.e., throughput per time unit (# Agents/sec), where the system is considered until the time when the system returns after disturbances to its normal state like before.

For this explanation of the robustness measurement, the words agent and vehicle can be used interchangeably.

1- Using cumulative system performance (cumulative throughput)

Figure 4-11 illustrates this comparison where t_1 is the time at which the disturbance (accident) occurs. The disturbance is assumed to remain active until the time t_2. This figure shows the cumulative performance (throughput) values of the system before and after the disturbance comparing the three mentioned cases.

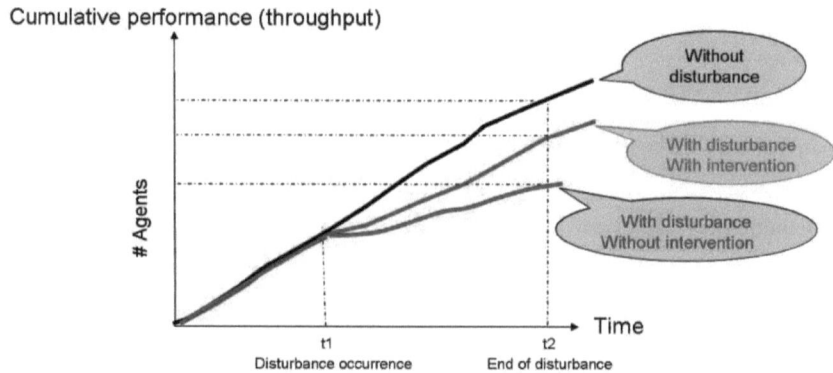

Figure 4-11: Comparison of cumulative system performance (throughput) for three situations

The black curve is the performance (throughput) of the system if no disturbance occurs. The green curve is the performance of the system when a disturbance at time t_1 occurs and the central planning intervenes on time. The system is considered until time t_2 when the disturbance ends. The red curve is the performance of the system when a disturbance at time t_1 occurs and the central planning does not intervene. Here, two areas can be distinguished: $Area_1$ and $Area_2$ in order to measure the robustness of RobustMAS as depicted in Figure 4-12.

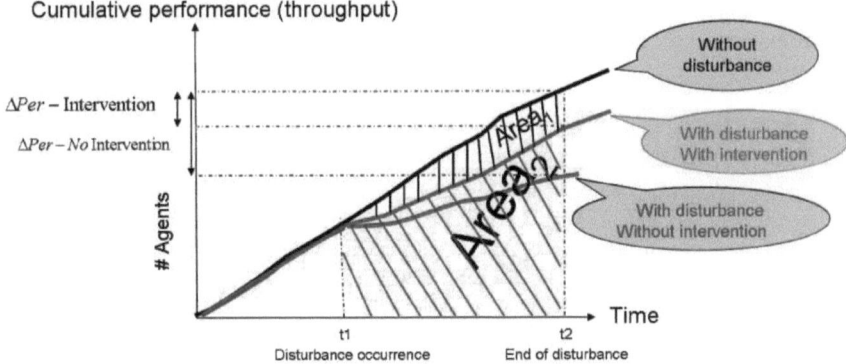

Figure 4-12: Measuring robustness and gain using cumulative system performance

Figure 4-12 shows the idea of how the robustness of the system as well as the gain of the system can be determined according to the RobustMAS concept.

The relative robustness (R) of a system (S) is determined as follows:

$$R = \frac{Area_2}{Area_1 + Area_2} = \frac{\int_{t1}^{t2} Per(t)_{(withIntervention)} d(t)}{\int_{t1}^{t2} Per(t)_{(NoDisturbance)} d(t)} \quad (4.6)$$

This means that the robustness is $Area_2$ divided by the sum of the two areas 1 and 2. $Area_2$ is the integral of the green curve (disturbance with intervention) between t_1 and t_2. The sum of $Area_1$ and $Area_2$ is the integral of the black curve (no disturbance) between t_1 and t_2.

Additionally, the gain of the system can be used as a secondary measure. In this context, the gain of a system can be defined as follows:

Definition 9: Gain

"The gain of a system is the benefit of the system through central planning (compared to decentral planning). Accordingly, the gain of a system represents the difference between the system performance (throughput) in the two cases, with and without intervention of the central planning algorithm".

This issue is expressed by the following equation:

$$Gain = \Delta Per_{(NoIntervention)} - \Delta Per_{(Intervention)} \quad (4.7)$$

As depicted in Figure 4-12, the gain of the system can be calculated using the values of the system performance (throughput values) at the time t_2. Here, *Per(Intervention)* represents the difference between the system performance in the two cases, without disturbance and disturbance with intervention of the central planning algorithm; whereas

Per(NoIntervention) represents the difference between the system performance in the two cases, disturbance with and without intervention of the central planning algorithm.

2- Using system performance (throughput per time unit)

In this case, the system performance, i.e., throughput per time unit (# Agents/sec) is used. Additionally, the system is considered longer than in the case of the cumulative performance (cumulative throughput) values. Therefore, compared to that case that defines time t_1, the occurrence time of disturbance, and time t_2, the end time of disturbance, the times t_3 and t_4 will also be defined. Here, t_3 is the time at which the system returns to its normal state with minimal central planning intervention, while t_4 is the time at which the system returns to its normal state without central planning intervention. In this regard, the normal state represents the system performance level at its best when no disturbances occur (under normal operating conditions).

Here, we use the following functions:

- $P_0(t)$: represents the system performance when no disturbances occur (normal state).

- $P_{d, ni}(t)$: represents the system performance with a disturbance with no intervention by the central planning.

- $P_{d, i}(t)$: represents the system performance with a disturbance with an intervention of the central planning.

Figure 4-13 shows the performance (throughput per time unit) values of the system before and after the disturbance until the time when the system returns to its normal state like before comparing the three mentioned cases.

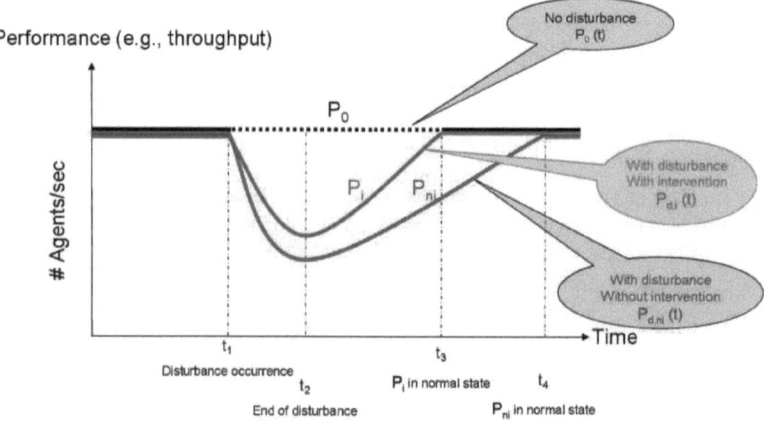

Figure 4-13: Comparison of system performance (throughput per time unit) for three situations

Chapter 4. Design and architecture for robust multi-agent systems

In accordance with the definition 8 mentioned above, the relative robustness (R) of a system (S) is determined as follows:

$$R = \frac{\int_{t1}^{t4} P_{d,i}(t)\,d(t)}{\int_{t1}^{t4} P_0(t)\,d(t)} \quad ; \quad 0 \le R \le 1 \tag{4.8}$$

Here, the lower and upper boundaries can be set as follows:

- $R = 0$ represents the lower boundary case of the relative robustness, where the system is considered as non-robust against disturbances (very poor performance). It appears when $P_{d,i}(t) \ll P_0(t)$, i.e., the performance degradation is very strong due to the disturbance in spite of the intervention, compared to the performance when no disturbance occurs. Thus, the system behaviour is not acceptable in the face of disturbances.

- $R = 1$ represents the upper boundary case of the relative robustness, where the system is considered as strongly robust against disturbances (an optimal performance, an ideal behaviour). It occurs, when $P_{d,i}(t) = P_0(t)$, i.e., there is no performance degradation due to the intervention despite the presence of disturbances.

Furthermore, the system could be also weakly robust if its performance level is acceptable but not optimal in the presence of disturbances. Therefore, the system behaviour is acceptable but not ideal.

Similar to the definition 9 mentioned above, the gain of a system is determined as the difference between the performance in both cases, disturbances with and without intervention:

$$\begin{aligned}Gain(i \rightarrow ni) &= \#Agents(i) - \#Agents(ni) \\ &= \int_{t1}^{t4} [P_{d,i}(t) - P_{d,ni}(t)]\,d(t)\end{aligned} \tag{4.9}$$

Consequently, the loss of a system is determined as the difference between the performance in both cases, no disturbance and disturbances with intervention:

$$Loss = \int_{t1}^{t4} [P_0(t) - P_{d,i}(t)]\,d(t) \tag{4.10}$$

The discussion of the robustness measurement using the system throughput metric will be based on the parameter *disturbance strength* (see the definition in section 4.4.4.5). In the traffic scenario, the disturbance strength represents the size of the accident in the traffic intersection. Accordingly, the robustness measurement was repeated in the cases that the disturbance strength is 1, 2, and 4. That means, the accident occupies an area of size 1, 2 and 4 cells in the traffic intersection as depicted in Figure 4-14.

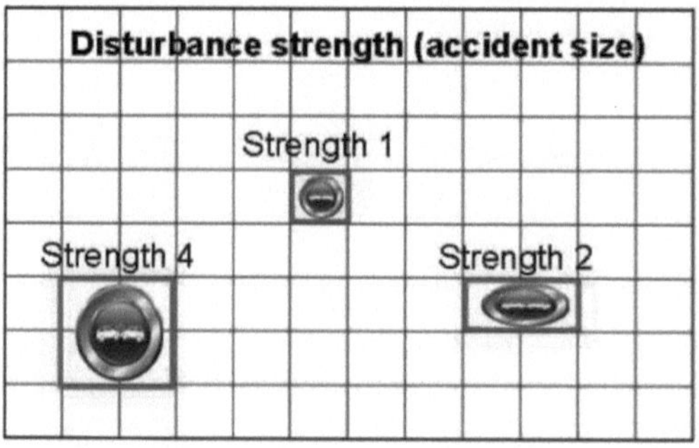

Figure 4-14: The disturbance strength (the accident size) in three cases: 1, 2, and 4 cells in the traffic intersection

Obviously the disturbance strength influences the system performance, which in turn leads to different degrees of system robustness. When the disturbance strength is increased, then the system performance will be reduced. This means that the increase of the disturbance strength is inversely proportional to the degree of the system performance.

However, the definition of system robustness can be extended to include the strength of disturbances experienced (amount of disturbances applied). Accordingly, the robustness (Rob) of a given system depending on the disturbance strength ($Dist_{str}$) can be determined as follows:

$$Rob = \underbrace{\frac{\int_{Start\ dist.}^{End\ dist.} P_{d,i}(t)d(t)}{\int_{Start\ dist.}^{End\ dist.} P_0(t)d(t)}}_{R} * Dist_{str} \qquad (4.11)$$

This means that $Rob = R * Dist_{str}$, where R is the relative robustness defined above. In this case, the integral will be between the time t_1 at which the disturbance begins, and time t_2, at which the disturbance ends. This formula implies that a system shows varying degrees of robustness (Rob) while the disturbance strength is varied. For the evaluation of the RobustMAS concept, the relative robustness R will be used later in section 6.3.4.1 (Measuring robustness and gain).

According to the used application scenario "RobustMAS Traffic", the size of the accident influences the intersection throughput (the number of vehicles that have left the intersection area), which in turn leads to different degrees of the robustness of the intersection. When the size of the accident increases, then the intersection performance will decrease. This can be justified simply on the ground that accidents will cause obstacles for the vehicles in the intersection. These obstacles will impede the movement of vehicles which are behind the accident location. Additionally, the central plan algorithm considers the accidents as virtual obstacles (restricted areas) and therefore it limits the planned trajectories of potential traffic. The autonomous vehicles which do not obey their planned trajectories have to avoid the accident location by performing a lane change (to the right or to the left of the accident location) if it is possible as depicted in Figure 4-15. Certainly, autonomous vehicles have to check the possibility to avoid the accident by pulling into another lane before they take this evasive action.

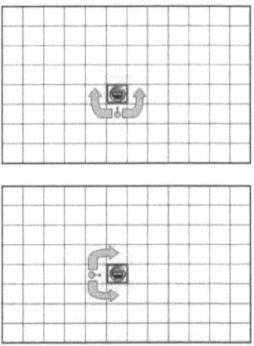

Figure 4-15: The evasive action of autonomous vehicles that check the possibility (right or left) to avoid the accident by pulling into another lane

Figure 4-15 shows the evasive action of autonomous vehicles according to "RobustMAS Traffic". Here, the vehicle behind the accident location tries to overtake the accident location on the right if the intended position is not occupied by another vehicle. Otherwise, if the intended position is occupied by another vehicle, then the vehicle tries to overtake the accident location on the left if the intended position is not occupied by another vehicle. If all potential intended positions are occupied, then the vehicle stops (doesn't change its position) and repeats this behaviour (the evasive action) again in the next simulation step.

4.5 Summary

This chapter discussed the RobustMAS methodology, followed by a detailed explanation of concept, objectives, agent classes and the proposed architecture and its components. The resulting concept allows building robust multi-agent systems in presence of disturbances. RobustMAS uses a hybrid approach (a combination of central and self-organising form) that is robust enough against disturbances. In this way, RobustMAS guarantees an acceptable system performance by limiting the degradation of the performance in the presence of disturbances. In other words, RobustMAS combines the use of a central O/C architecture, autonomous agents, disturbances and deviations from the planned behaviour aiming to solve coordination problems in multi-agent systems. In this context, RobustMAS solves the conflict between a central controller (i.e., a coordination algorithm) and the autonomy of agents so

Chapter 4. Design and architecture for robust multi-agent systems 88

that the system robustness can be achieved. More accurately, RobustMAS introduces a hybrid coordination of a multi-agent system. This hybrid coordination takes place in three steps: path planning, observation, controlling (for details see chapter 5).

Furthermore, this chapter presented the general problem domain of RobustMAS, the resource sharing problem (resource allocation problem), followed by the proposed solution to cope with it. This problem appears in a multi-agent system wherever multiple agents move in a shared environment. In this context, agents struggle to get resources (the shared environment) in order to move over it quickly. Therefore, RobustMAS provides a coordination mechanism to prevent a potential resource sharing conflict. This mechanism uses a concept of path planning so that the required resource allocation is planned over time. Accordingly, the resource allocation is made by a central controller, while the agents employ these resources. The resource planning is done in the configuration space-time (x, y, t), so that the agents can move reliably in their environment. We use the term "Spatial-dependent resource assignment" to denote the fact that the next needed resource at the next time-step is nearby (successive time-steps).

On the other hand, this chapter proposed "RobustMAS Traffic" as a special problem domain of the RobustMAS concept. "RobustMAS Traffic" focuses on the traffic problem in an intersection without physical traffic lights. Here, vehicles are modelled as autonomous (semi-autonomous) agents with limited local capabilities. These vehicles try as quickly as possible to cross the intersection. "RobustMAS Traffic" aims to design a robust traffic intersection in the presence of disturbances (e.g., accidents) and deviations (e.g., unplanned autonomous behaviour).

Finally, the measurement of robustness and gain of a multi-agent system was presented in this chapter. Subsequently, a method to measure robustness and gain of multi-agent systems was proposed.

The next chapter explains the realisation of RobustMAS investigating which techniques cab be applied to accomplish the three steps of the RobustMAS concept: path planning, observation, and controlling.

5 Realisation of RobustMAS

After the concept and objectives of RobustMAS have been presented in section 4, the realisation of RobustMAS will be explained in the next sections. The realisation of the three steps of the concept of RobustMAS (path planning, observation, controlling) will be explained respectively.

5.1 First step: Path planning

For the explanation of the algorithms, the words agent and vehicle are used interchangeably. Also, the term "shared environment" is used interchangeably for "centre of the intersection".

This section presents the realisation and requirement of path planning in RobustMAS and illustrates the resulting trajectories. Accordingly, the adapted A*- algorithm to calculate collision-free trajectories for all agents is introduced using virtual obstacles. This section gives also a summary of the path planning process.

When every agent has its unique path from one point to another, no conflict is possible when no unexpected errors or disturbances occur during movement of agents. In order to plan such unique paths for multiple agents that move in a shared space (centre of the intersection area), global knowledge and centralised control will be needed so that it will be easy to prevent conflicts.

Path planning in this work is the applied coordination mechanism to solve the problem of resource sharing wherever multiple agents cross the shared environment avoiding collisions. Path planning delivers collision-free trajectories for all participants in this multi-agent system. The behaviour of an agent outside the shared environment do not need path planning, because an agent outside the shared environment has only local rules (as described later), through which it tries to move forward avoiding collisions with other agents. Path planning has to be done only for agents inside the shared environment.

When an agent arrives at a border of the shared environment (Figure 5-1), it sends a message (request) to the controller (intersection). The path planning unit of the controller (path planning unit of the intersection) has to reply to this message thereby the agent can cross the shared environment safely provided no unexpected errors or deviations from the plan occur within this process.

Figure 5-1: The traffic intersection without traffic lights

When the path planning unit of the controller receives a request from an agent (vehicle), it simulates the trip of that agent through the shared environment taking into consideration the presence of other agents and the geometry of the shared environment (intersection) in the configuration time-spaces. It calculates an appropriate trajectory and sends it to the agent. Furthermore, the calculated trajectory is stored in the trajectory memory.

The enquiring agent gets its trajectory, which guarantees a coordinated behaviour with the other agents in order to avoid traffic jams in the intersection.

It can be assumed that every agent obeys its trajectory in the case that all agents are non-autonomous and that the circumstances of the system operation are ideal (no disturbances). But this is not guaranteed in dynamic and disturbed environments, where autonomous agents are of significant importance so that each one can choose its own actions. Therefore the observer of the intersection (the observer of the O/C architecture) observes whether the current travelled path of an agent in the shared environment corresponds to the planned trajectory of this agent in the trajectory memory. If this is not the case, then the intersection controller is informed so that it could intervene on time if necessary.

The problem of path planning for multiple agents (robots) has been discussed in various papers in order to coordinate the movements of the agents [11] [2] [5]. There are various approaches to solve this problem. Two well-known approaches are: the coordination technique and an A*-based path planning technique [2]. The first approach (**coordination technique**) [8] arranges and discovers the optimal paths of the individual agents (robots) and then computes a schedule how the robots have to traverse these trajectories. The second approach (**A*-based technique**) applies the A* search algorithm (a graph search algorithm that finds the least-cost path from a given initial node to one goal node) to work out independent planning of the paths for the individual robots in their configuration time-spaces, which extends the configuration space of the robot by a time axis. In [2], a series of experiments have been performed to compare these approaches. These experiments demonstrate that the A*-based technique significantly outperforms the coordination technique. It shows that the A*-based technique is much more efficient because of the independent planning of the paths for the individual robots in the time-spaces configuration. These experiments demonstrate also that the A*-based approach is well suited to control the motions of a team of robots in various environments and illustrate its advantages over the coordination technique.

5.1.1 A*-algorithm

Since RobustMAS uses the A*-based technique, which employs the A*-algorithm, this section presents the A* procedure described by Nilsson et al. in [134]. As mentioned above, A*-algorithm is a search algorithm to obtain the optimal path (minimum-cost path according to a given cost function) from a given start state to a target state in a graph. In order to build only paths that lead towards the target state, A* uses priorities assigned to each path. The priority of a path n is determined by the cost function: $f(n) = g(n) + h(n)$. It should be mentioned that using a priority queue to store paths through the graph (already visited nodes) together with their related A* costs is the most common implementation of the A*-algorithm. For this purpose, the lower the A* cost, i.e., the $f(n)$ cost, of the node n, the higher the priority assigned to this node.

Here, $f(n)$ is the total A* cost of the path from the start state (start node) until the current state (current node) n, where $f(n)$ is composed of $g(n)$ and $h(n)$. First, $g(n)$ represents the accumulated costs of reaching the state n from the start state. Second, $h(n)$ is the estimated cost of reaching the goal state from the state n. The estimated cost is called heuristics. The cost function $f(n)$ plays a main role in finding optimal paths, because A* takes into account the distance already travelled, the $g(n)$ function. Therefore, A* will certainly obtain the shortest path, if it exists, when a good heuristics is selected. The algorithm 5.1 gives an overview of how the A*-algorithm works.

Algorithm 5.1: Overview of the A*-algorithm

```
A-Star (startNode, goalNode)
BEGIN
// G: graph of all nodes, Q: priority queue of nodes to be traversed,
// startNode: initial state.
Initialise (G, Q, startNode);

CostUntilNow [startNode] = 0;
optimalPathUntilNow [startNode] = startNode;

// Insert the start node in the priority queue Q with the initial cost f=0.
Q = addToQueue (startNode), f (startNode) = 0;

while not isEmpty (Q) do
      bestNode = returnFirstElementOfQueue (Q);
      if (bestNode = = goalNode) then
            // optimal path from startNode to goalNode is given by
            // optimalPathUntilNow [].
            return optimalPathUntilNow [];
      end if
      // for each neighbour n of bestNode.
      for all n in successors (bestNode) do
            // Check if the path through bestNode to n is shorter than the
            // current way.
            if (CostUntilNow[n] > CostUntilNow [bestNode] +
            CostDistBetweenNeighbour (bestNode, n)) then

                  // Update the costs due to the cost between two neighbours.
```

```
            // These costs are given by the function
            // CostDistBetweenNeighbour
            CostUntilNow [n] = CostUntilNow [bestNode] +
            CostDistBetweenNeighbour (bestNode, n);
            optimalPathUntilNow [n] = bestNode;
                if (n in Q) then
                        // update the A* cost f(n) of the node n. This cost
                        // is composed of the accumulated costs g(n) =
                        // CostUntilNow [n] of reaching the node n from the
                        // start node, and the estimated cost h (n,
                        // goalNode) of reaching the goal node from the
                        // node n (the estimated cost is called
                        // heuristics).
                        update f(n)= CostUntilNow[n] + h(n, goalNode) in Q;
                else
                        // Insert the node n in priority queue Q with the
                        // cost f(n).
                        Q = addToQueue (n), f(n) = CostUntilNow [n] + h (n,
                        goalNode);
                end if
        end if
    end for
end while
// No path could be found between startNode and goalNode.
return failure;
END
```

5.1.2 Trajectories

A trajectory in RobustMAS represents the path of an agent only inside the shared environment (inside the intersection). The controller plans trajectories for all agents in the system, which have to be collision-free. If all agents comply with their planned trajectories, then the throughput of the system would be better (the intersection will be covered optimally by the vehicles), because RobustMAS uses a central algorithm in order to plan the trajectories. Here, the central planning algorithm (A*-algorithm) has a global view of all available resources (cells in the intersection) that can be allocated to the agents.

The agents get its planned trajectories only as recommendation from the controller, because they can behave in a fully autonomous way.

The memory of all trajectories serves the observer to detect any deviations from the planned trajectories occurred in the system, where the observer compares the actual travelled trajectories to this memory.

A trajectory is modelled as a vector (n-tupel) of space-time points, where each point has its coordinates (x_i, y_i) that can be reserved at time t_i:

$$trajectory = \{(x_1, y_1, t_1), \ldots, (x_n, y_n, t_n)\} \text{ with } 1 \leq i \leq n;\ i, n \in \mathbb{N} \quad (5.1)$$

5.1.3 An adapted A*-algorithm

In RobustMAS, the A*-procedure for path planning of agents is applied and the minimum-cost path in its three-dimensional configuration time-space is searched. However this A*-based procedure has been adapted for the requirements of the used application scenario "intersection without traffic lights", because a vehicle can only take a "rational" path, whereas an agent (e.g., robot) can take any calculated path. Here, the term "rational" denotes the fact that a vehicle carries out a goal-directed motion along a rational (most reasonable) path in the intersection when it moves towards its target. This path will be a straight or concave trajectory (or sections of a trajectory) with respect to the travel direction as depicted in Figure 5-2.

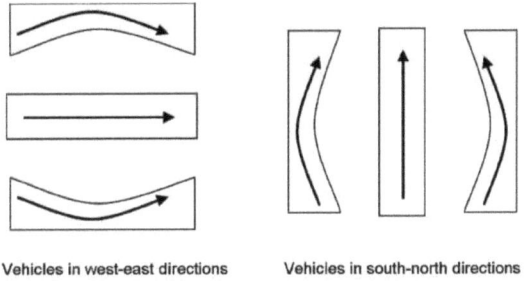

Vehicles in west-east directions   Vehicles in south-north directions

Figure 5-2: Rational paths of vehicles with respect to the travel direction

However, robots can follow an arbitrary (winding) path. As a result, due to the use of the A*-algorithm not adapted to a traffic intersection, "non-rational" path (or sections of the path) from one waypoint to the target can be built and consequently used, where vehicles can not take such paths in the centre of an intersection to reach their targets. Examples of "irrational" paths are due to repeated zigzag movements, or back and forth movements (crisscross).

Figure 5-3 shows how A* is used for the problem supported by an example. Here, the trajectory of the vehicle consists of six points. Every point has its (x, y, t) in the three-dimensional configuration time-space as follows:

Trajectory = [(x_1,y_1,t_1) , (x_2,y_2,t_2) , (x_3,y_3,t_3) , (x_4,y_4,t_4) , (x_5,y_5,t_5) , (x_6,y_6,t_6)]   (5.2)

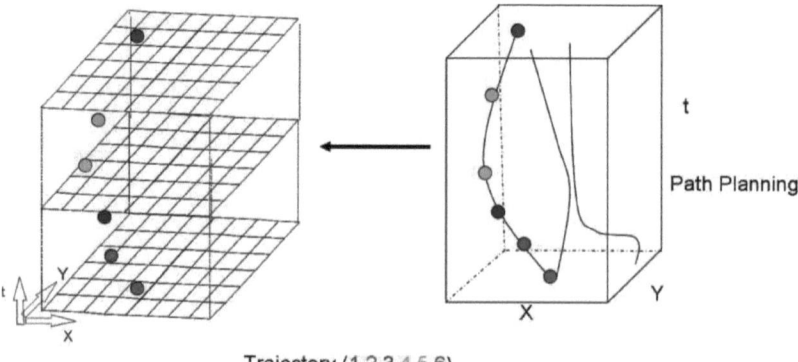

Trajectory (1,2,3,4,5,6)

Figure 5-3: An adapted A*-algorithm used for the problem of path planning in the three-dimensional configuration time-space.

Compared to the A*-algorithm described above, the adapted A*-algorithm, which is used in RobustMAS, has the following features:

- The function **BuildVirtualObstacles (n):** It uses this function in order to build virtual obstacles into the path from the current node n to the goal node, because a vehicle can only follow a "rational" path as explained above. Virtual obstacles are blocked areas, which can not be crossed by vehicles. For details see section 5.1.4 (Virtual obstacles).

- It plans independent paths for the individual vehicles in their three dimensional configuration time-spaces. Thus, reservation of space-time points (x_i, y_i, t_i) is the key step of the adapted A*, where each node (space-time point, tile or cell in the intersection) of the graph that has its coordinates (x_i, y_i) can be reserved by one agent A_i at time t_i. For this purpose, the adapted A*-algorithm uses the function **isCellReserved (n, time)**. This function tests whether the node n(x, y) has been already reserved for an other agent for a specific time, where the parameter "time" represents the time at which the agent, for which A* is looking for the best trajectory, will reach the node n(x, y) according to its planned trajectory so far. So, RobustMAS considers the problem of path planning for teams of agents.

- It provides the possibility to react to potential deviations of the agents from their planned trajectories during the plan execution. Deviations from the planned trajectories are detected by the observer of the O/C architecture, where the controller is informed of it. Consequently, the adapted A* re-plans the affected trajectories using the function **replanNewTrajectoriesOfAffectedAgents ()**. Moreover, it takes into account the presence of disturbances (i.e., accidents in the intersections) by computing the paths.

- The heuristics used in the adapted algorithm for the estimated cost of reaching the goal state is based on the straight-line distance from any given state (a node in the graph) to the goal state:

Chapter 5. Realisation of RobustMAS 95

$$\min \| (x_s, y_s) - (x_g, y_g) \| \; ; (x_s, y_s): \text{start state}, (x_g, y_g): \text{goal state} \quad (5.3)$$

This heuristics (a heuristic estimation of the distance in the case of path planning) will enable definitely A* finding the shortest path, if it exists, where the search will be limited to selected collections of the state space. Thus, a heuristic estimate of the distance to be travelled may be the straight-line distance between two states in a shared environment, so that optimal paths can be planned.

5.1.4 Virtual obstacles

The implementation of the adapted A*-algorithm in RobustMAS has been carried out under consideration of virtual obstacles. Virtual obstacles have been adopted, where blocked surfaces should not be considered by the planner. Virtual obstacles model blocked surfaces, restricted areas, which may arise as a result of reservations, accidents or other obstructions. In addition, virtual obstacles can be used for traffic control. Figure 5-4 shows the shape of the blocking surfaces (virtual obstacles), which are used by RobustMAS in order to plan trajectories using an adapted A*-algorithm.

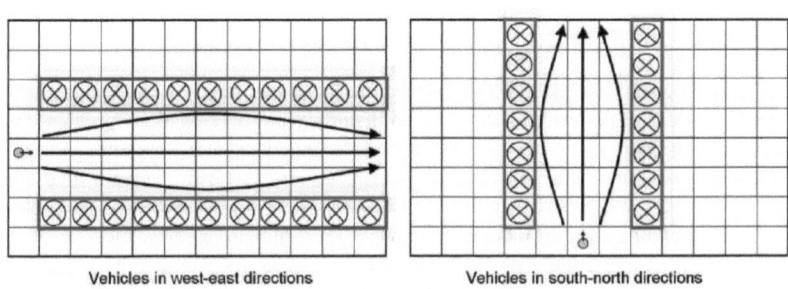

Vehicles in west-east directions   Vehicles in south-north directions

Figure 5-4: Blocking surfaces (virtual obstacles) used by RobustMAS

Such virtual obstacles are necessary and save time while searching for a suitable trajectory. E.g., if a vehicle coming from the south wants to turn right, the planner excludes a large area from the intersection, which should not be used. Thus, a vehicle takes only a "reasonable" or "rational" way.

5.1.5 Summary: Path planning

The path planning by RobustMAS is the applied coordination mechanism to solve the problem of resource sharing wherever multiple agents (vehicles) cross the shared environment (centre of the intersection) avoiding collisions.

Path planning serves to compute collision-free trajectories and to arrange the agents (vehicles). The controller performs the path planning using a central planning algorithm and sends the planned trajectories to the agents (vehicles) only as recommendation, whereas the agents can behave in a fully autonomous way (obey the plan or deviate from it or the agents are completely outside of the plan).

A trajectory in RobustMAS represents the path of an agent (vehicle) only inside the shared environment (inside the intersection).

An adapted A*-algorithm for path planning of agents (vehicles) has been applied. The adaptation was necessary for the requirements of the used application scenario "intersection without traffic lights", because a vehicle can only take a "rational" path. A*-algorithm searches the minimum-cost path in its three dimensional configuration time-spaces. The implementation has been carried out under consideration of virtual obstacles that model blocked surfaces, restricted areas, which may arise as a result of reservations, accidents or other obstructions.

5.2 Second step: Observation

This section describes the realisation of the second step of the concept of RobustMAS, the observation. Furthermore, it presents the classes of deviations, the detection of deviations, an example of the detection of deviations, and the situation parameters, which will be collected including the specification of deviations and disturbances (accidents) occurred in the system under observation. Finally, it gives a summary of the observation process.

The main goal of RobustMAS introduced in sections 4.2 and 4.3 is keeping a multi-agent system at a desired performance level when disturbances and deviations occur in the system behaviour. Agents (vehicles) have to be observed within the shared environment (intersection) through an observer (the observer of the O/C architecture), because the agents are autonomous (decentral) and they are allowed to behave in a completely autonomous way, therefore deviations from the planned trajectories (central plan) are possible.

The A*-based path planning algorithm considered here provides no means to react to possible deviations of agents from their planned trajectories during the plan execution. For example, if one agent is delayed because unforeseen objects block its path, alternative plans for the agents might be more efficient. In such situations, it is important to have means for detecting such opportunities and to re-plan dynamically [2].

5.2.1 Deviation classes

The observer is able to detect when something has gone wrong. In order to detect the deviation class, which occurred in the shared environment, the second detector of the observer (the collision detector) is used. It discovers the deviation class and whether the deviation led to a collision. There are a large number of possible classes of deviations. We use the following ones, where these selected classes aim to illustrate the possibilities of deviations but the deviation class does not affect the functioning of the algorithm:

1. The first class of deviations is a deviation through the unplanned behaviour of an agent (driver agent of a vehicle). This class could emerge due to the deviation of this or another driver, who has deviated either because of an obligatory reason, or because the driver is an egoistic (autonomous) driver and does not obey his prescribed trajectory aiming to move more speedily than planned if it is possible.

Chapter 5. Realisation of RobustMAS 97

2. The second class of deviations is a deviation through the hardware of an agent (vehicle). This class could emerge due to any error in vehicles, e.g., a deviation because of an error in the vehicle's sensors.
3. The third class of deviation is a deviation through the environment (road of vehicles). This class could emerge due to any errors, disturbances in the road or the environment of the system, e.g., a deviation because of a slippery patch in the road or a deviation because of a disturbance in the environment (an accident in the intersection).

Furthermore, there are many classes of deviation, which emerge due to mechanical failures. These classes of deviation are not in the concern of RobustMAS, e.g. deviation because of a flat tire, failed brakes or other causes that lead to a severe catastrophic event. However, since mechanical failures can happen any time, RobustMAS assumes that the worst-case deviation (failure) will lead to an accident.

5.2.2 Detection of deviations

The observer concentrates only on the agents (vehicles) within the shared environment. Therefore, other observers in order to observe the agents outside of the shared environment (on the way to the intersection) are not considered in RobustMAS.

Figure 5-5 shows how such deviations are detected through the observer (through the deviation detector and collision detector) in the system.

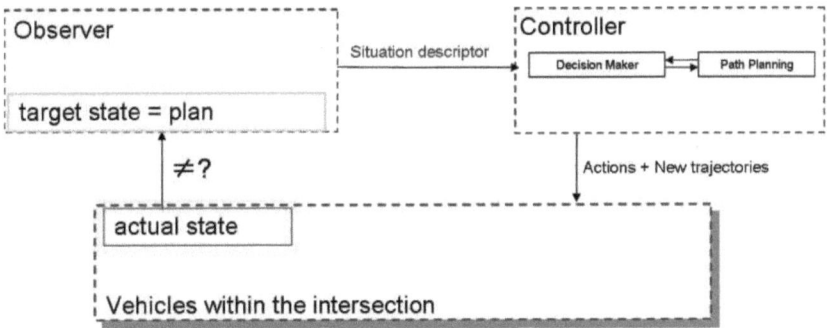

Figure 5-5: Detection of deviation

The observer reads the planned trajectory of an agent (vehicle) from the trajectory memory (target state), only when this agent is located within the shared environment (within the intersection). At the same time, it reads also the current travelled trajectory (actual state) of this agent, including (x_i, y_i, t_i), as well as other observations (see section 5.2.4 Situation Parameters). The deviation detector in the observer compares the two states (target and actual states) of every agent in order to detect whether any deviation from the plan occurred as in the next equation:

$$\text{deviation} = \text{if (target state)} \quad \text{(actual state)} \tag{5.4}$$

Nevertheless, this should not be considered as absolute correspondence of both states, because RobustMAS has the deviation-tolerance capability, so that some deviations from the desired (planned) behaviour can be tolerated as described later (see section 5.2.2.1 Neighbourhood).

When any deviation from the plan occurs, the collision detector performs the next process. This process detects whether the deviation led to a collision and finds the deviation class. The possible deviation classes, which could be detected through the observer in this system, are: autonomy (a deviation from plan), accident (a disturbance) or autonomy with accident (a deviation with a disturbance). We assume that the observer is able to perceive such deviations using surveillance cameras or other sensors, as well as by automatic notification systems, such as: Automatic Collision Notification (ACN) or Advanced Automatic Collision Notification (AACN). A device, like to that used on cars to trigger an airbag, is required to send an emergency signal to the intersection in the case of an accident. In an analogous manner, devices in aircraft are used to send distress signals and locator beacons in the case of a crash [6].

Afterwards, the observer aggregates its observations as a vector of situation parameters (for details see section 5.2.4 Situation Parameters) describing the actual states and sends it to the controller, which selects the more suitable actions and sends it to the system with the new trajectories.

It is important to mention that the controller decides whether the detected deviations can be tolerated with respect to the safety distance around the agents as described in section 5.3.1.

The deviation detector uses the idea of neighbourhood in order to compare the two states (target and actual states) of every agent (vehicle) as described in 5.2.2.1.

5.2.2.1 Neighbourhood

The term neighbourhood is used in this thesis wherever multiple agents (e.g., robots, vehicles, etc.) move in a common environment (intersection). It designates the places of occurred deviations: 1-step neighbourhood (the direct neighbourhood), 2-step neighbourhood, etc).

Here, the neighbourhood is a square-shaped area, which can be used to define a set of cells (C) surrounding a given cell c_0 (x_0, y_0); whereas the common environment (the intersection) is a square grid.

When an agent A is located in a cell c_0 (x_0, y_0) of the intersection, then the neighbourhood $N(c_0)$ of this cell is the set of cells $C = \{c_i (x_i, y_i)\}$ that can be "seen" by this agent from the central cell c_0 (x_0, y_0). Consequently, the neighbours of this agent A are defined as a set of agents A_i, which are located in this neighbourhood $N(c_0)$.

The neighbourhood has a distance (radius), which determines its borders. This extent represents the view of an agent. In a metric space of cells $M = (C, d)$, where d is a distance function or simply the distance, a set $N_r(c_0)$ is a neighbourhood of a cell c_0 if there exists a set of cells with centre c_0 and radius r, so that

$$N_r(c_0) = N(c_0; r) = \{c \in C \mid d(c, c_0) < r\} \tag{5.5}$$

Figure 5-6 shows the idea of neighbourhood, which is used in RobustMAS.

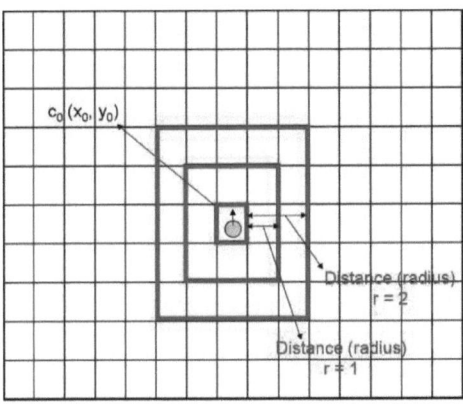

Figure 5-6: The used neighbourhood in RobustMAS

This definition of neighbourhood can be seen as the well-known Moore neighbourhood (also known as the 8-neighbours) where the distance (radius) is 1. In reference [21], the Moore neighbourhood of range r is defined by:

$$N^M_{(x_0, y_0)} = \{(x, y) : |x - x_0| \le r, |y - y_0| \le r\} \tag{5.6}$$

Here, the neighbourhood is a set of cells surrounding a given cell (x_0, y_0). Moore neighbourhoods for ranges r = 0, 1, and 2 are illustrated in Figure 5-6. It can be inferred that the number of cells in the Moore neighbourhood of range r is the odd squares $(2r + 1)^2$.

It can be seen that the number of cells in the Moore neighbourhood of range r=0 is 1, i.e., it contains only the cell $c_0(x_0, y_0)$ where the agent, whose neighbourhood is under search, is located. However, it contains 9 cells in the Moore neighbourhood of range r=1, i.e., it contains 8 neighbours and the cell $c_0(x_0, y_0)$ itself. In this case of Moore neighbourhood (r=1), the neighbourhood can be called the 1-step neighbourhood (first or direct neighbourhood). The 1-step neighbourhood is used in RobustMAS as depicted in Figure 5-7.

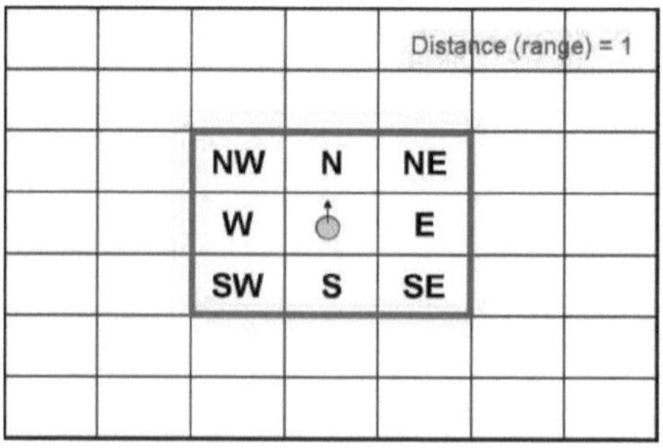

				Distance (range) = 1	
		NW	N	NE	
		W	⊙	E	
		SW	S	SE	

Figure 5-7: The 1-step neighbourhood (direct or first neighbourhood) in RobustMAS

Here, the agent is located in the central cell and the 8 neighbours of this agent are named according to the direction, in which there are the following neighbours:

N: North, E: East, S: South, W: West.

NW: North West, NE: North East, SE: South East, SW: South West.

Therefore, the neighbourhood of the central cell c_0, where the agent is located, can be defined as follows:

$$N_1(c_0) = N(c_0; 1) = \{c \in C \mid d(c, c_0) < 1\} \quad (5.7)$$

$$N_1(c_0) = \{c_0, N, E, S, W, NW, NE, SE, SW\} \quad (5.8)$$

By the range r=2, the Moore neighbourhood contains 24 neighbours and the cell c_0 (x_0, y_0) itself (the 2-step neighbourhood).

When the observer detects that an agent is located (the actual state) in a cell (e.g., the cell N), which belongs to the 1-step neighbourhood $N_1(c_0)$, instead of in their planned cell (e.g., the central cell c_0 that is the target state), then it informs the controller that the deviation of the agent is within the 1-step neighbourhood $N_1(c_0)$. In a similar way, the observer informs the controller that the deviation of the agent is within the 2-step neighbourhood, if it detects that the agent is located in a cell, which belongs to the 2-step neighbourhood $N_2(c_0)$ instead of in their planned cell c_0.

5.2.3 Detection of deviations (an example)

In order to simplify it, an example for the detection of deviations is given in three situations as depicted in Figure 5-8.

Chapter 5. Realisation of RobustMAS   101

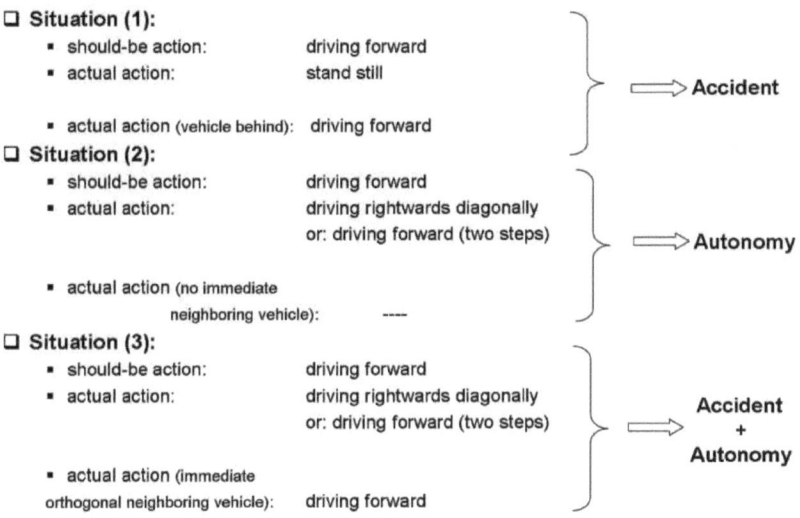

❑ **Situation (1):**
- should-be action: driving forward
- actual action: stand still
- actual action (vehicle behind): driving forward

❑ **Situation (2):**
- should-be action: driving forward
- actual action: driving rightwards diagonally or: driving forward (two steps)
- actual action (no immediate neighboring vehicle): ----

❑ **Situation (3):**
- should-be action: driving forward
- actual action: driving rightwards diagonally or: driving forward (two steps)
- actual action (immediate orthogonal neighboring vehicle): driving forward

Figure 5-8: Detection of deviation (Example)

Situation (1):
- Vehicle (1) should drive forward.
- But this vehicle has stopped.
- Vehicle (2) which is behind vehicle (1) has driven forward.
- I.e. an accident happened and the deviation class is (accident).

Situation (2):
- Vehicle (1) should drive forward.
- But this vehicle has driven rightwards diagonally or has driven forward (two steps) instead of one step.
- And there were no immediate neighbouring vehicles next to it.
- I.e. vehicle (1) is egoistic (autonomous) and the deviation class is (autonomy).

Situation (3):
- Vehicle (1) should drive forward.
- But this vehicle has driven rightwards (or leftwards) diagonally or has driven forward (two steps) instead of one step.
- And there was an immediate orthogonally neighbouring vehicle (2).

- I.e. vehicle (1) is egoistic (autonomous), an accident happened and the deviation class is (accident and autonomy).

5.2.4 Situation Parameters

The situation parameters contain the class of the detected deviation and the coordinates of the deviation (the new state), if the observer has detected a deviation. When the controller gets the situation parameters containing a deviation message, then it activates the decision maker and plans new trajectories, if needed, and sends to the system the more suitable actions with the new trajectories.

The situation parameters represent the global description of the current situation of the system under observation and include five parameters:

$$[\text{deviations, accidents, exceptions, predictions, confidence interval}] \quad (5.9)$$

1- Specification of the detected deviations (unplanned autonomous behaviour).
2- Specification of the detected disturbances (accidents).
3- Exceptions: e.g., an emergency car.
4- Predictions: e.g. the arrival time of the emergency car to the intersection (that is future consequences).
5- Confidence interval: e.g., currently normal planning but after two minutes, a special plan for the emergency car shall be activated (that is future consequences).

5.2.4.1 Deviation and disturbance (accident) specification

Figure 5-9 shows the specification of deviations and disturbances (accidents) which can occur in the intersection system.

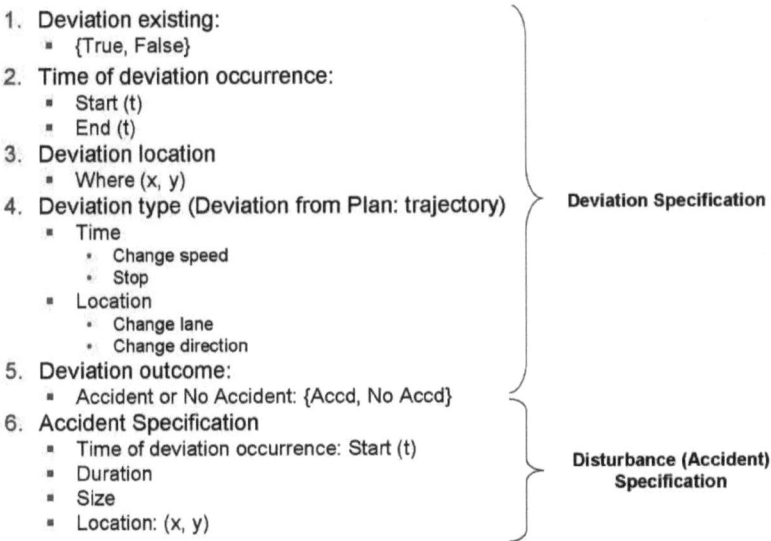

1. Deviation existing:
   - {True, False}
2. Time of deviation occurrence:
   - Start (t)
   - End (t)
3. Deviation location
   - Where (x, y)
4. Deviation type (Deviation from Plan: trajectory)
   - Time
     - Change speed
     - Stop
   - Location
     - Change lane
     - Change direction
5. Deviation outcome:
   - Accident or No Accident: {Accd, No Accd}
6. Accident Specification
   - Time of deviation occurrence: Start (t)
   - Duration
   - Size
   - Location: (x, y)

Figure 5-9: Deviation and disturbance (accident) specification

The specification of the deviations includes the following features:

1- Deviation existing: if any deviation from plan was detected: {true, false}.

2- Time of the deviation occurrence: if a deviation has occurred (true), then the begin time of the deviation occurrence, Start (t) and the end time, End (t).

3- Deviation location: the location of the deviation, the coordinates (x, y).

4- Deviation type: the type of the deviation (deviation from the planned trajectories). Here, there are four possible deviation types. According to the time of the deviation occurrence, it can recognise two deviation types. First, vehicles can change their speed (change speed) trying for example to cross the intersection more quickly than planned. Second, vehicles can stop trying to avoid a potential collision with another vehicle in the intersection. However, according to the location of the deviation, two other deviation types can be recognised. First, vehicles can change their lane (change lane) trying for example to leave a full lane of vehicles in order to move quickly as long as possible. Second, vehicles can change their direction (change direction) trying for example to avoid a potential collision with another vehicles in the intersection or trying to avoid a traffic jam in the intersection.

5- Deviation outcome: the result of the deviation. If the deviation caused an accident or not: {Accd, No. Accd}.

6- Disturbance (accident) specification: The specification of the disturbance (accident) includes the following features:

a) If any accident was detected: {true, false}.
b) If an accident occurred (true), then the time of the accident occurrence, Start (t).
c) The duration of the accident, if it is predictable.
d) The size of the accident: the size of the blocked area in the intersection.
e) The location of the accident where it occurred, the coordinates (x, y).

5.2.4.2 Exceptions

Traffic Signal Priority deals with the utilisation of priority-based concepts, so that both maximum benefits for public transport and minimum effect of intervening with individual traffic can be guaranteed. So, various existing technologies provide priorities to favour public transport vehicles. Transit Signal Priority (TSP) is a solution, which tries to speed up public transport vehicles (e.g., buses and trams) at intersections, as well as to maintain the public transit systems on schedule. In this context, several technologies can be used, e.g., induction loops, signposts/roadside beacons, optical emitters, data radio, etc [120].

Public transport vehicles signify their impending arrival to an intersection when they approach it. For this purpose, they send audio, optical, or radio signal asking for their priorities. The signal controller provides priorities for the transit vehicles announced their arrival, and transmits the high-priority traffic first. Here, a green phase will be extended or the red phase will be early terminated, as required, to enable the transit vehicles to cross speedily. Subsequently, to minimise the effect on the individual traffic, the priority granted will be terminated directly subsequent to the vehicle crossing [120].

Similar to Transit Signal Priority (TSP), Emergency Vehicle Preemption (EVP) is a preferential strategy adequate for a safe and expeditious transit of emergency vehicles through intersections. EVP enables such vehicles to move quickly as possible. Emergency vehicles send an advance request for high priority movement to the intersection controller that prioritises the flow of them. Compared to EVP, TSP has a lower priority to change the traffic light phases, i.e., to extend the green phase or to truncate the red one [118].

In this regard, RobustMAS uses a priority-based concept, where the situation parameters, which are sent from the observer to the controller, contain "exceptions". This means, there are situations where the system has to change its traditional strategy in order to accommodate new circumstances. In the intersection application scenario, all normal vehicles have the same priority when the controller plans the trajectories using the traditional strategy. When an emergency car announces its coming to the intersection, then the system will select another strategy, because the emergency car has a high-priority.

An emergency car (e.g., fire engine, police car, or an ambulance) sends a signal to the intersection requesting priority. The observer forwards it to the controller with the needed information about the expected state endowing preference to this emergency car. The controller uses a special strategy (alley strategy) forming an alley, a narrow street, so that the vehicles keep the way free for the emergency car so that it can cross over the intersection quickly.

Another required strategy is the special strategy for public transport (e.g., a bus) which has a high-priority and need to cross the intersection without long waiting time. Here, the controller considers the public transport to be urgent and consequently gives the public transport a higher priority than the other vehicles by the trajectories planning using a special strategy (public transport strategy). However, in this thesis, the priority concept has been designed but not implemented.

In contrast to RobustMAS, both TSP and EVP systems use the priority-based concept to modify the traffic light phases by extending green or early termination of red phase. However, RobustMAS takes into account the transit priority by the trajectories planning for all vehicles based on the received priority requests. Thus, the trajectory plan is adapted by a traffic public transport (or emergency vehicles) priority module, so that public transit vehicles (or emergency vehicles) can be given higher priorities.

5.2.5 Summary: Observation

The observation of compliance with the planned trajectories (the central plan) is needed; because the agents (vehicles) are autonomous (decentralised in the sense of having local rules) and thus deviations from the plan are possible. Therefore, agents (vehicles) are observed within the shared environment (intersection) through an observer (the observer of the O/C architecture) using the memory of all planned trajectories.

Different types of deviations from the plan were introduced. The deviation detector in the observer compares the two states (target and actual states) of every agent in order to detect whether any deviation from the plan occurred. The collision detector detects whether the deviation led to a collision.

Afterwards, the observer aggregates its observations as a vector of situation parameters including the specification of deviations and disturbances (accidents) occurred in the system under observation. Finally, the observer sends the situation parameters to the controller.

5.3 Third step: Controlling

This section describes the realisation of the third step of the RobustMAS concept, the controlling, focusing on the control process of the system to deal with the occurred deviations or disturbances (accidents). Furthermore, it presents the decision making (decision maker), the controller algorithm, the actions table of the controller and decision making under certainty and under uncertainty. Finally, it summarises the tasks of the decision maker and gives a summary of the controlling process.

When deviations in the system behaviour (unplanned autonomous behaviour) from the central plan or disturbances in the system environment (an accident in the intersection) were detected (through the observer), then RobustMAS tries to make the system capable to return to its normal state like before with minimal central planning intervention (through the controller). This means that the main goal of the O/C architecture of RobustMAS is the monitoring and coordination of the participants in conflict achieving a robust multi-agent system.

5.3.1 Decision making

The decision maker is the central part of the controller (see Figure 4-10). The controller uses the decision maker to take a decision how it can intervene most suitably when it is necessary so that the system can be influenced with respect to the given goal by the user. The given goal of the user in the introduced application scenario (the intersection) is to keep the system at a nominal performance level in spite of fully autonomous behaviour (causes deviations from plan) and disturbances (accidents) which could appear in the intersection system. In addition, it aims to allow for autonomous traffic with minimal delays.

The decision maker is activated when the controller gets the situation parameters from the observer containing a deviation message. On the other side, when there is no deviation, this means that everything is as planned and the decision maker will not be used.

The controller has to intervene on time if it is necessary (decision maker unit) and to select the best corrective action (it makes a decision whether a replanning is required and it uses also the path planning unit if needed) that corresponds to the current situation so that the system performance remains acceptable and the target performance of the system is maintained. Here, the controller has the capability of fault-tolerance (deviation-tolerance) and consequently it decides whether the detected deviations can be tolerated with respect to the free positions (safety distance) around the agents (vehicles). It tolerates a deviation unless the limit of the safety distance is exceeded through the deviated agent (vehicle). The controller sends to the system the appropriate actions with the new planned trajectories according to the actions table.

5.3.2 Controller algorithm

The algorithm 5.2 serves to give an overview of how the controller algorithm works and cooperates with the observer. This algorithm allows the controller to intervene dynamically through replanning all trajectories of the affected agents, when the observer has detected deviations from the planned trajectories.

The controller algorithm is based on two terms, Deviation Detector (DD) and Emergency Threshold (ET). The Deviation Detector (DD) represents the number of the detected deviations from the planned trajectories, whereas the Emergency Threshold (ET) represents the degree of the system sensitivity to the deviations that occur, at which the controller should change its normal strategy to the emergency strategy. The Emergency Threshold (ET) can be adjusted according to the used application scenario. E.g., when the application scenario is risky (vehicles application scenario), the ET can be adjusted to a very low value. Otherwise, ET can be adjusted to a higher value. Another possibility, ET can be adjusted dynamically taking into consideration the changing circumstances in the used application scenario. That means, ET will be adjusted and changed dynamically in run-time.

Algorithm 5.2: Overview of the controller algorithm with the aid of the observer

---

```
O/C (trajectory memory)
BEGIN
The observer compares the actual travelled trajectories
(actual state) of all agents A to the planned
trajectories (target state)using the trajectory memory.
```

```
for t = 1 to A do
        - identify eventual deviations δ from the plan.
        δ ← (target state) XOR (actual state)

        The observer checks δ:
        if (δ = 0) then
                - Do nothing. There is no deviation, and
                Everything is as planned, and the decision
                maker will not be used here.
        else
                - there is a deviation from the plan (δ ≠ 0).
                - if the detected deviation δ is in the
                tolerance range (TR), then this deviation
                from the planned behaviour can be tolerated.
                The tolerance range is the defined safety
                distance (free positions) around the agents
                in their shared environment.

                if (deviation δ ∈ tolerance range TR)
                        - the deviation δ will be tolerated.
                else
                        - there is a deviation δ from the plan
                        and replanning is necessary.
                        - increase the counter of the Deviation Detector:
                        (DD = DD + 1).
                        if (DD ≥ ET)
                        then
                                activate the state of emergency.
                        end if
                        - the observer finds the deviation class, and
                        stores it in the deviation message.
                end if
        end if
end for

- the observer sends its observations (deviation
message) to the controller.
- the controller reads the deviation message
and re-plans the trajectories of the affected
agents (vehicles), and sends it to the system.
END
```

When the value of DD reaches the Threshold (ET), the controller activates the emergency state. In the emergency state, the controller behaves as follows. First, all the planned trajectories are no longer valid and will be deleted informing all agents (vehicles) to stop. Second, the controller will stop the distribution of new trajectories to other agents until end of the emergency state. Third, the controller uses only step by step (successive) planning of the new trajectories. This means, it plans only the next step for the agents (the next iteration, tick, of the simulation). Then, it lets the agents perform their actions waiting for the next observations of the observer (i.e., no more planning trajectories). According to the new observed situations the controller plans for the next step, and so on.

There are two methods in order to re-plan new trajectories (i.e., the rescheduling of the trajectories), namely the complete test and the limited test.

- In the first one, the complete test, the trajectories of all agents will be tested always after the agents have carried out their actions. This method will be performed at the state of emergency, where the situation is critical and the attention is big.
- In the second method, the limited test, only the trajectories of the deviated agents will be tested, which could be in conflict with other agents. This method will be performed in the normal strategy of the system, where the situation is normal and the attention is low because there are only little deviations from the plan.

5.3.3 Action table of the controller

Section 5.3.1 mentioned that the controller sends to the system under observation and control the most suitable actions with the new planned trajectories according to the actions table. The actions table distinguishes between four situations (a deviation, a disturbance: an accident, a high priority agent: an emergency-car, and above emergency-threshold) as described in Table 5-1.

Condition	**Behaviour**
Deviation	• Re-plan trajectories of affected vehicles • Deviation Detector (DD) = DD+1 • If (DD > ET) then Emergency-State (ET: Emergency Threshold)
Disturbance (accident)	• Allow the vehicles behind the accident place trying to pass the place of accident on the right or left (agent behaviour) • Stop all vehicles which have the location of the accident as part of their planned trajectory • Re-plan trajectories of affected vehicles • Plan new trajectories of the accident vehicles when the accident duration is over
High Priority Agent (Emergency car)	• Special strategy: (Alley: narrow street). • Re-plan trajectories of vehicles in front of the emergency car so that this car can cross over the intersection quickly
Above emergency threshold	• Switch to emergency-operation (single-step mode) • Delete all planned trajectories • Plan (step by step) • Switch to normal-operation (trajectory mode), if no deviation is detected

Table 5-1: The actions table of the controller

5.3.4 Decision making (under certainty & under uncertainty)

There are two situations, in which decisions must be made, decision making under certainty (DMUC) and decision making under uncertainty (DMUU).

Decision Making under Certainty: This means that everything is clear and decisions can be made under certainty or assurance. This can be seen in situations, in which there is only one outcome for each action (for each decision alternative).

In this case, the decision maker in the controller assumes that everything he sends as control signals (actions) to the system will certainly be executed correctly, e.g., the vehicles follow surely the new action from the controller. For this case, the approach (look-up table) can be used as solution which is simple (if - then) statements.

Decision Making under Uncertainty: This means that not everything is clear and decisions have to be made under uncertainty or unconfidence. This can be seen in situations, in which there is more than one outcome for each action.

In this case, the decision maker in the controller assumes that everything he sends as control signals (actions) to the system will not necessarily be executed correctly, e.g. the vehicles may either follow the new action from the controller or may not.

Here, there are several solutions to make decisions under uncertainty. The decision theory has been proposed for this problem; exactly the Expected Utility Theory (EUT) [155] can be applied here as solution. If an agent makes a decision under uncertainty, then the probability plays a role in that decision. The decision theory consists of two theories: the probability theory and the utility theory. The decision theory is used to build a system that makes decisions by considering all possible actions and choosing the one that leads to the best expected outcome. In this context, the expected utilities (EU) of all possible actions are evaluated and then compared with each other to choose the best suitable action. The general formula of the expected utilities (EU) is described in the next equation:

$$EU(Action_i) = P_1.U(X_1) + P_2.U(X_2) + \ldots + P_N.U(X_N) \quad (5.10)$$

Suppose that there are N possible outcomes $\{X_1, X_2, .., X_N\}$, when $Action_i$ was selected and executed. Where $\{U(X_1), U(X_2), .., U(X_N)\}$ are the utilities of these N possible outcomes, and where $\{P_1, P_2, .., P_N\}$ are the probabilities of occurrence of these N possible outcomes. It can be generalised as follows:

$$EU(Action) = \sum P.U \quad (5.11)$$

This means, the expected utility of an ($Action_i$) is an aggregation value of all expected utility values of every possible outcome.

An example: There are two possible actions. $Action_1$: stop all vehicles, which are in the immediate neighbourhood of an egoistic (autonomous) vehicle; whereas, $Action_2$: do not stop them. To choose one of these two possible actions, either $Action_1$ or $Action_2$, the expected utilities (EU) of every action are evaluated using the following formulas:

$$EU(Action_1) = P.U(Outcome\_A) + (1 - P).U(Outcome\_B) \quad (5.12)$$

$$EU(Action_2) = P.U(Outcome\_X) + (1 - P).U(Outcome\_Y) \quad (5.13)$$

Suppose that there are only two possible outcomes for every action, Outcome_A: when the agents (vehicles) surely follow the new action (Action$_1$) from the decision maker in the controller; whereas Outcome_B: when the agents (vehicles) do not follow the new action (Action$_1$) from the decision maker in the controller. Here, (P) is the probability that the vehicles surely follow the new action from the decision maker; whereas, (1-P) is the possibility that the vehicles do not follow the new action from the decision maker. Similarly, it is Outcome_X and Outcome_Y for the Action$_2$. Recalling, that the expected utility of the Action$_1$ is the sum of the expected utility of Outcome_A and the expected utility of Outcome_B; whereas the expected utility of the Action$_2$ is the sum of the expected utility of the Outcome_X and the expected utility of the Outcome_Y. At the end, the best action is selected and executed Action$_1$ or Action$_2$, which is most suitable and leads to the best expected outcome.

In these cases, probabilities P_i can be estimated through experience, because P_i represents the likelihood that an event will occur. In the traffic scenario, it depends on the likelihood that the intersection encounters a particular hazard, e.g., a disturbance increases beyond a certain threshold (the accident size is enormous) leading to slow response to strong disturbance.

5.3.5 Uncertainty of sensor values

Accuracy of sensors is crucial to the system performance and its components. The sensor accuracy represents the maximum difference between the measured value at its output and the actual value. Based on this, inaccuracy in sensor values may lead to an incomplete description of the system and its environment. Real sensors may return uncertain and probably invalid values, because real sensors can not typically be modelled completely.

Sensors may malfunction and consequently return incorrect sensor values, so that the system may go into a fault state and not work properly. Furthermore, sensors may fail to send the value information that may lead in turn to unwanted consequences, especially, when the value information should be delivered at the right time to support the system to make the right decision.

In the traffic scenario, the sensors accuracy is important to perform the observation and consequently the control of the traffic intersection successfully. In this scenario, sensors are mainly needed to observe continuously the locations of the vehicles in the intersection. For vehicle observations, the sensor values are measured and used to report the vehicle locations to the deviation detector (DD component in the observer) for detecting potential deviations from the planned trajectories.

However, since the vehicle locations (sensor values) being observed are continuously changing, the reported sensor values may be different from the exact actual values of the vehicle locations. Consequently, comparing the measured sensor values to the values of the planned trajectories stored in the trajectory memory can create faulty results. For example, the result of the comparison is that one or more deviations occurred despite the fact that there are no deviations, or vice versa.

From the point of view of dealing with uncertainty of sensor values, the aim in the traffic scenario is to minimise the variance of both measured and actual sensor values. For this purpose, safety distance is considered in order to make the aggregate results of observations more tolerant to faulty sensor values. The safety distance represents free positions, which should be left around vehicles, so that uncertain sensor readings can be handled and tolerated

Chapter 5. Realisation of RobustMAS 111

by avoiding any potential collision. Sensor uncertainty can be traced back to the fact that each measured value (i.e., a vehicle location) is only an approximate value of the actual vehicle location being observed in the intersection.

5.3.6 Tasks of the decision maker

The tasks of the decision maker in the controller of the O/C architecture can be summarised

- It makes a decision whether replanning is required according to the detected deviations. It decides whether the detected deviations can be tolerated utilising the capability of fault-tolerance (deviation-tolerance).
- It uses also the path planning unit if needed and sends the new planned trajectories to the system.
- It selects the most appropriate actions and sends them to the system according to the actions table.
- It adjusts and changes the Emergency Threshold (ET) dynamically in run-time according to the new circumstances.
- It activates emergency-operation (single-step mode) when the value of Deviation Detector (DD) reaches the value of ET.
- It switches to Special strategy (e.g., Alley: narrow street) when there is a high priority agent (e.g., an Emergency-Car).
- It selects the appropriate method (complete test or limited test) to re-plan new trajectories (i.e., the rescheduling of the trajectories) determining the affected agents (vehicles).
- In the emergency-state, it plans step by step instead of trajectories.
- It lets free positions (safety distance) around the agents (vehicles) that behave as if they owned the place according to the number of their deviations. I.e., the agents, which frequently deviate from the plan, need a greater safety distance than the agent, which rarely deviate.
- In the case of uncertainty, the expected utilities (EU) of all possible actions are evaluated and then compared with each other to choose the best suitable action.

5.3.7 Summary: Controlling

The decision maker is activated when the controller gets the situation parameters from the observer containing a deviation message. On the other side, when there is no deviation, this means that everything is as planned and the decision maker will not be used in this case.

When the controller gets the situation parameters from the observer containing a deviation message (deviations or disturbances were detected), it follows the next course of action:

1- It activates the decision maker unit.
2- It plans new trajectories (if needed) using the path planning unit.

3- It sends the appropriate actions with the new planned trajectories according to the actions table of the controller to the system under observation and control.

This means, the controller selects an appropriate corrective intervention corresponding to the current situation according to its actions table taking into account the given goal by the user. Of particular interest is that the system returns after disturbances to the normal state with minimal central planning intervention.

5.4 Summary

This chapter discussed the realisation of RobustMAS including the three steps of the RobustMAS concept: path planning, observation, controlling. Additionally, it summarised each of the three steps mentioned separately after an extended explanation of each one of them (see section 5.1.5, section 5.2.5 and section 5.3.7).

The path planning was the applied coordination mechanism. It contributes to solve the resource sharing problem wherever multiple agents (vehicles) cross the shared environment (centre of the intersection) avoiding collisions. In this regard, an adapted A*-algorithm for path planning of agents was applied. This algorithm computes collision-free trajectories for all agents. The controller completes the path planning using a central planning algorithm. Accordingly, the agents get the planned trajectories only as recommendation.

The observation process is designed to detect deviations from the planned trajectories (desired behaviour), because agents are autonomous and consequently deviations from such a plan are possible. In this context, diverse types of deviations from the plan were presented, followed by determining the situation parameters. These parameters contain the specification of deviations and disturbances (accidents) occurred in the system under observation.

The controlling step concentrated on the control process of the system to cope with the occurred deviations or disturbances (accidents). For this purpose, a decision maker was used. This decision maker will be activated when the controller gets a deviation message from the observer. Based on this, the controller algorithm was developed and discussed, followed by the actions table of the controller. The actions table was structured to achieve a desired strategy distinguishing between four different situations (a deviation, a disturbance: an accident, a high priority agent: an emergency-car, and above emergency-threshold). Based on this, the controller decides on an appropriate corrective intervention. In this way, the controller aims to allow the system to return after deviations or disturbances to its normal state with minimal central planning intervention.

The next chapter addresses the evaluation of the previously suggested RobustMAS concept using three different metrics.

6 Evaluation

The traffic intersection without traffic lights from Chapter 2 served as a testbed for the evaluation of the RobustMAS concept proposed in this thesis. The next sections will prove the performance of RobustMAS presenting an empirical evaluation including experiments with three metrics: throughput, waiting time and response time. Here, the first metric, the throughput, is required for estimating the overall reduction of the system's performance, in which deviations from the plan of the controller occur. Furthermore, it presents two modes of the trajectories-reservation algorithm. The evaluation was made using four test situations. Additionally, the robustness measurement of RobustMAS was carried out, where a new concept was introduced in order to define the robustness of multi-agent systems. The gain of RobustMAS was used as another metric. This chapter gives also a summary of the evaluation process for every used test situation.

6.1 Experimental setup and the simulation environment

Once the model of the system, intersection without traffic lights, has been designed and developed, it is possible to implement and simulate its behaviour over time. The Recursive Porous Agent Simulation Toolkit (RePast) [12] has been used in this thesis as the simulation engine to perform discrete event driven simulations. Simulation consists of repeating steps (ticks) until a preset limit is reached or the user clicks on the stop button. It provides a fully concurrent discrete event scheduler so that agents can be triggered to execute their predefined behaviour in each time step. Furthermore, Repast provides functionalities such as pause and stop which make it easy to control a simulation when it is running.

The intersection without traffic lights in this thesis has been modelled as a grid-based layout (grid environment), i.e., the intersection is divided into a number of cells (see Figure 6-1) so that neighbourhoods can be defined in different ways. Vehicles in this environment try to cross the intersection as quickly as possible.

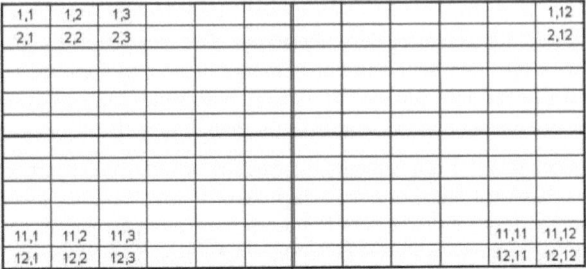

Figure 6-1: The traffic intersection as cells

The main agents of a multi-agent traffic simulation are the vehicles. Every vehicle is controlled by an individual agent as described below. Other important elements of the simulated environment can also be modelled as agents, for example a no-road agent that forms cells of the simulation area which are not defined as road (yellow cells in Figure 6-2). A traffic light agent would be another example however is not used in this system.

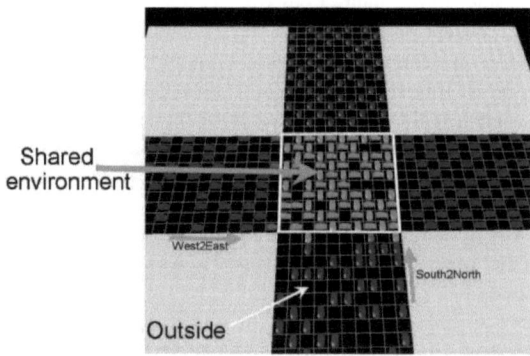

Figure 6-2: The traffic intersection without traffic lights

The behaviour of a vehicle outside the centre of the intersection (blue vehicles in Figure 6-2) is simple so that a vehicle tries to move forward avoiding collisions with other vehicles. That means, a vehicle moves forward, if there is no vehicle in front of it. Otherwise, if the position is occupied by another vehicle, it stops and doesn't change its position. The vehicle inside the centre of the intersection (green vehicles in Figure 6-2) may obey (if no deviations occurred) its calculated trajectory, which is planned through the path planning unit that is located in the controller of the O/C architecture (a calculated trajectory will be given as recommendation); or may not obey it making deviations (e.g., to cross more quickly than planned). That means, a trajectory of a vehicle represents the calculated path of this vehicle only inside the centre of the intersection.

In Figure 6-2, there are two traffic flows with orthogonal directions. The first traffic flow has vehicles that enter the intersection from the west direction and move into east direction (West2East) across the centre of the intersection. The second traffic flow has vehicles that enter the intersection from the south direction and move into north direction (South2North) across the centre of the intersection. The maximum possible number of vehicles that enter the intersection in one direction at the same time (at each tick) is 10 vehicles.

When the simulation is run without any planning or intervention (without the central path planning unit of the controller), e.g. the behaviour of a vehicle outside and inside the centre of the intersection is fully autonomous, it has been observed that vehicles with different driving directions block each other in the centre of the intersection. That is because every vehicle has only a goal to maximise its own gain by crossing over the intersection as fast as possible. That means that competition situations arise due to the egoistic behaviour (competition-based behaviour) of vehicles, which in turn lead to a traffic jam in the centre of the intersection when more than one vehicle may want to occupy the same position at the same time.

6.2 System performance metrics

A classification of metrics, which can be used to measure the system performance, is here first discussed.

High performance is always required and expected in traffic engineering; therefore appropriate metrics to evaluate the performance of the RobustMAS system are needed. The measurement of the system performance quantitatively should rely on well-known metrics. This can be broken down into two fundamental performance metrics in traffic engineering: a high throughput and a low waiting time (a low latency). Accordingly, the goal of the implemented O/C architecture can be defined as minimising the waiting time and maximising the throughput, because RobustMAS uses a traffic application scenario to analyse these two common performance metrics in traffic engineering.

Another metric is response time, which is very important for real time systems, because in those systems short response time is required. Response time (it will be precisely defined later) is the time which takes a system to react to a given input. A short response time is also necessary in RobustMAS, because vehicles approaching the intersection need trajectories (plan). Moreover, the reservation algorithm for the trajectories of vehicles has been implemented in two ways: "AllTrajectoriesVector" and "PhotoOfGrid" trying to get better response time of the system.

Throughput, mean waiting time and mean response time are also measured in this work. Throughput here is the total number of vehicles that left the intersection (simulation area) over time, whereas the mean waiting time is the average time (ticks or iterations) needed by vehicles to traverse the intersection. Therefore, each vehicle has an internal counter to keep track of its own waiting time. The counter is increased each time the vehicle cannot move and remains unchanged otherwise. Consequently, mean waiting time MWT here is the sum of all waiting times of all vehicles, which are located in the simulation area (inside and outside the intersection), divided by the total amount of those vehicles.

$$MWT_i = \frac{1}{v} \sum_{k=1}^{v} W_{k,i} \qquad (6.1)$$

Where:

MWT_i is the mean waiting time of the system at the time (tick) i.

$W_{k,i}$ is the waiting time of the vehicle k at the time i.

v is the total amount of vehicles.

The response time RT has two parts. Firstly, the path planning time T_{pp}: It is the time to search for trajectories, i.e., the time between the moment when the path planning unit in the controller of the O/C architecture gets messages (requests) from the system (vehicles) and the moment when it sends appropriate trajectories to the system (vehicles). Secondly, the observation/controlling time (T_{oc}): It is the needed

- time by the observer $T_{observer}$ to detect a deviation and the needed
- time by the controller $T_{controller}$ to re-plan the affected trajectories.

$$RT = T_{pp} + \underbrace{T_{observer} + T_{controller}}_{T_{oc}} \tag{6.2}$$

In this application scenario, the system with the O/C architecture will provide a better system performance if the response time is shorter.

The application of path planning of the O/C architecture to the system facilitates the collaboration between the vehicles, and this in turn leads to larger throughput and lower waiting time in the centre of the intersection. Therefore, throughput is used in order to show collaborative group behaviour in the traffic application scenario. In this application scenario, the system with the O/C architecture will provide a better system performance if the throughput is larger.

Other common metrics used in traffic engineering to measure the system performance are not used in this thesis like the travel time, the difference between the minimum possible travel time and actual travel time, percentage of stopped vehicles and density of vehicles. However, RobustMAS concentrates on metrics, which have greater relevance to traffic engineering, i.e., the fundamental performance metrics: throughput and waiting time (as mentioned above).

6.2.1 Modes of the reservation algorithm for trajectories

The reservation algorithm for the trajectories of vehicles has been implemented in two ways (modes): "AllTrajectoriesVector" and "PhotoOfGrid" in order to find the more appropriate way that needs shorter response time of the system.

The first mode is "AllTrajectoriesVector". Here, every cell in the intersection is an object (instance) of the class SpaceTimePoint (x, y, time). Each trajectory in turn is a vector (a vector defined in Java). This vector contains all points (SpaceTimePoints) which represent a trajectory. Accordingly, the AllTrajectoriesVector is a vector that contains all trajectories of vehicles.

Figure 6-3 shows the structure of the AllTrajectoriesVector mode that can be used in the reservation algorithm for the trajectories of vehicles.

Figure 6-3: The structure of the AllTrajectoriesVector mode

The second mode is "PhotoOfGrid". Here, for each tick (each unit of time) in the simulation a "photo" for the whole area of the intersection will be stored. Therefore, in every cell an "AgentID" (VehicleID) is saved if this cell at this time (at this tick) for this agent (vehicle) is reserved. Each level represents a photo of a specific tick of the simulation. Thus, a

Chapter 6. Evaluation

photo represents the coordinates (x, y), whereas a level represents the third axis (time), so that the configuration time-space is formed. Each photo is implemented as a HashMap (in Java), where the keys are the ticks and the values are the photos according to the next equation:

$$(key, value) = (Tick, PhotoOf\ Grid) \tag{6.3}$$

Figure 6-4 shows the structure of the PhotoOfGrid mode that can be used in the reservation algorithm for the trajectories of vehicles.

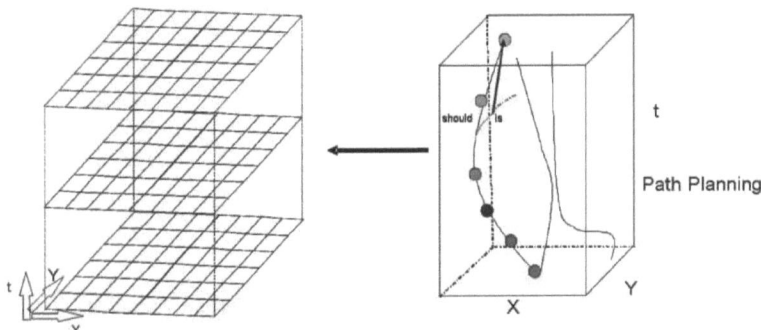

Figure 6-4: The structure of the PhotoOfGrid mode

Here, the configuration time-space can be seen, in which all points (x, y) of all trajectories of vehicles at a specific time (t) will form one level (one photo) in the three dimensional configuration.

6.3 Test situations

According to the goal of the RobustMAS system, four different test situations were used in order to measure the performance of the RobustMAS system. The goal of the RobustMAS system is to build a robust intersection without traffic lights when disturbances (e.g., accidents) and deviations (e.g., unplanned autonomous behaviour) occur. Consequently, these four test situations are:

- First test situation: Si1 (Plan): No Deviations, No Disturbances (No Accidents): There are no deviations from the plan and there are also no accidents in the intersection.
- Second test situation: Si2 (Deviation): Deviations, No Disturbances (No Accidents): There are deviations from the plan but there are no accidents in the intersection.
- Third test situation: Si3 (Plan, Disturbance): No Deviations, Disturbances (Accidents): There are accidents in the intersection but there are no deviations from the plan.
- Fourth test situation: Si4 (Deviation, Disturbance): Deviations, Disturbances (Accidents): There are deviations from the plan and also accidents in the intersection.

It is noteworthy to mention here that despite the presence of an accident by Si3, all vehicles comply with the new planned trajectories and consequently no deviations will occur.

For each test situation, the three metrics (throughput, mean waiting time and mean response time) are measured, as shown in Table 6-1.

		Metrics		
		Throughput (Vehicles)	Mean Waiting Time (Ticks=Iterations)	Mean Response Time (m.sec)
Situations	Si1 (Plan)			
	Si2 (Deviation)			
	Si3 (Plan -Disturbance)			
	Si4 (Deviation - Disturbance)			

Table 6-1: The four test situations with the three used metrics

Test environment

As a test environment, a Pentium 4 personal computer with 2.8 GHz speed and 2 GB RAM has been used to perform the simulation of the traffic application scenario of the RobustMAS system.

6.3.1 First test situation: Si1 (Plan)

In this test situation, all vehicles obey their planned trajectories (plan) and thus no deviations from the plan will occur. In addition, there are no accidents in the intersection. This means that everything is as planned (full central plan) and the decision maker will not be used here.

Since the path planning algorithm plays an important role in the RobustMAS system to achieve high performance, an evaluation of this algorithm is required under different test scenarios considering various loads of vehicles, where no deviations and accidents occur in the system.

Evaluation scenarios:

Four different evaluation scenarios are used to measure and compare the system performance, which results from change of values of the following two simulation parameters. The first simulation parameter is the maximum number of vehicles in each direction. The second simulation parameter is the production rate of vehicles in each direction (traffic level or traffic flow rate). The four different evaluation scenarios ensure that the system performance in various combinations of the parameter remains effective even when

Chapter 6. Evaluation 119

the intersection is very busy, especially during rush hour (during morning and afternoon peak traffic).

The simulation parameter V_{max} "the maximum number of vehicles" in one direction represents the theoretical maximum capacity of vehicles in this direction (vehicles moving in one direction at once). However, the simulation parameter TL "the traffic level" (i.e., the production rate of vehicles) in one direction represents the rate at which vehicles enter this direction. This parameter describes the effect of changes in traffic streams (traffic congestion). In other words, it influences the headway of vehicles, especially in the centre of the intersection, where vehicles from all directions converge to cross over.

Table 6-2 shows the resulting four evaluation scenarios. Here, "equal TL" means that the traffic flow rates of vehicles in each direction are the same, while these rates in each direction are different in the case of "not equal TL". Similarly, the "equal V_{max}" and "not equal V_{max}" can be expressed by the parameter "maximum number of vehicles".

		Traffic Levels (TL)	
		Equal	Not Equal
Max. Num. of Vehicles (V_{max})	Equal	*Scenario I*	*Scenario II*
	Not Equal	*Scenario III*	*Scenario IV*

Table 6-2: The four evaluation scenarios

For each evaluation scenario, the three metrics (throughput, mean waiting time and mean response time) are measured, as shown in Table 6-3.

		Metrics		
		Throughput (Vehicles)	Mean Waiting Time (Ticks=Iterations)	Mean Response Time (m.sec)
Evaluation Scenarios	S1 (Equal-Equal)			
	S2 (Equal-Not Equal)			
	S3 (Not Equal-Equal)			
	S4 (Not Equal-Not Equal)			

Table 6-3: The four evaluation scenarios with the three used metrics

Chapter 6. Evaluation

The three used metrics of RobustMAS have been measured in an interval between 0 und 3000 ticks (time steps in simulator). The results of the simulation of these three metrics were discussed also after 3000 ticks. As shown in Figure 6-2, two traffic flows with orthogonal directions are taken into account: W2E (West2East) and S2N (South2North).

According to the size of the traffic intersection implemented in this work (see Figure 6-2), the study of intersections with very low traffic volumes will be clearly a trivial case. Therefore, the values of both simulation parameters, mentioned above, were chosen in such a way that a wide spectrum of traffic volumes can be covered (low, medium, high and extreme traffic volumes).

Table 6-4 shows the four different evaluation scenarios.

Scenarios	#Max. Number of Vehicles (V_{max})	#Traffic levels (TL) (Traffic flow rates)
S1 (Equal-Equal)	N2S = W2E	N2S = W2E
S2 (Equal-Not Equal)	N2S = W2E	N2S ≠ W2E
S3 (Not Equal-Equal)	N2S ≠ W2E	N2S = W2E
S4 (Not Equal-Not Equal)	N2S ≠ W2E	N2S ≠ W2E

Table 6-4: The four evaluation scenarios (two traffic flows with orthogonal directions)

Evaluation scenario I (Equal-Equal):

In evaluation scenario I (Equal V_{max} – Equal TL), the throughput and the mean waiting time of the system have been measured in the case that the traffic flow rates (traffic levels) of vehicles in south-north and west-east directions is equal, namely 5 vehicles/tick, where the measurement has been repeated in the cases that the maximum number of vehicles in each direction is equal, namely 20, 40, 80, 100, and 500 vehicles. The case of 500 vehicles in every direction is an extreme case, where the maximum number of vehicles is greater than the capacity of the intersection (very busy intersection).

Evaluation scenario II (Equal-not Equal):

In evaluation scenario II (Equal V_{max} – not Equal TL), the throughput and the mean waiting time of the system have been measured in the case that the traffic level of vehicles in each direction is different, namely in south-north direction 5 vehicles/tick and in west-east direction 8 vehicles/tick, where the measurement has been repeated in the cases that the maximum number of vehicles in each direction is equal, 20, 40, 80 and 100 vehicles.

Evaluation scenario III (not Equal-Equal):

In evaluation scenario III (not Equal V_{max} – Equal TL), the throughput and the mean waiting time of the system have been measured in the case that the traffic level of vehicles in south-north and west-east directions is equal, namely 5 vehicles/tick, where the measurement has been repeated in the cases that the maximum number of vehicles in each direction is different, namely in south-north direction 20, and in west-east direction 20, 40, 80 and 100 vehicles.

Chapter 6. Evaluation 121

Evaluation scenario IV (not Equal-not Equal):

In evaluation scenario IV (not Equal V_{max} – not Equal TL), the throughput and the mean waiting time of the system have been measured in the case that the traffic level of vehicles in each direction is different, namely in south-north direction 5 vehicles/tick, and in west-east direction 8 vehicles/tick, where the measurement has been repeated in the cases that the maximum number of vehicles in each direction is different, namely in south-north direction 20, and in west-east direction 20, 40, 80 and 100 vehicles.

The next part of this discussion shows the results of the evaluation of RobustMAS in the traffic application scenario using the three metrics described above, where no deviations and accidents occur (first situation: Si1: Plan).

6.3.1.1 Results of throughput measurement

Section 6.2 has mentioned that the throughput used in the traffic application scenario is the total amount of vehicles that left the intersection over time. Here, the path planning of the O/C architecture has been implemented assuming that no deviations and accidents occur in the system according to requirements of the first situation (Si1: Plan).

Figure 6-5 shows the cumulative system throughput (# Vehicles) for each evaluation scenario that was measured in an interval between 0 und 3000 ticks. Furthermore, Figure 6-6 shows the same as Figure 6-5 using the throughput per time unit (# Vehicles/tick). Recalling, that one tick in the simulator means one time step.

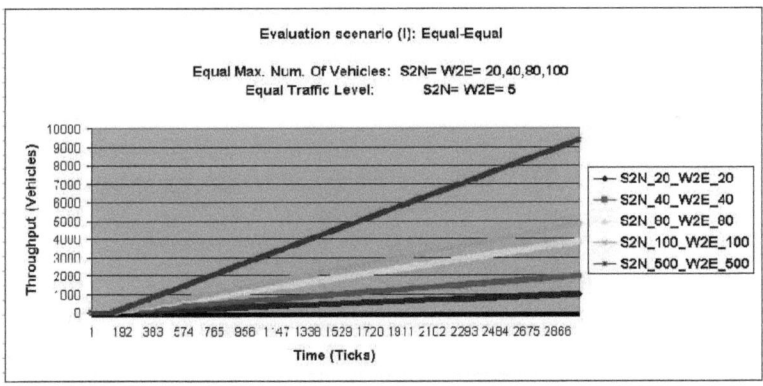

Chapter 6. Evaluation

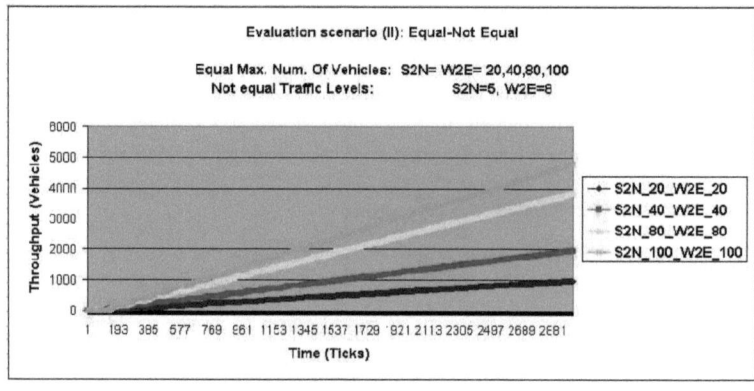

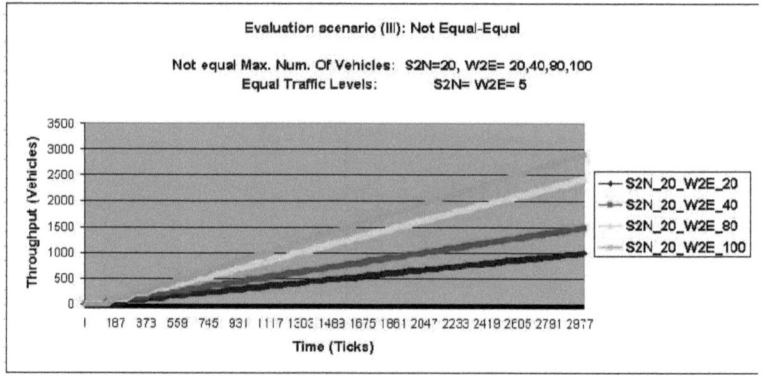

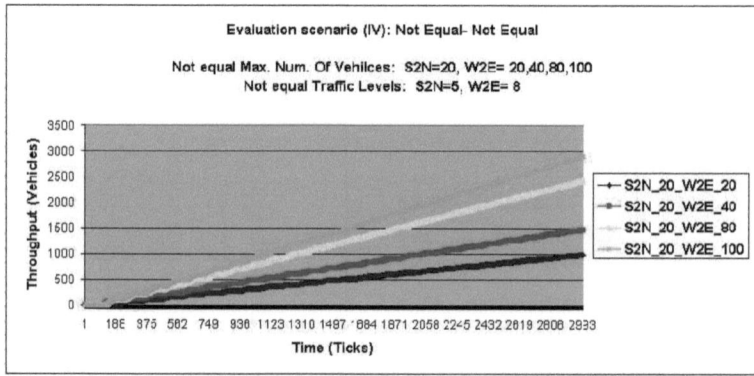

Figure 6-5: The cumulative system throughput (# Vehicles) for each evaluation scenario (I, II, III, and IV) in an interval between 0 und 3000 ticks

Chapter 6. Evaluation 123

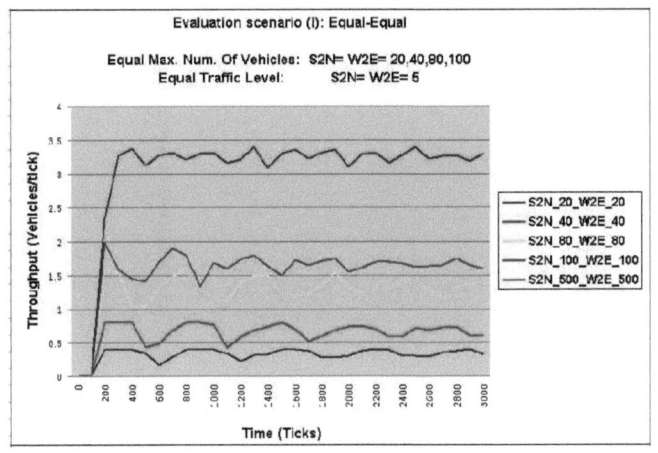

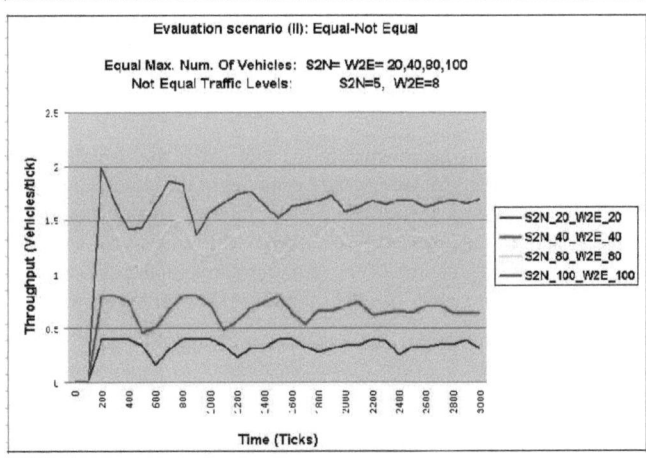

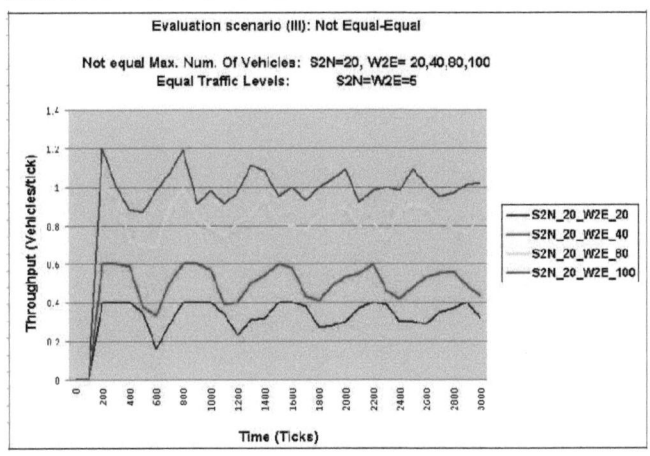

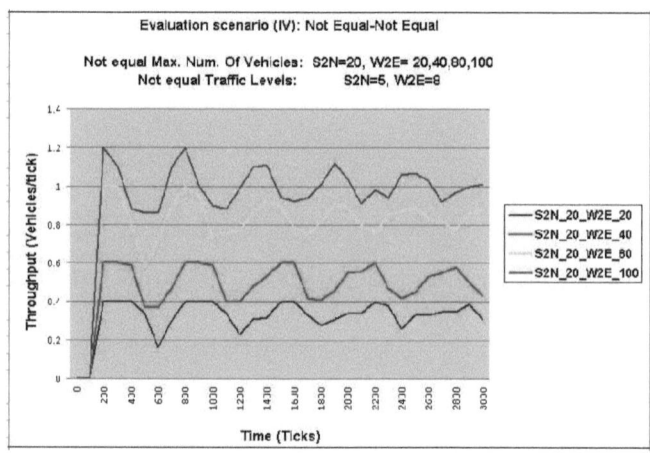

Figure 6-6: The system throughput (# Vehicles/tick) for each evaluation scenario (I, II, III, and IV) in an interval between 0 und 3000 ticks

It can be seen that from approximately the tick (120) the vehicles begin to leave the intersection (simulation area), because at the beginning of the simulation the intersection was empty. Therefore, the system throughput in this interval (0 until ca. 120 ticks) is zero. Thereafter, the system throughput increases always with time in the case of the cumulative curve, or it is at its best (i.e., approximately constant throughput per time unit) in the case of the throughput per time unit curve. This note applies to the four evaluation scenarios.

Figure 6-7 shows the system throughput comparing the four evaluation scenarios according to varying the value of the maximum number of vehicles in each direction after 3000 ticks; whereas Figure 6-8 shows the same but including the extreme case (500 vehicles in every direction and consequently 1000 vehicles in both directions). Here, on the x-axis is the maximum number of vehicles together in both directions W2E and S2N. Due to the extreme case, the maximum number of vehicles on the x-axis in Figure 6-8 has 1000 as maximum value; whereas in Figure 6-7 has 200 as maximum value.

Chapter 6. Evaluation

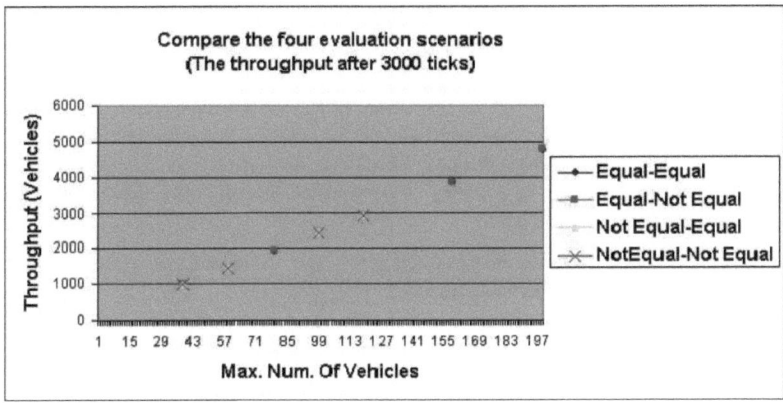

Figure 6-7: The throughput of system in the four evaluation scenarios after 3000 ticks

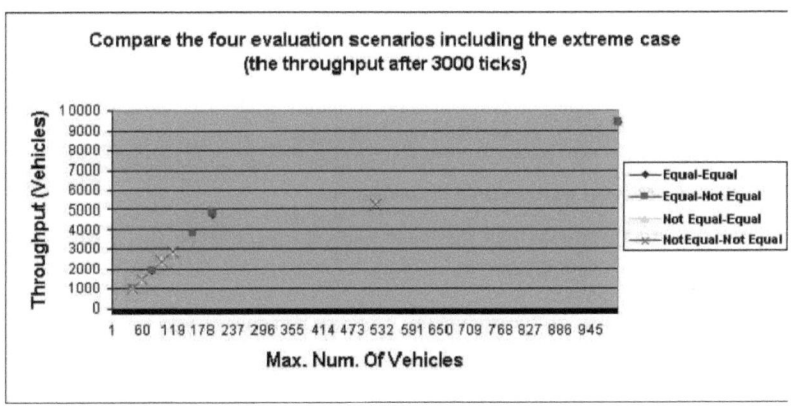

Figure 6-8: The throughput of system in the four evaluation scenarios including the extreme case after 3000 ticks

In evaluation scenario (I) (Equal-Equal), the system throughput achieves a value of around 1000 vehicles after 3000 ticks when the maximum number of vehicles in each direction is (20-20), whereas it achieves a value of around 2000 by (40-40) vehicles and a value of around 5000 vehicles by (100-100) vehicles. This means that the system throughput increases almost always linearly with the number of vehicles. In a similar manner, the same behaviour of the system throughput applies to the other evaluation scenarios (see Figure 6-7). However, this behaviour of the system throughput will be changed only in the extreme case (see Figure 6-8).

In the extreme case (500-500) vehicles and consequently 1000 vehicles in both directions, the system performance achieves a value of around 9500 vehicles, because the maximum number of vehicles here is greater than the capacity of the intersection. Thus, it can be concluded that the system throughput within the capacity of the intersection increases almost always linearly with the number of vehicles.

In evaluation scenarios I and II, the values of the system throughput are approximately identical. This means that the maximum number of vehicles in each direction is relevant, not the traffic levels (traffic flow rates) of vehicles in each direction. The system achieves a throughput of around 5000 vehicles by (100) vehicles in every direction in both evaluation scenarios I and II (see Figure 6-8).

A similar conclusion can be obtained when the values of the system throughput in evaluation scenarios III and IV are compared.

However, it is obvious that the values of the system throughput in evaluation scenario III are not similar to the values in the evaluation scenario I and II, because the total amount of vehicles in both directions in evaluation scenario III is less than the amount in evaluation scenarios I or II. Here, in evaluation scenario III, the maximum number of vehicles are (20, 20) then (20,40) then (20,80) then (20,100); whereas in evaluation scenarios I or II the maximum number of vehicles are (20,20) then (40,40) then (80, 80) then (100,100). Therefore, the values of the system throughput in evaluation scenario III or IV is lower than in evaluation scenario I or II.

In general, it can be noted that the system throughput increases almost always linearly with the number of vehicles in all evaluation scenarios (I, II, III, and IV) as long as the maximum number of vehicles is not greater than the capacity of the intersection.

6.3.1.2 Results of mean waiting time measurement

Section 6.2 has mentioned that the mean waiting time used in the traffic application scenario is the mean waiting time (ticks or iterations) needed by vehicles to traverse the intersection. This can be done using the internal counter of each vehicle including its own waiting time.

Figure 6-9 shows the mean waiting time for each evaluation scenario that was measured in an interval between 0 und 3000 ticks.

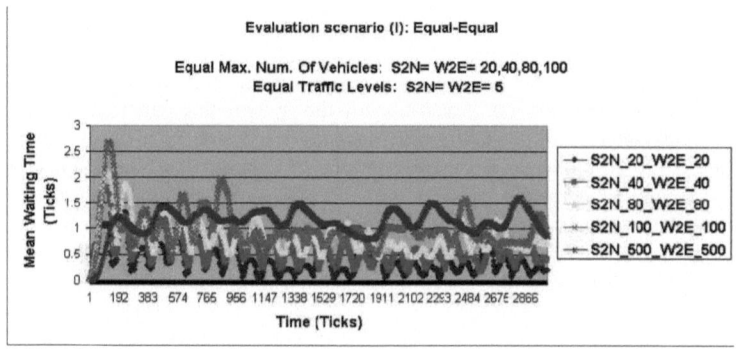

Chapter 6. Evaluation _____ 127

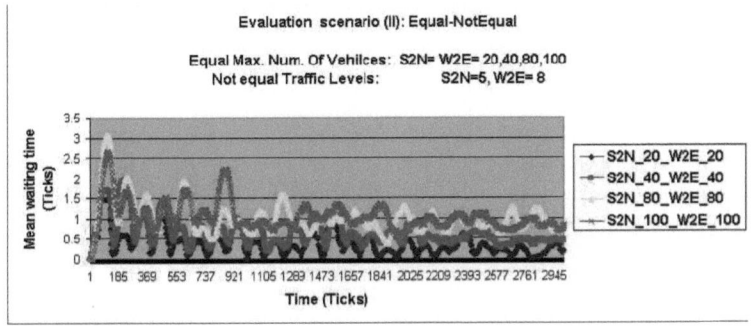

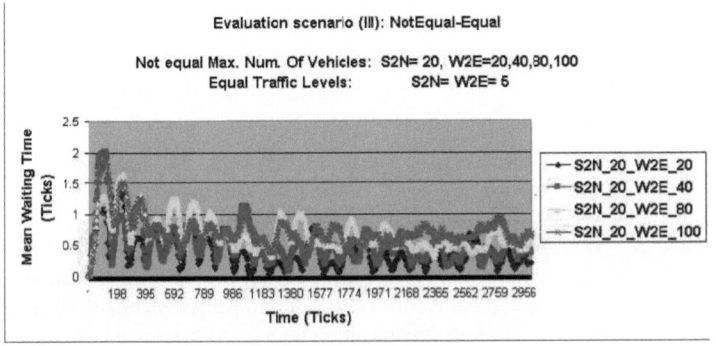

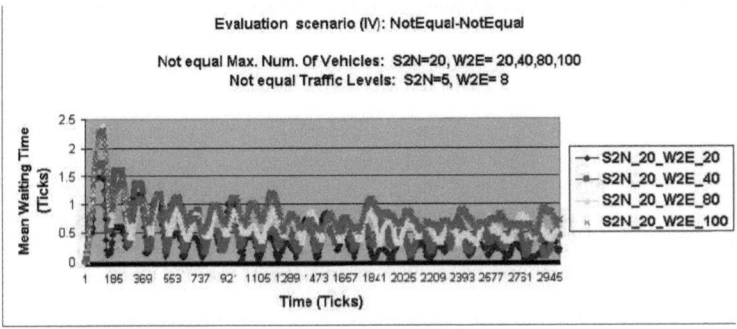

Figure 6-9: The mean waiting time for each evaluation scenario (I, II, III, and IV) in an interval between 0 und 3000 ticks

It can be seen that from the beginning of the simulation up to approximately the tick 100, a short threshold (the initially effect where time < 100 ticks) is formed. That is because the intersection was empty at the beginning of the simulation and the vehicles of both directions

Chapter 6. Evaluation

W2E and S2N arrive roughly together at the borders of the central area of the intersection. Therefore, several conflicts (competitions) arise at these times which increase in turn the waiting time for multiple vehicles. The maximum value of the mean waiting time of the system by this threshold is around 3 ticks when the maximum number of vehicles in each direction is (100,100) vehicles, which is a low value of waiting time. After this, the threshold disappears and the mean waiting time will be lower. Thereafter, the more the total amount of vehicles in the intersection, the greater the mean waiting time of the system. This observation applies to the four evaluation scenarios.

In evaluation scenario (I) (Equal-Equal), for an example, the maximum value of the mean waiting time is around 1 tick when the maximum number of vehicles in each direction is (20-20) and (40-40) and (80,80) vehicles; whereas around 2 ticks by (100,100) vehicles. However, it is slightly different in the extreme case (500,500) vehicles. Here, due to the large number of vehicles the maximum value of the mean waiting time is around 1.5 ticks and the mean waiting time of the whole system will be reduced.

In evaluation scenarios I and II, the values of the mean waiting time of the system are approximately identical. The same can be concluded when the values of the mean waiting time of the system in evaluation scenarios III and IV are compared.

However, it can be seen that the values of the mean waiting time of the system in evaluation scenario III are not the same as the values in the evaluation scenario I and II, because the total amount of vehicles in both directions in evaluation scenario III is less than the amount in evaluation scenarios I or II. Here, in evaluation scenario III, the maximum number of vehicles are (20,20) then (20,40) then (20, 80) then (20,100); whereas in evaluation scenarios I or II the maximum number of vehicles are (20,20) then (40,40) then (80, 80) then (100,100). Therefore, the values of mean waiting time of the system in evaluation scenario III or IV is lower than in evaluation scenario I or II.

Now, the results of the mean waiting time metric will be discussed for the extreme case, (500) vehicles in every direction, where the maximum number of vehicles is greater than the capacity of the intersection (very busy intersection). That is done in order to show the longest waiting time at all with its standard deviation.

For this purpose, the measurements were repeated in the cases that the traffic levels of vehicles in south-north and west-east directions are: (1,1), (1,8), (5,5), (5,8), (8,8) vehicles/tick. The different rates at which vehicles enter each of the directions are chosen to investigate the effect of traffic streams with equal/unequal strength on the mean waiting time which vehicles experience as depicted in Table 6-5. Additionally, Figure 6-10 shows the same as Table 6-5 using a box plot. The mean waiting times and the standard deviations of all vehicles, that left the intersection, have been registered after 3000 ticks in the extreme case.

Chapter 6. Evaluation   129

S2N (Vehicles/Tick)	W2E (Vehicles/Tick)	Mean Waiting Time (Ticks)	Std. Deviation
1	1	0.59	0.80
1	8	3.81	1.55
5	5	3.57	1.49
5	8	3.57	1.48
8	8	4.07	1.19

Table 6-5: The mean waiting time and the standard deviation of all vehicles that left the intersection after 3000 ticks in the extreme case (1000 vehicles)

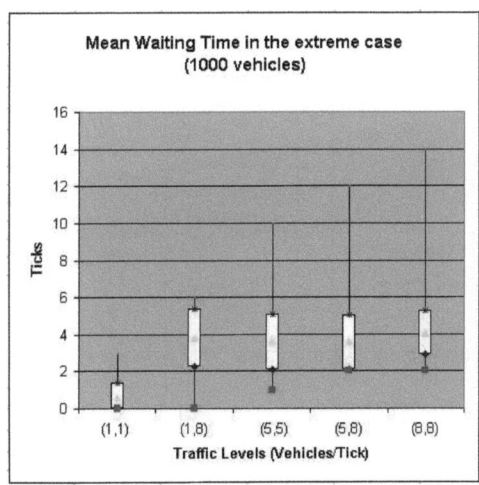

Figure 6-10: The mean waiting time in the extreme case (1000 vehicles)

Despite the huge number of vehicles, which is greater than the capacity of the intersection, the resulting mean waiting times were low values with small standard deviations in all different traffic flow rates (traffic levels). The largest mean waiting time is by traffic rate (8,8) around 4 ± 1.19.

6.3.1.3 Results of mean response time measurement

Section 6.2 has mentioned that the response time used in the traffic application scenario has two parts: the path planning time and the observation/controlling time. Additionally, the reservation algorithm for the trajectories of vehicles has been implemented in two ways (modes): "AllTrajectoriesVector" and "PhotoOfGrid" trying to get better response time of the system.

According to the first situation (Si1: Plan), no deviations and accidents will occur in the system, the mean response time here is the mean computation time of the search for the best appropriate trajectories of vehicles.

In order to compare the two proposed ways of the reservation algorithm for trajectories, the mean response time of the system has been measured for both reservation ways after 3000 ticks in two selected scenarios. Scenario I is a simple scenario in terms of a small number of vehicles. In this scenario, the mean response time of the system has been measured considering that the traffic level of vehicles in south-north and west-east directions is only 1 vehicles/tick, whereas the maximum number of vehicles in each direction is only 20 vehicles. Scenario II is a complex scenario in terms of a large number of vehicles. In this scenario, the mean response time of the system has been measured with a traffic level of vehicles in south-north and west-east directions of 4 vehicles/tick, whereas the maximum number of vehicles in each direction is 100 vehicles.

Table 6-6 shows the resulting mean response times comparing both reservation ways in simple and complex case.

	Scenario I (simple case) (m.sec)	Scenario II (complex case) (m.sec)
AllTrajectoriesVector	0.167	0.930
PhotoOfGrid	1.062	12.447

Table 6-6: The mean response times after 3000 ticks comparing both reservation ways

According to the resulting values in Table 6-6, it can be concluded that the second reservation mode (PhotoOfGrid) requires about 6 times longer time than the first reservation mode (AllTrajectoriesVector) in the scenario I (simple case), whereas it is about 13 times longer in the scenario II (complex case). Accordingly, the reservation mode (AllTrajectoriesVector) has approximately a quadratic complexity, $O(n^2)$, whereas the reservation mode (PhotoOfGrid) has approximately a cubic complexity, $O(n^3)$. That is because time is additional to the (x, y) form in this 3-D configuration.

Since the reservation mode (AllTrajectoriesVector) outperforms significantly the other reservation mode (PhotoOfGrid) by computation time in several situations, only the former (AllTrajectoriesVector) will be further measured and discussed.

Figure 6-11 shows the system performance (mean response times) for the evaluation scenario I (Equal-Equal) after 3000 ticks using the reservation mode (AllTrajectoriesVector).

Chapter 6. Evaluation

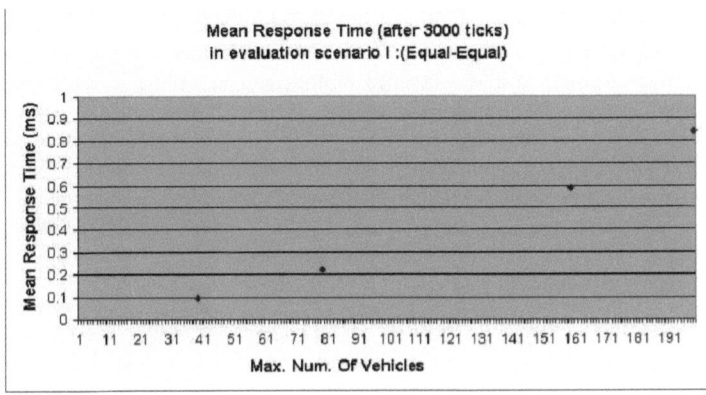

Figure 6-11: The mean response times of system in scenario I (Equal-Equal) after 3000 ticks using the reservation mode AllTrajectoriesVector

Here, on the x-axis the maximum number of vehicles together in both directions W2E and S2N is shown. The mean response time of the system in this scenario has an approximate value of 0.1 ms when the total number of vehicles in both directions is 40 vehicles, whereas an approximate value of 0.83 ms by 200 vehicles. That means, the mean response time of the system increases approximately quadratically with the total number of vehicles requiring less than 1 ms when the total number of vehicles in both directions is 200 vehicles.

Real world

The simulation has been made by the simulation framework RePast, but what about the real world? In order to make the traffic system in this work realistic as a practical and implementable system in the real world, it has to be tested assuming a variety of conditions. Therefore the following assumptions were taken into account:

- Each cell in the simulation area has a length of 10 meters.
- The total length of the simulation area is 40 cells, i.e. 400 meters.
- The total width of the simulation area is 40 cells, i.e. 400 meters.
- The speed of a vehicle is 10 meters per second, i.e. 1 cell per second, i.e. 36 km/h.
- The shortest time to cross the simulation area is 400/10 = 40 seconds.
- In each tick one vehicle can move only 1 cell, i.e. each 1 tick in the simulation represents 1 second in reality.

In evaluation scenario I (Equal-Equal), the measured mean response time of the system after 3000 ticks using the reservation mode (AllTrajectoriesVector) is 0.845 ms, where the total amount of vehicles in south-north and west-east directions together is 200 vehicles and the total traffic level of vehicles in both directions together is 10 vehicles/tick. This value is less than 1 ms. According to the assumptions described above, that is feasible, because it was assumed that each tick represents 1 second.

Since communication delays C_d in the delivery of messages or control actions may be present, the consideration of the communication delay is normally required. C_d may range from some microseconds to a few hundred milliseconds according to the communication networks used. In this work, communications are considered to be under no delay condition. Thus, C_d has not been computed assuming that the underlying communication network ensures the required level of communication (C_d may assumed to be constant). Therefore, it is essential to provide the minimum required bandwidth to send messages (communication). An example, a message m that has the maximum size of 688 byte is sent by the use of an IEEE 802.11 network, which has 5.5 Mbps data rate transmission. Here, the transmission time to send the message m is around 1 ms.

Content Addressable Memory (CAM)

If the system has to be even more effective with respect to the short response time capability, then the reaction time of the system has to be improved. One of several ways to achieve this goal is the associative memory (Content Addressable Memory, CAM). The CAM provides a performance advantage over other memory search algorithms in the search time. The associative memory is used in real-time systems, in two cases: First, as hardware associative memory [19]. It is a memory for search applications that require a very high speed. A typical application area for this memory is a fast cache memory, memory tables that often are accessed and data structures in artificial intelligence [20]. All cells of this memory can be tested in one operation due to the hardware design. That leads to very fast search operations. This achieves in turn an advantage for the system performance. The penalty of using a hardware associative memory is the cost, because it is designed in hardware. However, this form of memory is today replaced largely by hashing techniques, which work with the conventional memory and are therefore much cheaper to implement. This second variant is called a software associative memory (associative array). It is slower than the hardware associative memory, but it costs actually much less than the hardware one. Accordingly, a CAM is the hardware embodiment of what in software terms would be called an associative array. Finally, it can be concluded, that the use of hardware associative memory can improve the system performance assuring a faster reaction time of the system in order to keep it at a desired performance level when errors, disturbances and deviations occur in the system behaviour, particularly in the cases, in which a short response time capability is required. However, a special study has to be made to assess the actual improvement of the system performance that can be achieved using a hardware associative memory.

6.3.1.4 Summary: First test situation: Si1 (Plan)

In this test situation, no deviations from the plan will occur and consequently there are no accidents in the intersection. That means, all vehicles obey their planned trajectories (full central plan) and the decision maker will not be used here.

Four different evaluation scenarios were used to measure and compare the system performance.

- Evaluation scenario I (Equal-Equal)
- Evaluation scenario II (Equal-not Equal)
- Evaluation scenario III (not Equal-Equal)

- Evaluation scenario IV (not Equal-not Equal)

The three used metrics of RobustMAS have been measured in interval between 0 und 3000 ticks (time steps in simulator): throughput, mean waiting time and mean response time. Also, a discussion of the measured values for this three metrics after 3000 ticks was managed.

1) Throughput:

As long as the maximum number of vehicles is not greater than the capacity of the intersection, the system throughput increases almost always linearly with the number of vehicles.

2) Mean waiting time:

Despite of the huge number of vehicles which is greater than the capacity of the intersection, the resulting mean waiting times were low with small standard deviations in all different traffic flow rates (traffic levels). The largest mean waiting time is by traffic rate (8,8) around 4 ± 1.19.

3) Mean response time:

According to the first situation (Si1: Plan), no deviations and accidents will occur in the system, the mean response time here is the mean used computation time of the search for the best appropriate trajectories of vehicles.

The reservation mode (AllTrajectoriesVector) outperforms significantly the other reservation mode (PhotoOfGrid) by computation time in several situations.

The mean response time of the system increases approximately quadratically with the total number of vehicles requiring less than 1 ms when the total number of vehicles in the both directions is 200 vehicles.

Assumptions, that are required, have been discussed in order to make the traffic system realistic in the real world. Additionally, a hardware associative memory can assure a faster reaction time of the system.

6.3.2 Second test situation: Si2 (Deviation)

In this test situation, the vehicles do not obey their planned trajectories (plan) and thus deviations from the plan will occur but there are no accidents in the intersection.

Of course, an observation of actual trajectories by the observer component has to be made in order to identify any deviations from plan allowing replanning all affected trajectories by the controller using the path planning algorithm.

Here, the desired type of potential deviations in the simulation of the traffic system is change speed. That means, vehicles can change their speed trying for example to cross the intersection more quickly than planned. With respect to this type of deviations, vehicles that can only make one move (its planned speed is one move) in one tick (a single time step) are trying to make two moves in the same length of simulation time (one tick). For example, a vehicle moves two steps forward, if there is no vehicle in the next two cells in front of it in the intersection. Otherwise, it moves only one step (as its planned speed) if there is no vehicle only in the next cell in front of it. However, deviations do not cause any accident.

Here, a comparison between the first test situation Si1 (Plan), see section 6.3.1, and the second test situation Si2 (Deviation) is of particular interest. The values which are results of throughput measurement, see section 6.3.1.1, and results of mean waiting time measurement, see section 6.3.1.2, and results of mean response time measurement, see section 6.3.1.3, will be compared with their corresponding values obtained from the measurement of throughput, mean waiting time and mean response time by the test situation Si2 (Deviation). This comparison can lead to discover the effect of non-compliance with the central plan (planned trajectories of vehicles). Consequently, the comparison here is between the first test situation Si1 (Plan) which is the fully central plan and the second test situation Si2 (Deviation) which is the hybrid coordination (central and decentral).

The measurement of the three metrics will be made using several values of the simulation parameter, the maximum number of vehicles, employing the evaluation scenario I (Equal-Equal). Accordingly, the traffic flow rates (traffic levels) of vehicles in south-north and west-east directions is equal, namely 5 vehicles/tick. However, the measurement has been repeated in the cases that the maximum number of vehicles in each direction is equal, namely 20, 40, 80, and 100 vehicles (40, 80, 160, 200 vehicles in both directions). The three used metrics have been measured after 3000 ticks.

Here, the comparison was managed between the measured values of the first test situation Si1 (Plan) and the measured values of the second test situation Si2 (Deviation) using the three metrics: throughput, mean waiting time and mean response time.

6.3.2.1 Results of throughput measurement

Table 6-7 shows the comparison of the system throughput measured after 3000 ticks between the first test situation Si1 (plan) and the second test situation Si2 (Deviation) with varying amounts of the maximum number of vehicles in both directions from 40 to 200 vehicles. Additionally, Figure 6-12 shows the same comparison of the system throughput as diagram.

# Vehicles (Max. Number of Vehicles)	Si1 Without Deviations (vehicles)	Si2 With Deviations (vehicles)
40	989	989
80	1950	1951
160	3849	3864
200	4800	4786

Table 6-7: The comparison of the system throughput after 3000 ticks between the first and second test situations

Chapter 6. Evaluation

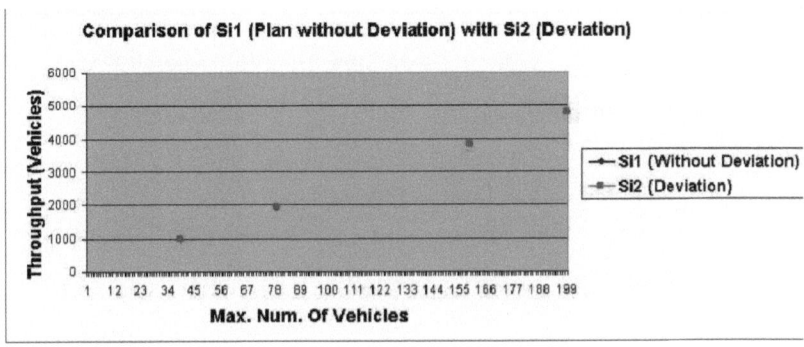

Figure 6-12: The comparison of the system throughput after 3000 ticks between the first and second test situations

In this regard, the same behaviour of the system throughput applies to both test situations Si1 (plan) and Si2 (Deviation) can be seen. Consequently, the values are roughly identical by both test situations Si1 (plan) and Si2 (Deviation). Here, the system throughput by Si1 or Si2 achieves a value of around 990 vehicles after 3000 ticks when the maximum number of vehicles in each direction is (20-20), whereas it achieves a value of around 1950 by (40-40) vehicles and by (100-100) vehicles a value of around 4800 vehicles. That means, the system throughput by the second test situation Si2 (Deviation) increases almost always linearly with the number of vehicles despite deviations from the planned trajectories (due to the autonomous vehicles).

This emphasises that no degradation of the system throughput was observed when vehicles make deviations (move more speedily than the plan) and thus do not obey their planned trajectories. Therefore, it is inferred that the central plan (the path planning by means of a central planning algorithm) was optimal. However, no improvement of the system throughput was found. The reason for this is that the vehicles which move more speedily than planned block other vehicles in the neighbourhood to obey their planned trajectories. Therefore, a speed increase of a vehicle will be at the expense of the speed of other vehicles in the next neighbourhood and thus it may lead to delays of these vehicles.

6.3.2.2 Results of mean waiting time measurement

Table 6-8 shows the comparison of the mean waiting times and the standard deviations of all vehicles, that left the intersection measured after 3000 ticks between the first test situation Si1 (plan) and the second test situation Si2 (Deviation) with varying amounts of the maximum number of vehicles in both directions from 40 to 200 vehicles. Additionally, Figure 6-14 shows the same comparison of the mean waiting time as diagram, whereas Figure 6-13 illustrates the box plot output for Si1 and Si2 combined.

	Si1 Without Deviations		Si2 With Deviations	
# Vehicles	Mean Waiting Time (Ticks)	Std. Deviation	Mean Waiting Time (Ticks)	Std. Deviation
40	0.59	0.80	0.59	0.80
80	0.84	0.53	0.89	1.09
160	1.13	1.16	1.21	1.23
200	1.43	1.39	1.50	1.32

Table 6-8: The comparison of the mean waiting times and the standard deviation of all vehicles that left the intersection after 3000 ticks between the first and second test situations

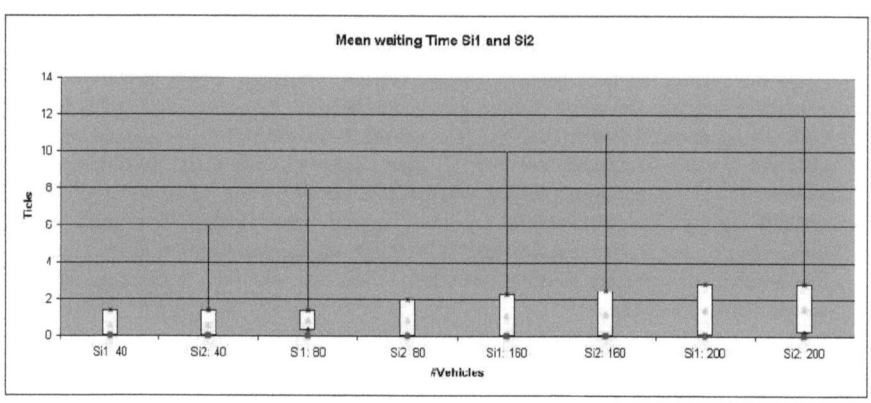

Figure 6-13: The comparison of the mean waiting times between Si1 and Si2

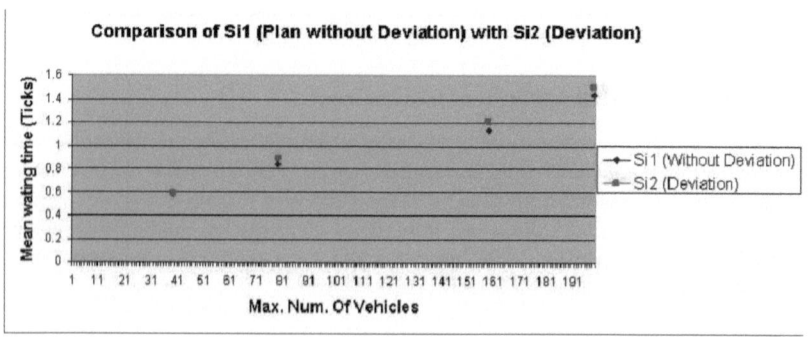

Figure 6-14: The comparison of the mean waiting times and the standard deviation of all vehicles that left the intersection after 3000 ticks between the first and second test situations

Chapter 6. Evaluation

Here, it can be seen that the same behaviour of the waiting times applies to both test situations Si1 (plan) and Si2 (Deviation). Consequently, the mean waiting times are roughly identical by both test situations Si1 (plan) and Si2 (Deviation). More accurately, there is very small increase by Si2 due to deviations. For example, the mean waiting times by Si1 and Si2 is the same (0.59 ± 0.80) when the maximum number of vehicles in each direction is (20-20), i.e., no increase of the waiting times; whereas Si2 (Deviation) has a very low increase (0.04 ticks, from 0.84 to 0.89 ticks) by (40-40) vehicles. However, Si2 has a very low increase (0.08 ticks, from 1.13 to 1.21 ticks) by (80-80) vehicles; whereas Si2 has a very low increase (0.07 ticks, from 1.43 to 1.50 ticks) by (100-100) vehicles. That means, the mean waiting times by the second test situation Si2 (Deviation) increase very slightly despite the deviations from the planned trajectories (due to the autonomous vehicles).

The very small increase of the mean waiting times by Si2 (Deviations) can be traced back to the deviations of vehicles (move more speedily than planned) which lead in turn to block other vehicles in the neighbourhood causing longer delays than those intended (planned). This confirms the conclusion that the central plan (the path planning for the vehicles) was optimal.

6.3.2.3 Results of mean response time measurement

Section 6.2 has mentioned that the response time used in the traffic application scenario has two parts: the path planning time and the observation/controlling time. According to the second situation (Si2: Deviation), deviations but no accidents will occur in the system, the response time here has the two parts.

Table 6-9 shows the comparison of the mean response time between the first test situation Si1 (plan) and the second test situation Si2 (Deviation) with varying amounts of the maximum number of vehicles in both directions from 40 to 200 vehicles. Additionally, Figure 6-15 shows the same comparison of the mean waiting time as diagram. This comparison was made by the evaluation scenario I (Equal-Equal) after 3000 ticks using the reservation mode (AllTrajectoriesVector).

# Vehicles	Si1 Without Deviations (m.sec)	Si2 With Deviations (m.sec)
40	0.267	2.709
80	0.258	5.329
160	0.323	7.065
200	0.486	14.465

Table 6-9: The comparison of the mean response time after 3000 ticks between the first and second test situations

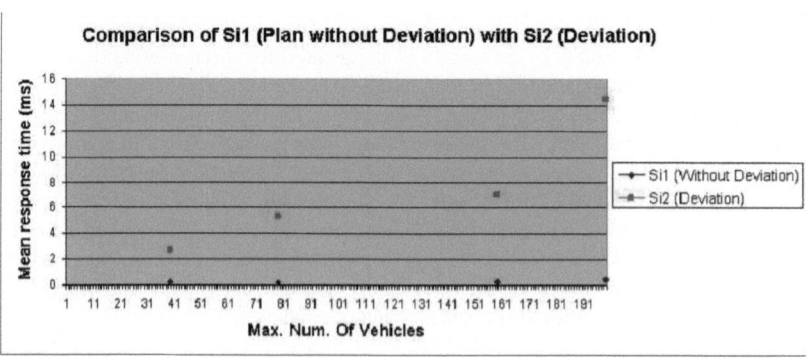

Figure 6-15: The comparison of the mean response time after 3000 ticks between the first and second test situations

Here, a different behaviour of the response times between the test situations Si1 (plan) and Si2 (Deviation) is clearly seen. More accurately, there is an increase by Si2 due to deviations. For example, the mean response time by Si2 (Deviation) increases slightly (about 2.50 ms, from 0.267 to 2.709 ms) when the maximum number of vehicles in each direction is (20-20); whereas Si2 (Deviation) increases more (about 5 ms, from 0.258 to 5.329 ms) by (40-40) vehicles. However, Si2 increases even more (about 7 ms, from 0.323 to 7.065 ms) by (80-80) vehicles; whereas Si2 increases most (about 14 ms, from 0.486 to 14.465 ms) by (100-100) vehicles. That means, the mean response times by the second test situation Si2 (Deviation) increase clearly but reasonably despite deviations from the planned trajectories (due to the autonomous vehicles).

The reasonable increase of the mean response times by Si2 (Deviations) can be attributed to the long time (comparing with the Si1: Plan without deviations) needed to detect deviations occurred in the system and to re-plan all affected trajectories. It can be seen that by (100-100) vehicles in the intersection the mean response time is less than 15 ms, which can be considered a reasonable value for the today's modern computing devices.

6.3.2.4 Summary: Second test situation: Si2 (Deviation)

In this test situation, deviations from the plan will occur but there are no accidents in the intersection. That means, vehicles do not obey their planned trajectories (i.e., decentral due to autonomous vehicles). Here, actual trajectories of vehicles will be observed identifying any deviations from plan in order to make replanning by means of the path planning algorithm. Here, vehicles try to change their speed crossing the intersection more quickly than planned (deviation type is change speed).

In this regard, a comparison was made between the first test situation Si1 (Plan) and the second test situation Si2 (Deviation). So, the comparison here is between the first test situation Si1 (Plan) which is full central plan and the second test situation Si2 (Deviation) which is hybrid coordination (central and decentral).

Chapter 6. Evaluation   139

The three used metrics of RobustMAS have been measured after 3000 ticks (time steps in simulator): throughput, mean waiting time and mean response time. The measurement of this metrics was made using the evaluation scenario I (Equal-Equal).

1) Throughput:
- There was no degradation of the system throughput in spite of deviations which made by vehicles in the intersection (move more speedily than planned) and consequently do not obey their planned trajectories.
- There was no improvement of the system throughput, because the vehicles which move more speedily than their plan block other vehicles in the neighbourhood to obey their planned trajectories.
- The central plan (the path planning of the central planning algorithm) was optimal.

2) Mean waiting time:
- There is very slight increase in the mean waiting time by Si2 (Deviation) due to deviations from the planned trajectories (due to the autonomous vehicles). These deviations of vehicles lead in turn to block other vehicles in the neighbourhood causing longer delays than planned.
- The central plan was optimal.

3) Mean response time:
- There is a clear but acceptable increase of the mean response time by Si2 (Deviation) due to deviations from the planned trajectories. Longer times are needed by Si2 than by Si1 (Plan without deviations) in order to detect deviations occurred in the system and to re-plan all affected trajectories.
- By 200 vehicles in the intersection, the mean response time is less than 15 ms.

Conclusion:

Consequently, the conclusion of this comparison between the first test situation Si1 (Plan) and the second test situation Si2 (Deviation) was the following:
- The system of central planning shows approximately the same performance as the system of decentral planning when only deviations from the central plan occur but no accidents (disturbances) occur.
- A local problem (e.g., small deviation) can be solved at local level.

6.3.3 Third test situation: Si3 (Plan, Disturbance)

In this test situation, all vehicles obey their planned trajectories (plan) and thus no deviations from the plan will occur. However, there are accidents in the intersection because of unforeseen mechanical failures.

Because there is not much difference between the test situations Si3 and Si4, and because the test situation Si4 is more applicable (it contains both deviations and accidents), the discussion will be limited to the test situation Si4.

6.3.4 Fourth test situation: Si4 (Deviation, Disturbance)

In this test situation, the vehicles do not obey their planned trajectories (the central plan) and thus deviations from the plan will occur as well as accidents in the intersection.

In this regard, an observation of actual trajectories by the observer will be made in order to detect any deviations from plan and to detect potential accidents in the intersection allowing the controller to make replanning for all affected trajectories using the path planning algorithm.

It can be recalled here that the identification of deviations from planned trajectories will be carried out via the deviation detector component in the observer; whereas the identification of disturbances (accidents) will be detected via the collision or accident detector component in the observer. Section 5.2.4.1 describes the specification of deviations and disturbances (accidents) which can occur in the intersection system.

Here, deviations will occur when autonomous vehicles change their speed trying to move more speedily than planned (change speed is the type of deviations). The vehicles that can make only one move (according to the planned trajectories) in one tick (a single time step in the simulation) are allowed to make two moves in the same length of simulation time (one tick) if it is possible.

The test situation Si4 serves to measure the robustness of the traffic intersection system and to assess the degree of the robustness of RobustMAS during disturbances (e.g., accidents) and deviations (e.g., unplanned autonomous behaviour). In order to achieve that, the simulation of the test situation Si4 was carried out under two conditions. First, disturbances (accidents) without intervention. In this case, disturbances (accidents) and deviations occur and no corrective intervention by central planning will be performed. That means, the autonomous agents (vehicles) were instructed to continue their usual local behaviour avoiding the accident position in order to move farther without any centralised interventions (without the O/C architecture). Second, disturbances (accidents) with intervention. In this case, disturbances (accidents) and deviations occur but replanning and corrective intervention by central planning will be performed (by means of the O/C architecture). This means that the autonomous agents (vehicles) will get a new planning (new trajectories) after accidents and deviations. The new planning takes into account the accident positions (as obstacles) allowing the agents (vehicles) to avoid it with the most appropriate way taking the advantage of the centralised interventions.

Here, a comparison between the first test situation Si1 (Plan), see section 6.3.1, and the fourth test situation Si4 (Deviation, Disturbance) in the first case (without intervention) and second case (with intervention) described above, is of particular interest. This comparison serves to illustrate the benefits of using a centralised intervention (i.e., the second case) compared to using only local behaviour (i.e., the first case) after disturbances (accidents), where the results of Si1 is used as comparison reference values for both cases.

6.3.4.1 Measuring robustness and gain

In order to measure the robustness of RobustMAS in the traffic intersection system, the throughput metric is used to determine the reduction of the performance (system throughput) of RobustMAS after disturbances (accidents) and deviations from the planned trajectories occur. That is because throughput is one of the most commonly used performance metrics. Therefore, the values resulting from the throughput measurement by the test situation Si1 (Plan), see section 6.3.1.1, will be compared with their corresponding values obtained from the measurement of the throughput by the test situation Si4 (Deviation, Disturbance) in both cases, with and without intervention from the central planning algorithm.

The discussion of the robustness measurement using the system throughput metric is based on the simulation parameter, the disturbance strength (the size of the accident). The measurement has been repeated in the cases that the disturbance strength is 1, 2, and 4. That means, the accident occupies an area of size 1, 2 and 4 cells in the traffic intersection as depicted in Figure 4-14. The results were obtained in an interval between 0 und 3000 ticks, where the maximum number of vehicles (Vmax) is 40 vehicles in both directions and the traffic level (TL) is 5 vehicles/tick in each direction.

It can be concluded that the increase in the size of the accident is inversely proportional to the degree of the intersection robustness.

RobustMAS tries to guarantee a relatively acceptable reduction of the intersection robustness when the size of the accident increases. RobustMAS ensures at least that increasing of size of the accident will not lead to failure of the intersection.

In the simulation, individual vehicles could cause accidents and consequently they could be crashed. If a vehicle is crashed, then they will directly stop moving and remain stopped. More accurately, autonomous and Non-Rational Vehicles (ANRV) make deviations from their planned trajectories and therefore they may cause accidents with other vehicles because of their non-rationality. These vehicles try to maximise only their own throughput in order to cross the intersection as quickly as possible.

Because the location of the accident within the intersection plays a major role in the performance of the intersection system, the simulation was repeated 10 times. Each time of repetition, an accident will be generated in a random position of the intersection by choosing a random (x, y) coordinate pair within the intersection. This (x, y) coordinate pair represents the central cell of the accident. The other cells which represent the whole accident location will be chosen also randomly depending on the value of the simulation parameter "size of the accident", so that the chosen cells will surround the central cell (x, y) of the accident. So, it can be ensured that accidents will be generated in different parts of the intersection achieving more realistic study. The average values of the system throughput will be calculated from several repetitions of the simulation (random accident locations), so that a picture of how an accident would affect the system performance is created.

The simulation parameter "Disturbance occurrence time" (Accident occurrence time) represents the time (the time step in the simulation) at which the accident will be generated. The time is measured in ticks. In the simulation, the "Accident tick" was adjusted to the value of the tick "1000", i.e., an accident should be generated at tick "1000". That means, the simulation has no accident in the interval [0-1000]; whereas it has an accident in the remaining simulation interval [1000-3000] as depicted in Figure 6-16.

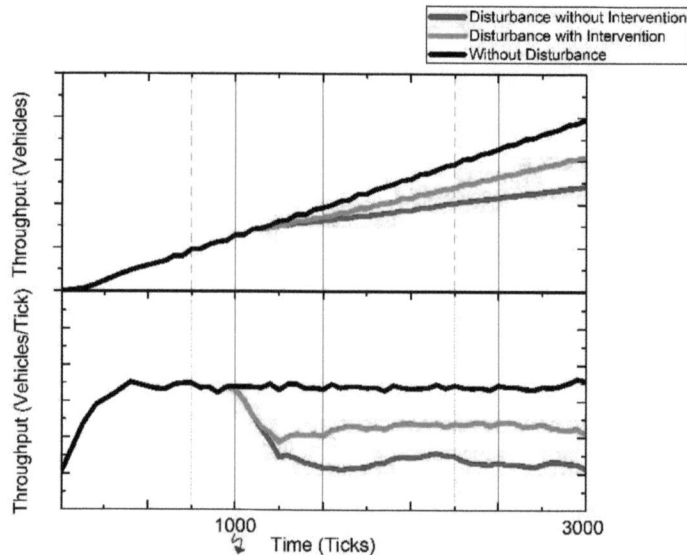

Figure 6-16: The "Disturbance occurrence time" adjusted to the tick 1000 and the simulation length is 3000 ticks (upper figure is cumulative throughput; lower figure is throughput per time unit)

Here, the system performance is the intersection throughput. The throughput is measured by the number of vehicles that left the intersection area (cumulative throughput values in the upper figure or throughput values per time unit in the lower figure).

The upper figure of Figure 6-17 shows the cumulative system performance values (throughput) of the intersection system in an interval between 0 und 3000 ticks comparing the three mentioned cases (without disturbance, disturbance without intervention and disturbance with intervention) using various values of the disturbance strength (size of the accident). Furthermore, the lower figure of Figure 6-17 shows the same as the upper figure using the throughput per time unit (# Vehicles/tick).

Chapter 6. Evaluation 143

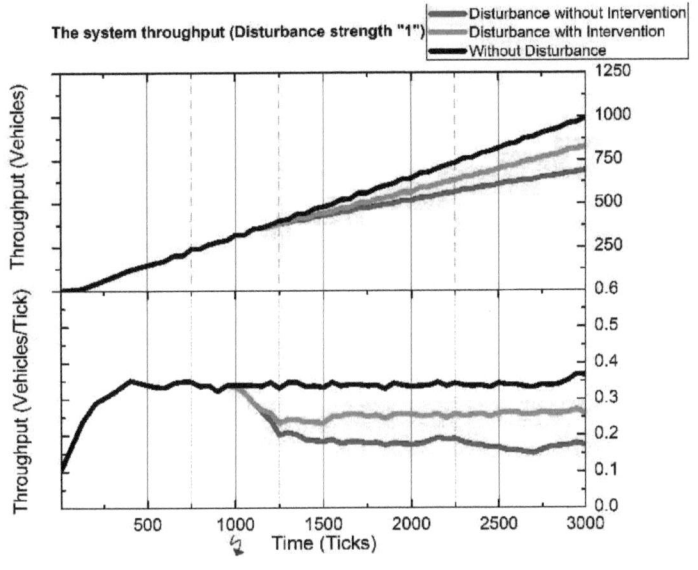

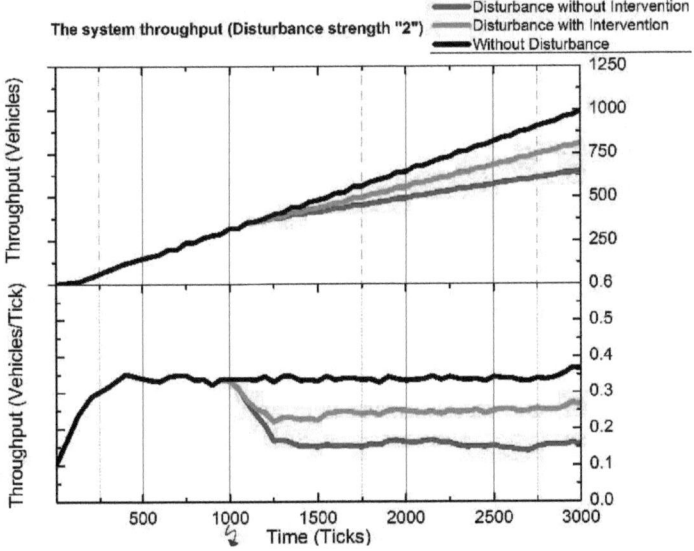

Chapter 6. Evaluation

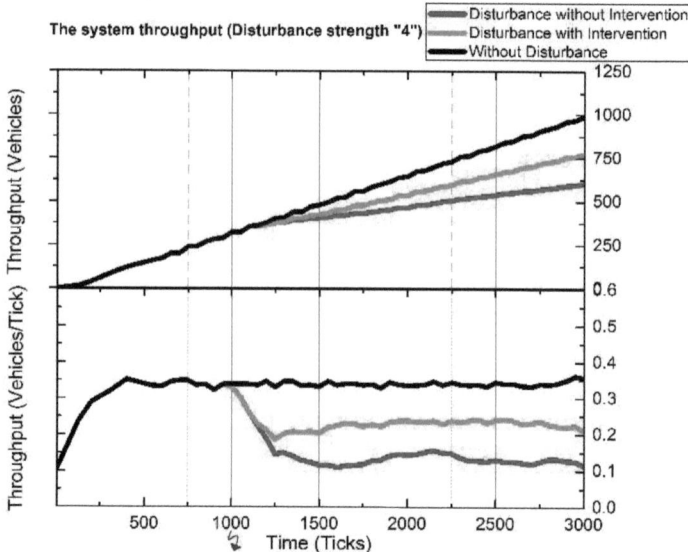

Figure 6-17: The system throughput per time unit (lower figure) and the cumulative system throughput (upper figure) using different values of the disturbance strength (size of the accident)

The robustness and the gain of the traffic intersection system can be determined using the two formulas of the relative robustness (R) and the gain of the system which were described in section 4.4.5. In order to see the effect of the disturbance strength (size of the accident), Table 6-10 compares the obtained results of the robustness and the gain of the system for various values of disturbance strength after 3000 ticks. The values of this table are based on the results of the system performance (throughput) that can be extracted from the three diagrams in Figure 6-17.

Disturbance strength (Accident size)	Robustness (R) (%)	Gain (Vehicles)
1	87	137
2	86	161
4	83	169

Table 6-10: The robustness and the gain of the system for various values of disturbance strength

So, when the disturbance strength is 1, then the robustness of the system was 87%; whereas it was 86% and 83% when the disturbance strength was 2 and 4 respectively. That means, when the disturbance strength increases, the robustness of the system decreases, but very slightly showing a high degree of robustness. This emphasises that a degradation of the system throughput was established when an accident has occurred in the intersection and the vehicles made deviations violating their planned trajectories. Therefore, in case of disturbances (accidents), the intervention of the central plan (a central planning algorithm) led to better system performance than the decentralised solution in which agents (vehicles) have to plan locally their trajectory.

However, when the disturbance strength is 1, then the gain of the system was 137 vehicles; whereas it was 161 and 169 vehicles when the disturbance strength was 2 and 4 respectively. That means, when the disturbance strength increases, the gain of the system increases. This confirms the conclusion that the intervention of the central plan was better demonstrating an improvement of the system throughput.

Therefore, it is inferred that a global problem (e.g., an accident in the intersection) should be solved at global level, because there is a central unit (the O/C architecture) that has the global view of the system. This central unit can plan better than a decentral unit. A central unit needs only longer time than a decentral unit. This issue can be solved simply by providing central units that have sufficient resources, e.g., CPU capacity (real-time requirements), memory capacity, etc, as well as the management of these resources.

6.3.4.2 Summary: Fourth test situation: Si4 (Deviation, Disturbance)

In this test situation, deviations from the plan occurred and accidents also took place in the intersection. That means, vehicles may violate their planned trajectories, because of their autonomy.

The identification of deviations from planned trajectories was carried out via the deviation detector component in the observer; whereas the identification of disturbances (accidents) was detected via the collision or accident detector component in the observer.

This test situation Si4 has served to measure the robustness of the traffic intersection system assessing the degree of the robustness of RobustMAS after disturbances (e.g., accidents) and deviations (e.g., unplanned autonomous behaviour) occur.

The simulation of Si4 was carried out in two cases: disturbances (accidents) with and without intervention (corrective intervention by central planning).

A comparison between the first test situation Si1 (Plan) and the fourth test situation Si4 (Deviation, Disturbance) was made with and without intervention. This comparison has served to illustrate the benefits of using a centralised intervention compared to using only local behaviour after disturbances (accidents).

The robustness of a multi-agent system has been defined according to the RobustMAS concept as a degradation of the system performance under disturbances and under deviations from the plan.

Since throughput is one of the most commonly used performance metrics, it was used to determine the reduction of the system performance of RobustMAS after disturbances (accidents).

Additionally, the gain of the system has been used as a measure. It has been defined according to the RobustMAS concept as a benefit of the system through central planning compared to decentral planning.

The analysis of the robustness measurement using the system throughput metric was based on the simulation parameter, the disturbance strength (size of the accident). The cumulative system performance (throughput) of the intersection system in an interval between 0 und 3000 ticks was measured to compare the three mentioned cases (without disturbance, disturbance without intervention and disturbance with intervention) by using various values of the disturbance strength (1, 2 and 4 cells as the size of the accident).

The disturbance occurrence time (accident occurrence time) was adjusted to the value of the tick "1000", so that the accident remains until the end of the simulation (the tick "3000").

The robustness and the gain of the traffic intersection system were determined using the two formulas of the robustness and the gain of the system, which were developed by this thesis.

1) Robustness:
- There was a degradation of the system throughput due to the accident in the intersection.
- When the disturbance strength (accident size) increases, the robustness of the system decreases, but very slightly showing a high degree of robustness, i.e., the increase of the disturbance strength is inversely proportional to the degree of the system robustness.
- Therefore, in case of disturbances (accidents), the intervention of the central plan (a central planning algorithm) led to better system performance than the decentralised planning.

2) Gain:
- When the disturbance strength increases, the gain of the system increases. This confirms that the central plan has demonstrated an improvement of the system throughput.

Conclusion:
- The system of central planning shows better performance than the system of decentral planning when accidents (disturbances) occur.
- A global problem (e.g., an accident in the intersection) should be solved at global level, because a central unit has a global view of the system.
- RobustMAS is characterised by a relatively acceptable level of reduction of the system robustness when the disturbance strength is increased in the system.

6.4 Summary

This chapter presented the evaluation of RobustMAS. It described the experimental setup and the simulation environment. For this purpose, the three metrics: throughput, waiting time and response time were used. This chapter discussed the four test situations proposed to perform the evaluation with respect to the goal of the RobustMAS system. The four test situations are:
- Si1 (Plan): No Deviations, No Disturbances (No Accidents).
- Si2 (Deviation): Deviations, No Disturbances (No Accidents).

Chapter 6. Evaluation

- Si3 (Plan, Disturbance): No Deviations, Disturbances (Accidents).
- Si4 (Deviation, Disturbance): Deviations, Disturbances (Accidents).

Additionally, this chapter summarised each of the four test situations mentioned separately after an extended explanation of each one of them (see section 6.3.1.4, section 6.3.2.4 and section 6.3.4.2).

The first test situation (Si1) declared the benefits of employing coordination mechanisms (central path planning) among fully autonomous vehicles. Moreover, this chapter presented two modes of the trajectories-reservation algorithm. As a result, the reservation mode (AllTrajectoriesVector) outperforms notably the other reservation mode (PhotoOfGrid) by computation time in numerous conditions.

Next, the second test situation (Si2) proved that a local problem (e.g., small deviations from central plan) can be solved at local level. However, the fourth test situation (Si4) confirmed that a global problem (disturbances, e.g., accidents in the intersection) should be solved at global level.

Additionally, the fourth test situation (Si4) was used to measure the robustness and gain of RobustMAS. For this purpose, the simulation was accomplished by Si4 in two cases: disturbances (accidents) with and without centralised intervention. Subsequently, a comparison between Si1 and the Si4 (with and without intervention) was performed to show the advantages of using a centralised intervention compared to using only local rules in the presence of disturbances (accidents). As a result, RobustMAS ensures an acceptable level of reduction of the system robustness against increasing of disturbance strength. On the other hand, the system gain increases when the disturbance strength increases. That means, the central plan expressed an improvement of the system throughput.

The next chapter contains the conclusion of this thesis and gives an overview of promising future projects.

7 Conclusion and future work

7.1 Conclusion and final words

The goal of Organic Computing (OC) is to develop robust, adaptive and flexible technical systems using several principles observed in natural systems like self-organisation. The robustness of OC systems represents a key property that should be investigated. This is particularly interesting for future systems which are complex enough so that the desired behaviour of such systems can not be guaranteed, or these systems are not able to withstand diverse disturbances, which may occur in systems or in their environments. This leads in turn to weakly robust systems or maybe even to not robust systems, especially in dynamic environments.

In this thesis, a new methodology called "Robust Multi-Agent System" (*RobustMAS*) was introduced. The focus of this methodology was the robustness of multi-agent systems in the context of organic computing. A traffic intersection without traffic lights was used as an application scenario for this thesis, where vehicles are driven by agents. In this traffic scenario, RobustMAS was proposed as a system for coordinating vehicles at traffic intersections using an O/C architecture. In this connection, the desired system architecture was presented together with the technique that is to be used to cope with this scenario. The traffic intersection is regulated by a controller, instead of having a traffic light.

RobustMAS is a new approach towards building a robust hybrid central/self-organising multi-agent system in intersections without traffic lights. This approach addresses the conflict between a central controller (e.g., a central planning algorithm) and the autonomy of the agents (vehicles). A hybrid central/self-organising multi-agent system was introduced to solve this conflict. It aims to keep a multi-agent system at a desired performance level in the presence of potential disturbances (accidents, unplanned autonomous behaviour). RobustMAS introduces a hybrid coordination of a multi-agent system (central and decentral). This hybrid coordination takes place in three steps: path planning, observation and controlling. Based on this, RobustMAS can be considered as a trajectory-based approach, which uses dynamic replanning in the presence of disturbances. Such a hybrid approach tolerates that agents (vehicles) behave in a fully autonomous way despite the central architecture. Also, the autonomy of the agents was recognised as a deviation from the central plan when the agents violate this plan. This leads in turn to an increase of the autonomy of agents in the fully central architecture

In this regard, the generic O/C architecture adapted to the intersection without traffic lights scenario was implemented. The goal of this architecture was to increase the system performance when there are no deviations from plan or disturbances. Certainly, the other goal was to maintain the system at a desired performance level when deviations from plan or disturbances occur. Additionally, the resource sharing conflict, which arises in the system wherever multiple agents move in a common environment, was discussed. The goal here was to avoid collisions in the centre of the intersection (a shared resource). Then, some coordination mechanisms to cope with this problem, resource sharing, were presented. These coordination mechanisms are based on the idea of path planning, which must be performed in the configuration space-time (x,y,t). Further, the A*-algorithm of path planning was adapted

Chapter 7. Conclusion and future work

for the requirements of the traffic intersection scenario. Then, the adapted A*- algorithm was applied in the search for the most appropriate trajectories for all vehicles aiming to coordinate them by crossing the centre of the intersection and consequently avoiding collisions. In this context, fully autonomous vehicles were used. Thereafter, the possibility how to observe these autonomous vehicles in an intersection without traffic lights was explained. This observation aims to detect deviations from the plan which represent unplanned autonomous behaviours of agents (vehicles), as well as to detect disturbances (accidents) which may occur in the system (intersection). Therefore, various classes of deviations from plan, which can be encountered, were defined. Subsequently, control features of the system designed to deal with these potential types of deviations or disturbances were introduced. That leads in turn to an intervention in time when it is necessary, so that the system remains demonstrating robustness.

The development and the evaluation of this interdisciplinary methodology (RobustMAS) were made concerning diverse evaluation scenarios by using different metrics of system performance. The empirical evaluation includes experiments with three metrics: throughput, mean waiting time and mean response time.

As evaluation metrics, the throughput was used to measure the system performance in four different evaluation scenarios in various combinations of system parameters. Moreover, throughput was required for estimating the overall reduction of the system's performance when deviations from plan or disturbances occur. Furthermore, two modes of the trajectories-reservation algorithm were presented ("AllTrajectoriesVector" and "PhotoOfGrid").

The robustness measurement of RobustMAS was made based on the new concept introduced to define the robustness of multi-agent systems. In this context, the robustness was defined as a degradation of the system performance under disturbances and under deviations from the plan. Moreover, the gain of RobustMAS was used as an additional metric. It was defined as a benefit of the system through central planning compared to decentral planning. In accordance with both definitions, two formulas of the robustness and the gain were developed and used.

The evaluation was made using four test situations with respect to the goal of the RobustMAS system. The first test situation is Si1 (Plan): No Deviations, No Disturbances (No Accidents). The second test situation is Si2 (Deviation): Deviations, No Disturbances (No Accidents). The third test situation is Si3 (Plan, Disturbance): No Deviations, Disturbances (Accidents). The fourth test situation is Si4 (Deviation, Disturbance): Deviations, Disturbances (Accidents). The three metrics (throughput, mean waiting time and mean response time) were measured for each test situation. Finally, a summary of the evaluation process for every used test situation was also given.

The experiments of the first test situation showed a high success potential by using fully autonomous vehicles and the coordination mechanisms (central path planning). Thus, it can be concluded that the application of path planning part of the O/C architecture to the system leads to a larger throughput and lower waiting time in the centre of the intersection.

On the other hand, the system performance by using central planning is roughly the same as by using decentral planning in the second test situation. This could indicate that a local problem (e.g., small deviation from plan) can be solved at local level.

However, the system performance by using central planning is better than the one by using decentral planning when disturbances (accidents) occur (i.e., the fourth test situation). This could point out that a global problem (a disturbance; e.g., an accident in the intersection) should be solved at global level. This can be traced back to the global view of the central unit on the system.

The experiments of the fourth test situation demonstrated that RobustMAS provides a high degree of robustness. Also, when the disturbance strength (accident size) increases, the robustness of the system decreases very slightly, but the gain of the system increases. Briefly, RobustMAS ensures a relatively acceptable level of reduction of the system robustness against increasing of disturbance strength.

7.2 A peek at future trends

It should be pointed out that only some of the aspects of the topic under study in this thesis could be taken into account and therefore they were included in the investigation. This can be traced back to the vastness of the topic. In this regard, robustness of hybrid multi-agent systems, especially in a traffic intersection without traffic lights, will play an important role in the future. That is because of the ever increasing development of autonomous vehicles, where vehicles can be driven by agents. Based on this, traffic intersections in the future will not require traffic lights, wherein such intersections of self-driving vehicles can be developed as a multi-agent system. Accordingly, safety and robustness of this desired system will remain key features, because the system's agents (vehicles) work autonomously and consequently they are faced with challenges in the presence of disturbances (e.g., accidents).

One aspect that may be of interest for follow-up research projects is the fairness between the system's agents (vehicles). In order to achieve this fairness, there are different approaches that deal with this issue. In this context, the fairness approach has to deliver promised results so that the system's performance remains effectively adequate for the requirements of the application scenario. According to the applied traffic scenario in this thesis, a fairly straightforward approach can be incorporated into the plan algorithm. Such approach aims to maximise the fairness between the vehicles so that all vehicles in the intersection encounter similar delays. This will surely be required where traffic levels are high. Conversely, in cases where traffic levels are very low, there's no need to a fairness approach. That is because of the adequate efficiency of traffic in low amounts of vehicles, where the average delay of vehicles can be employed as objective function.

The other aspect that will be an important issue for researchers in future is the coordination and cooperation of multiple intersections without traffic lights. The system can be considered as a network of nodes where every node represents an intersection with traffic lights. Consequently, the existing system will be extended and improved with a traffic information component. In this regard, a global optimisation of the whole traffic network could be reached by allowing these intersections to communicate with each other. For this reason, the intersections exchange information on traffic conditions, current and predicted traffic situations. This information can be used to cover a bigger area for optimisation. Based on this, the intersections cooperate to find their optimal strategies aiming to achieve global optimisations.

Finally, the presented thesis leaves space for the applicability of the RobustMAS concept for shared spaces. The current traffic scenario introduced in this work has similarities to shared spaces in the working environments and conditions, where vehicles move autonomously in a shared environment.

8 Bibliography

[1] Michael Beigl and et al. "Grand Challenges der Technischen Informatik". Technical Report Fachausschuss 3.1/6.1, Gesellschaft f¨ur Informatik e.V, March 2008.

[2] Maren Bennewitz and Wolfram Burgard. An Experimental Comparison of Path Planning Techniques for Teams of Mobile Robots. In In Autonome Mobile Systeme. Springer-Verlag, 2000.

[3] Emre Cakar, Jörg Hähner, and Christian Müller-Schloer. Creating collaboration patterns in multi-agent systems with generic observer/controller architectures. In Autonomics '08: Proceedings of the 2nd International Conference on Autonomic Computing and Communication Systems, pages 1–9, ICST, Brussels, Belgium, Belgium, 2008. ICST (Institute for Computer Sciences, Social-Informatics and Telecommunications Engineering).

[4] Y. Uny Cao, Alex S. Fukunaga, and Andrew B. Kahng. Cooperative Mobile Robotics: Antecedents and Directions. Autonomous Robots, 4:226–234, 1997.

[5] Kurt Dresner and Peter Stone. Multiagent Traffic Management: An Improved Intersection Control Mechanism. In The Fourth International Joint Conference on Autonomous Agents and Multiagent Systems, pages 471– 477. ACM Press, July 2005.

[6] Kurt Dresner and Peter Stone. Mitigating catastrophic failure at intersections of autonomous vehicles. In AAMAS '08: Proceedings of the 7th international joint conference on Autonomous agents and multiagent systems, pages 1393–1396, Richland, SC, 2008. International Foundation for Autonomous Agents and Multiagent Systems.

[7] Shin Kato, Sakae Nishiyama, and JunŠichi Takeno. Coordinating mobile robots by applying traffic rules. In Proceedings of the 1992 IEEE/RSJ, International Conference on Intelligent Robots and Systems, volume 3, pages 1535–1541. IEEE/RSJ, 1992.

[8] S. Leroy, J. P. Laumond, and T. Simeon. Multiple Path Coordination for Mobile Robots: A Geometric Algorithm. In In Proc. of the International Joint Conference on Artificial Intelligence (IJCAI), pages 1118–1123, 1999.

[9] Christian Müller-Schloer, Hartmut Schmeck and Theo Ungerer. "Organic Computing — A Paradigm Shift for Complex Systems". Birkhäuser,Verlag 2011

[10] C. Müller-Schloer. Organic computing: on the feasibility of controlled emergence. In CODES+ISSS '04: Proceedings of the 2nd IEEE/ACM/IFIP international conference

on Hardware/software codesign and system synthesis, pages 2–5. ACM, 2004.

[11] Ralf Regele and Paul Levi. Cooperative Multi-Robot Path Planning by Heuristic Priority Adjustment. In Proceedings of the 2006 IEEE/RSJ International Conference on Intelligent Robots and Systems, pages 5954– 5959, Peking, October 2006. IEEE.

[12] RePast Simphony.
http://repast.sourceforge.net/
, [accessed, September 3, 2009].

[13] Urban Richter, Moez Mnif, Jürgen Branke, Christian Müller-Schloer, and Hartmut Schmeck. Towards a generic observer/controller architecture for organic computing. In Christian Hochberger and Rüdiger Liskowsky, editors, INFORMATIK 2006 - Informatik für Menschen!, volume P-93 of GI-Edition - Lecture Notes in Informatics (LNI), pages 112–119. Bonner Köllen Verlag, 2006.

[14] Tsuyoshi Ueyama, Toshio Fukuda, Fumihito Arai, Yoshio Kawauchi, Yuuhei Katou, Shiro Matsumura, and Takehiro Uesugi. Communication Architecture for Cellular Robotic System. JSME international journal. Ser. C, Dynamics, control, robotics, design and manufacturing, 36(3):353–360, 1993.

[15] The DARPA urban challenge.
http://www.darpa.mil/grandchallenge
, [accessed, September 3, 2009].

[16] W. W. Wierwille, R. J. Hanowski, J. M. Hankey, and et al. Identification and evaluation of driver errors: Overview and recommendations. Technical Report FHWA-RD-02-003, Virginia Tech Transportation Institute, Blacksburg, Virginia, USA, August 2002.

[17] Branke, J., Mnif, M., Müller-Schloer, C., Prothmann, H., Richter, U., Rochner, F., and Schmeck, H. (2006). Organic computing - addressing complexity by controlled self-organization. In ISoLA, pages 185–191.

[18] Cakar, E., Mnif, M., Müller-Schloer, C., Richter, U., and Schmeck, H. (2007). Towards a quantitative notion of self-organisation. In IEEE Congress on Evolutionary Computation.

[19] Midas Peng and Sherri Azgomi. Content-Addressable memory (CAM) and its network applications, International IC- Taipei, Conference Proceedings, Altera International Ltd.

[20] Content-addressable memory at Wikipedia,
http://de.wikipedia.org/wiki/Assoziativspeicher

,[accessed, September 3, 2009]

[21] Moore Neighborhood in the WolframMathworld.
http://mathworld.wolfram.com/MooreNeighborhood.html
, [accessed, September 12, 2010]

[22] Examples for Robustness Requirements.
http://www.it-checklists.com/Examples_Robustness_Requirements.html
,[accessed, September 15, 2010]

[23] H. Schmeck, C. Müller-Schloer, E. Cakar, M. Mnif, U. Richter "Adaptivity and Self-organisation in Organic Computing Systems" ACM Transactions on Autonomous and Adaptive Systems, 2009, pp. 10:1-10:32.

[24] Waldschmidt, K., Damm, M., "Robustness in SOC Design", Digital System Design: Architectures, Methods and Tools, 2006. DSD 2006. 9th EUROMICRO Conference on, On page(s): 27 - 36, Volume: Issue: , 0-0 0.

[25] Knoll, F., Vogel, T.: Design for Robustness. Introductory paper to the JCSS and IABSE WC 1 Workshop, BRE, Garston UK 2005 (http://www.iabse.org).

[26] Knoll, F.; Vogel, T. (2009). Design for Robustness; Structural Engineering Documents No. 11. 2009, IABSE Zurich.

[27] Robust design of Bridges, Robustness analysis of Sjölundaviadukt Bridge, Ívar Björnsson, Division of Structural Engineering, Lund Institute of Technology, Lund University, 2010.

[28] Starossek, U.; Haberland, M. "Measures of structural robustness – Requirements & applications." Proceedings, ASCE SEI 2008 Structures Congress – Crossing Borders, Vancouver, Canada, April 24-26, 2008.

[29] Yvonne Bernard, Lukas Klejnowski, Emre Cakar, Jörg Hähner and Christian Müller-Schloer, "Efficiency and robustness using Trusted Communities in a Trusted Desktop Grid", Proceedings of the 2011 Fifth IEEE International Conference on Self-Adaptive and Self-Organizing Systems Workshop (SASOW 2011).

[30] OC-Trust project (Organic Computing Trust).
http://www.sra.uni-hannover.de/forschung/projekte/aktuelle-projekte/oc-trust/
,[accessed, September 30, 2011]

[31] Josang, A.; , "Robustness of Trust and Reputation Systems," Self-Adaptive and Self-Organizing Systems Workshop (SASOW), 2010 Fourth IEEE International Conference on , vol., no., pp.159, 27-28 Sept. 2010
doi: 10.1109/SASOW.2010.33

[32] Audun Josang. Trust and Reputation Systems. In A. Aldini and R. Gorrieri (Eds.), Foundations of Security Analysis and Design IV, FOSAD 2006/2007 Tutorial Lectures. Springer LNCS 4677. ISBN 978-3-540-74809-0. Bertinoro, Italy, September 2007.

[33] Trustworthy Self-Organizing Systems.
http://swt.informatik.uni-augsburg.de/tsos/2010/abstract-josang.html
,[accessed, September 28, 2011]

[34] Gershenson, C. Design and Control of Self-organizing Systems. PhD Thesis. Vrije Universiteit Brussel, 2007.

[35] E.Jen (ed.). "Robust Design: A Repertoire of Biological, Ecological, and Engineering Case Studies", Santa Fe Institute Studies on the Sciences of Complexity. Oxford University Press, USA, 2005.

[36] WAGNER, A. Robustness and Evolvability in Living Systems. University Presses Of California, Columbia And Princeton, 2005.

[37] Watson, R. A. (2002) Compositional Evolution: Interdisciplinary Investigations in Evolvability, Modularity, and Symbiosis. PhD thesis, Brandeis University, MA. USA.

[38] Fernandez, P. and Sole, R. : The role of computation in complex regulatory networks. In Koonin, E. V., Wolf, Y. I., and Karev, G. P., editors, Power Laws, Scale-Free Networks and Genome Biology. Landes Bioscience, 2004.

[39] Wagner, A. (2005), Distributed robustness versus redundancy as causes of mutational robustness. BioEssays, 27: 176–188. doi: 10.1002/bies.20170.

[40] Gershenson, C., S. A. Kauffman, and I. Shmulevich (2006). The Role of Redundancy in the Robustness of Random Boolean Networks. In Rocha, L. M., L. S. Yaeger, M. A. Bedau, D. Floreano, R. L. Goldstone, and A. Vespignani (Eds.), Artificial Life X, Proceedings of the Tenth International Conference on the Simulation and Synthesis of Living Systems. pp. 35-42. MIT Press.

[41] Whitacre, James M, and Axel Bender. "Degeneracy: a design principle for achieving robustness and evolvability." Journal of Theoretical Biology 263.1 (2009) : 143-153.

[42] Javier Macia and Ricard V Solé. "Distributed robustness in cellular networks: insights from synthetic evolved circuits". J R Soc Interface (2009) 6: 393-400

[43] Robust yet flexible. available from EMBO reports (2009):
http://www.nature.com/embor/journal/v10/n9/full/embor2009196.html
,[accessed, September 30, 2011]

[44] Wikipedia: Modularity,

http://en.wikipedia.org/wiki/Modularity
,[accessed, September 30, 2011]

[45] Wikipedia: Degeneracy,
http://en.wikipedia.org/wiki/Degeneracy_%28mathematics%29
,[accessed, September 30, 2011]

[46] Wikipedia: Redundancy,
http://en.wikipedia.org/wiki/Redundancy_%28engineering%29
,[accessed, September 30, 2011]

[47] GERSHENSON, C. A general methodology for designing self-organizing systems. Tech. Rep. 2005-05, ECCO (2006). URL http://uk.arxiv.org/abs/nlin.AO/0505009.

[48] Marc Zeller, Fraunhofer Institute for Communication Systems ESK, Germany. IARIA Work Group Meeting: Autonomic and Autonomous, 1. PANEL ICAS, Topic: Robustness and Trust in Autonomic Systems. Panel @ ICAS 2010. The Sixth International Conference on Autonomic and Autonomous Systems ICAS 2010, March 7-13, 2010 - Cancun, Mexico.
http://www.iaria.org/conferences2010/filesICAS10/ICAS_2010_Panel.pdf

[49] Jan-Philipp Steghöfer, Rolf Kiefhaber, Karin Leichtenstern, Yvonne Bernard, Lukas Klejnowski, Wolfgang Reif, Theo Ungerer, Elisabeth André, Jörg Hähner, and Christian Müller-Schloer, "Trustworthy Organic Computing Systems: Challenges and Perspectives", Proceedings of the 7th International Conference on Autonomic and Trusted Computing (ATC 2010), Springer

[50] Alderson, D.L., Doyle, J.C.: Can complexity science support the engineering of critical network infrastructures? In: IEEE International Conference on Systems, Man and Cybernetics, SCM 2007 (2007).

[51] G. Di Marzo Serugendo. "Robustness and Dependability of Self-Organising Systems – A Safety Engineering Perspective". The 11th International Symposium on Stabilization, Safety and Security of Distributed Systems (SSS 2009), Lyon, France, November 2009.

[52] Andy Snow, School of Information & Telecommunication Systems, Ohio University. Avoiding, Accepting and Influencing Complex System Behavior. IARIA Work Group Meeting: Advances on Systems, 1. PANEL ICONS, Topic: Robustness in Real-time Complex Systems. Panel @ ICONS 2010. The Fifth International Conference on Systems ICONS 2010, April 11-16, 2010 - Menuires, The Three Valleys, French Alps, France.

http://www.iaria.org/conferences2010/filesICONS10/ICONS_2010_PANEL.pdf

[53] Irving Wladawsky-Berger. Complex Organizational Systems. August, 2008. In Complex Systems, Innovation, Technology and Strategy.

http://blog.irvingwb.com/blog/2008/08/complex-organiz.html

[54] Wikipedia: System accident,

http://en.wikipedia.org/wiki/Normal_accidents

,[accessed, Oktober 06, 2011]

[55] Julie Cohen, Dan Plakosh and Kristi Keeler. „Robustness Testing of Software-Intensive Systems: Explanation and Guide". Technical Note, CMU/SEI-2005-TN-015, April 2005, Acquisition Support Program.

[56] Marko Jäntti, ITÄ-Suomen Yliopisto, University Of Eastern Finland. Robustness in Real-time Complex Systems: Testing-based approach. IARIA Work Group Meeting: Advances on Systems, 1. PANEL ICONS, Topic: Robustness in Real-time Complex Systems. Panel @ ICONS 2010. The Fifth International Conference on Systems ICONS 2010, April 11-16, 2010 - Menuires, The Three Valleys, French Alps, France.

http://www.iaria.org/conferences2010/filesICONS10/ICONS_2010_PANEL.pdf

[57] Anderson, T. (Editor). "Resilient Computing Systems", vol. 1,

http://dl.acm.org/citation.cfm?id=20598&preflayout=flat

Publisher John Wiley & Sons, Inc. New York, NY, USA 1986, ISBN 0-471-84518-3.

[58] Algirdas Avižienis, Jean C. Laprie, Brian Randell, Carl Landwehr. "Basic Concepts and Taxonomy of Dependable and Secure Computing". IEEE Transactions on Dependable and Secure Computing In Dependable and Secure Computing, IEEE Transactions on, Vol. 1, No. 1. (January 2004), pp. 11-33.

[59] Avizienis, A., Laprie, J. C., & Randell, B. (2004). Dependability and its threats: a taxonomy. System, 156 (July 1834), 91-120. Springer. Retrieved from

http://www.springerlink.com/index/P3278R4557H6578R.pdf

[60] D. Powell, G. Bonn, D. Seaton, P. Veríssimo, F. Waeselynck, "The Delta-4 approach to dependability in open distributed computing systems", in Proc. 18th IEEE Int. Symp. On Fault-Tolerant Computing (FTCS-18), Tokyo, Japan, June 1988, pp. 246-251.

[61] Christophe Dony, Jørgen Lindskov Knudsen, Alexander B. Romanovsky, and Anand Tripathi, editors. Advanced Topics in Exception Handling Techniques, volume 4119 of Lecture Notes in Computer Science. Springer, 2006. ISBN 978-3-540-37443-5

[62] Briot, J.P., Aknine, S., Alvarez, I., Guessoum, Z., Malenfant, J., Marin, O., Perrot,

J.F., Sens, P.: Multi-agent systems and fault-tolerance: State of the art elements. Technical report, LIP6 & MODECO-CReSTIC, 2007. Bibliographic Study.

[63] Sanjeev Kumar and Philip R. Cohen. Towards a Fault-Tolerant Multi-Agent System Architecture. In Proceedings of the fourth international conference on Autonomous agents, 2000. Pages: 459-466, ACM Press publisher.

[64] Sanjeev Kumar, Philip R, Cohen, and Hector J. Levesque. The Adaptive Agent Architecture: Achieving Fault-Tolerance Using Persistent Broker Teams. In Proceedings of the Fourth International Conference on Multi-Agent Systems (ICMAS-2000), Boston MA, USA, July 7-12, 2000.

[65] Steffen Becker, Wilhelm Hasselbring, Alexandra Paul, Marko Boskovic, Heiko Koziolek, Jan Ploski, Abhishek Dhama, Henrik Lipskoch, Matthias Rohr, Daniel Winteler, Simon Giesecke, Roland Meyer, Mani Swaminathan, Jens Happe, Margarete Muhle, and Timo Warns. 2006. "Trustworthy software systems: a discussion of basic concepts and terminology". SIGSOFT Software. Engineering. Notes 31, 6 (November 2006).

[66] Tor-Erik Hagen. An Architectural Process for Achieving Robustness. Master of Science in Informatics, Norwegian University of Science and Technology, Department of Computer and Information Science, December 2007

[67] V. Shestak, H. J. Siegel, A. A. Maciejewski, and S. Ali. The robustness of resource allocations in parallel and distributed computing systems. In Proceedings of the International Conference on Architecture of Computing Systems (ARCS 2006), pages 17–30, 2006.

[68] W. Heupke, C. Grimm, and K. Waldschmidt. Modeling uncertainty in nonlinear analog systems with affine arithmetic. Advances in Specification and Design Languages for SOCs Selected Contributions from FDL '05, 2005.

[69] D. England, J. Weissman, and J. Sadagopan. A new metric for robustness with application to job scheduling. In IEEE International Symposium on High Performance Distributed Computing 2005 (HPDC-14), Research Triangle Park, NC, July 24-27, 2005.

[70] D. S. Callaway, M. E. J. Newman, S. H. Strogatz, and D. J. Watts. Network robustness and fragility: Percolation on random graphs. Physical Review Letters, 85(25):5468–5471, 2000.

[71] Slotine JJE, Li W. Applied nonlinear control. Prentice Hall; 1991.

[72] Kouvelis P, Yu G. Robust discrete optimization and its applications. Nonconvex

optimization and its applications, vol. 14. Dordrecht (Boston): Kluwer Academic Publishers; 1997.

[73] Tabakov P.Y., Walker M. A technique for optimally designing engineering structures with manufacturing tolerances accounted for. Engineering Optimization, 39 (1), pp. 1-15, 2007.

[74] Nicola Policella. Robust Scheduling: Analysis and Synthesis of flexible solutions, PhD Thesis Proposal, Dipartimento di Informatica e Sistemistica, Universita' di Roma "La Sapienza", 2004.

[75] Simon Parsons and Mark Klein. Towards Robust Multi-Agent Systems: Handling Communication Exceptions in Double Auctions. Proceedings of the Third International Joint Conference on Autonomous Agents and Multi-agent Systems - Volume 3, New York, New York, 2004.

[76] M. Klein, J. A. Rodriguez-Aguilar, and C. Dellarocas. Using domain-independent exception handling services to enable robust open multi-agent systems: The case of agent death. Journal of Autonomous Agents and Multi-Agent Systems, 7(1/2), 2003.

[77] Amy Unruh, James Bailey, and Kotagiri Ramamohanarao. "A Logging-Based Approach for Building More Robust Multi-agent Systems". Intelligent Agent Technology, 2006. IAT '06. IEEE/WIC/ACM International Conference on , vol., no., pp.342-349, 18-22 Dec. 2006.

[78] Daniel Frey, Jens Nimis, Heinz Wörn and Peter Lockemann. Benchmarking and robust multi-agent-based production planning and control. Engineering Applications of Artificial Intelligence In Intelligent Manufacturing, Vol. 16, No. 4., pp. 307-320, June 2003.

[79] Daniel Frey and Heinz Wörn. Das Benchmarking und der robuste Betrieb eines MAS in der Produktionsplanung und –steuerung (in german). Institut für Prozessrechentechnik, Automation und Robotik; Universität Karlsruhe (TH), 2000.

[80] Jens Nimis and Peter C. Lockemann. Robust Multi-Agent Systems: The Transactional Conversation Approach. In: 1st International Workshop on Safety and Security in Multiagent Systems (SASEMAS04), 2004.

[81] Khaled Nagi. Transactional Agents: Towards A Robust Multi-Agent System. Referent/Korreferent: Lockemann, Deussen. Universität Karlsruhe, Ph.D., Lecture Notes in Computer Science, Springer, 2001.

[82] Khaled Nagi, Jens Nimis and Peter C. Lockemann. Transactional support for cooperation in multiagent-based information systems. In: Proceedings of the Joint

Conference on Distributed Information Systems on the basis of Objects, Components and Agents (VertIS), Bamberg, 2001.

[83] Michael Schillo, Hans-Jürgen Bürckert, Klaus Fischer, Matthias Klusch. .Towards a Definition of Robustness for Market-Style Open Multi-Agent Systems.
In: Proceedings of the Fifth International Conference on Autonomous Agents. International Conference on Autonomous Agents (AGENTS-01), May 28 - June 1, Montreal, Canada, Pages 75-76, ACM Press, New York, 2001.

[84] Michael Schillo, Ingo Zinnikus, and Klaus Fischer. Towards a Theory of Flexible Holons: Modelling Institutions for Making Multi-Agent Systems Robust. In Conte, R., and Dellarocas, C. Proceedings of the Workshop on Norms and Institutions at Agents 2001, Montreal.

[85] Michael Schillo, Bettina Fley, Michael Florian, Frank Hillebrandt, Daniela Hinck. Self-Organization in Multiagent Systems: From Agent Interaction to Agent Organization. In: Proceedings of the Third International Workshop on Modelling Artificial Societies and Hybrid Organizations (MASHO'02) at the 24th German Conference on Artificial Intelligence (KI2002), Aachen.

[86] Christian Hahn, Bettina Fley, Michael Schillo. Optimisation of Multiagent Organisation for Robustness. In: Sozionik aktuell, Vol. 3, pp. 1-13, 2003

[87] Wikipedia: Intelligent Transportation System (ITS),
http://en.wikipedia.org/wiki/Intelligent_transportation_system
,[accessed, November 30, 2011]

[88] Fritz Busch. Intelligent Transportation Systems – Opportunities and Challenges (Intelligente Verkehrssysteme – Neue Möglichkeiten und Fragestellungen) it - Information Technology: Vol. 50, Issue 4, pp. 217-221. (2008).

[89] Felix Schmidt-Eisenlohr and Moritz Killat. Vehicle-to-Vehicle Communications: Reception and Interference of Safety-Critical Messages (Fahrzeug-zu-Fahrzeug-Kommunikation: Empfang und Interferenz sicherheitskritischer Nachrichten) it - Information Technology: Vol. 50, Issue 4, pp. 230-236, (2008).

[90] Ana L. C. Bazzan and R. Junges. Traffic Network Equilibrium using Congestion Tolls: a case study. Proceedings of the 4th Workshop on Agents in Traffic and Transportation. May. 1-8, 2006.

[91] Julien Laumonier , Charles Desjardins , Brahim Chaib-draa. Cooperative adaptive cruise control: a reinforcement learning approach. In The Fourth Workshop on Agents in Traffic and Transportation, Japan, 2006.

[92] OTC project (Organic Traffic Control).
http://www.sra.uni-hannover.de/forschung/projekte/abgeschlossene-projekte/organic-traffic-control-otc/
,[accessed, December 12, 2011]

[93] OTC project (Organic Traffic Control).
http://projects.aifb.kit.edu/effalg/otcqe/otc/phase1.htm
,[accessed, December 12, 2011]

[94] OTCC project (Organic Traffic Control Collaborative).
http://www.sra.uni-hannover.de/forschung/projekte/aktuelle-projekte/organic-traffic-control-collaborative-otcc/
,[accessed, December 12, 2011]

[95] OTCC project (Organic Traffic Control Collaborative).
http://projects.aifb.kit.edu/effalg/otcqe/otc/phase2.htm
,[accessed, December 12, 2011]

[96] H. Prothmann, F. Rochner, S. Tomforde, J. Hähner, C. Müller-Schloer, H. Schmeck "Organic Control of Traffic Lights". Proceedings Autonomic and Trusted Computing 2008 (ATC 2008), Oslo, June 23 – 25, 2008, Springer LNCS.

[97] S. Tomforde, H. Prothmann, F. Rochner, J. Branke, J. Hähner, C. Müller-Schloer "Decentralised Progressive Signal Systems for Organic Traffic Control". SASO 2008, Venedig, 20. - 24.10.08, IEEE computer society, pp. 413-422.

[98] Holger Prothmann. Organic Traffic Control. KIT Scientific Publishing, PhD 2011.

[99] Tomforde, S.; Brameshuber, A.; Hahner, J.; Muller-Schloer, C.; , "Restricted on-line learning in real-world systems," Evolutionary Computation (CEC), 2011 IEEE Congress on , vol., no., pp.1628-1635, 5-8 June 201, CEC.2011.

[100] Sven Tomforde. An Architectural Framework for Self-configuration and Self-improvement at Runtime. Dissertation, Leibniz Universität Hannover, 2011.

[101] OTC^3 project (Organic Traffic Control^3).
http://projects.aifb.kit.edu/effalg/otcqe/otc/index.htm
,[accessed, December 12, 2011]

[102] Prothmann, Holger; Tomforde, Sven; Lyda, Johannes; Branke, Jürgen; Hähner, Jörg; Müller-Schloer, Christian; and Schmeck, Hartmut: "Decentralised Route Guidance in Organic Traffic Control". In: Proceeding of the 5th IEEE International Conference on Self-Adaption and Self-Organization (SASO'11), IEEE, 2011, pp.219-220, 3-7 Oct. 2011.

Chapter 8. Bibliography

[103] Brian Dong & Graham Roff. Adaptive Self-Configuring Traffic Control Systems. University of California San Diego, San Diego, USA, CSE237A Final Report, June 11, 2004.

[104] Kevin Stock. Autonomous Driving.
http://citeseerx.ist.psu.edu/viewdoc/summary?doi=10.1.1.128.3935

[105] Wikipedia: Autonomous cruise control system,
http://en.wikipedia.org/wiki/Adaptive_cruise_control
,[accessed, December 15, 2011]

[106] The "Center for Automotive Research" at the Ohio State University (OSU).
http://car.eng.ohio-state.edu/
,[accessed, December 19, 2011]

[107] The DARPA Grand challenge.
http://www.darpagrandchallenge.com/
,[accessed, December 19, 2011]

[108] The project "Autonomous Outdoor Robot RTS-HANNA" at the Real Time Systems Group (RTS) of the Leibniz University Hannover in Germany.
http://www.rts.uni-hannover.de/index.php/Autonomous_Outdoor_Robot_RTS-HANNA
,[accessed, December 19, 2011]

[109] Autonomo 2030 Concept. Posted by Jeff Darling on 21 November 2011.
http://www.diseno-art.com/news_content/2011/11/autonomo-2030-concept/
,[accessed, December 19, 2011]

[110] Autonomo - fully autonomous vehicle designed for the year 2030, by Jan Belezina on 26 November 2011
http://www.gizmag.com/autonomo-fully-autonomous-vehicle-designed-for-the-year-2030/20529/
,[accessed, December 19, 2011]

[111] Smolorz, S.; Wagner, B.: "Self-organized Distribution of Tasks inside an Autonomous Mobile Robotic System", 6th IEEE International Conference on Digital Ecosystem Technologies - Complex Environment Engineering (IEEE DEST-CEE), Campione d'Italia, Italy, June 2012.

[112] The project "Stadtpilot" at the Technical University Braunschweig in Germany.
http://stadtpilot.tu-bs.de/en/stadtpilot/project
,[accessed, December 19, 2011]

Chapter 8. Bibliography 164

[113] The project "CarOLO" at the Technical University Braunschweig in Germany.
http://www.carolo.tu-bs.de/
,[accessed, December 22, 2011]

[114] The project "AutoNOMOS" at the Free University Berlin in Germany.
http://autonomos.inf.fu-berlin.de/
,[accessed, December 22, 2011]

[115] The project "AutoNOMOS" by DARPA Urban Challenge.
http://autonomos.inf.fu-berlin.de/introduction/darpa-urban-challenge
,[accessed, December 22, 2011]

[116] The autonomous car "Spirit-of-Berlin" at the project "AutoNOMOS".
http://autonomos.inf.fu-berlin.de/technology/spirit-of-berlin
,[accessed, December 22, 2011]

[117] The autonomous car "Made-In-Germany" at the project "AutoNOMOS".
http://autonomos.inf.fu-berlin.de/technology/made-in-germany
,[accessed, December 22, 2011]

[118] Concept of Operations (ConOps) for: "Standard Traffic Signal". Minnesota Department of Transportation, document: January 26, 2010.

[119] Google's Autonomous Car Takes To The Streets, by Evan Ackerman on 12 Oktober 2010.
http://spectrum.ieee.org/automaton/robotics/artificial-intelligence/googles-autonomous-car-takes-to-the-streets
,[accessed, December 25, 2011]

[120] Greschner, J.T., Gerland, H.E.: Traffic Signal Priority: Tool To Increase Service Quality And Efficiency. In: Proceedings APTA Bus and Paratransit Conference, Houston, TX, pp. 138–143, 2000.

[121] ChipOnline - Report: Hightech im Auto „Autofahren 3.0". Spitzenforschung: KIT aus Karlsruhe, by Daniel Wolff, on 22 October 2009
http://www.chip.de/artikel/Report-Hightech-im-Auto-4_38097098.html
,[accessed, December 25, 2011]

[122] Gizmag News, Halo Interceptor concept would serve as car, boat, plane and helicopter.
http://www.gizmag.com/halo-interceptor-multivehicle-concept/16798/picture/123820/
,[accessed, December 25, 2011]

[123] Auto motor und sport, Halo Intersceptor: Auto, Jet, Helikopter und Boot in Einem, on 13 October 2010.
http://www.auto-motor-und-sport.de/news/halo-intersceptor-auto-jet-helikopter-und-boot-in-einem-2799082.html
,[accessed, December 25, 2011]

[124] Wikipedia: IEEE_802.11p.
http://en.wikipedia.org/wiki/IEEE_802.11p
,[accessed, December 26, 2011]

[125] The SimTD project at Fraunhofer SIT (car-to-X communication).
http://www.sit.fraunhofer.de/en/fields-of-expertise/projects/simtd.html
,[accessed, December 26, 2011]

[126] The "simTD: Safe and Intelligent Mobility Test Field Germany" project (car-to-X communication).
http://www.simtd.org/index.dhtml/344ef89cf97cd92375su/-/enEN/-/CS/-/
,[accessed, December 26, 2011]

[127] A. Festag, H. Füssler, H. Hartenstein, A. Sarma, and R. Schmitz. FleetNet: Bringing Car-to-Car Communication into the Real World. In 11th ITS World Congress and Exhibtion, October 2004.

[128] The project "Invent" (Car-to-Car) communication.
http://www.invent-online.de/en/projects.html
,[accessed, December 26, 2011]

[129] The project "NOW: Network On Wheels" (Car-to-Car) communication.
http://www.network-on-wheels.de/links.html
,[accessed, December 26, 2011]

[130] Wikipedia: Shared space.
http://en.wikipedia.org/wiki/Shared_space
,[accessed, September 10, 2012]

[131] Wikipedia: Autonomous car.
http://en.wikipedia.org/wiki/Autonomous_car
,[accessed, December 27, 2011]

[132] Sylvia Richter and Matthias Geue. „Autonome Autos", Seminar Automotiv 2, University Potsdam, Germany, winter semester 2007/08.

[133] Christopher Armbrust, Tim Braun, Tobias Föhst, Martin Proetzsch, Alexander Renner, Bernd-Helge Schäfer, Karsten Berns. RAVON - The Robust Autonomous

Vehicle for Off-road Navigation. Proceedings of the IARP International Workshop on Robotics for Risky Interventions and Environmental Surveillance 2009 (RISE 2009) - IARP January 12--14, 2009 - Brussels, Belgium.

[134] Nilsson, J. Nils: Principles of Artificial Intelligence; Springer Verlag, Berlin Heidelberg, 1982.

[135] Shladover, S., California., University of California, Berkeley., & Partners for Advanced Transit and Highways (Calif.). "Effects of cooperative adaptive cruise control on traffic flow: Testing drivers' choices of following distances". Berkeley, Calif: California PATH Program, Institute of Transportation Studies, University of California at Berkeley,2009.

[136] FOT-Net Wiki: SKY Project - Intersection Collision Avoidance.
http://wiki.fot-net.eu/index.php?title=SKY_Project_-_Intersection_Collision_Avoidance
,[accessed, January 5, 2012]

[137] Naumann, R.; Rasche, R.; Tacken, J.; Tahedl, C.: „Validation and Simulation of a Decentralized Intersection Collision Avoidance Algorithm", Proceedings of the IEEE Conference on Intelligent Transportation Systems (ITSC'97), Boston, MA, 1997.

[138] Naumann, R.; Rasche, R.; Tacken, J.: „Managing autonomous vehicles at intersections", IEEE Intelligent Systems & Their Applications, Vol. 13, No. 3, P. 82 – 86, May/June, 1998.

[139] Naumann, R.; Rasche, R.: "Intersection Collision Avoidance by Means of Decentralized Security and Communication Management of Autonomous Vehicles", Proceedings of the 30th ISATA Conference on Mechatronics, Florence, Italy, 1997.

[140] Reynolds, C. W. Steering Behaviors For Autonomous Characters. in the proceedings of Game Developers Conference 1999 held in San Jose, California. Miller Freeman Game Group, San Francisco, California. Pages 763-782, 1999.

[141] Kurt Dresner and Peter Stone. A Multiagent Approach to Autonomous Intersection Management. Journal of Artificial Intelligence Research, 31:591–656, March 2008.

[142] U.S. Department of Transportation, Intelligent transportation system, ITS Research Success Stories. Cooperative Intersection Collision Avoidance Systems (CICAS).
http://www.its.dot.gov/cicas/
,Updated January 12, 2012, [accessed, January 16, 2012]

[143] Mark VanMiddlesworth, Kurt Dresner, and Peter Stone. Replacing the Stop Sign: Unmanaged Intersection Control for Autonomous Vehicles. In The Fifth Workshop

Agents in Traffic and Transportation (ATT 08), Estoril, Portugal, May 2008.

[144] OCCS project (Observation and Control of Collaborative Systems).
http://www.sra.uni-hannover.de/index.php?id=603&L=2
,[accessed, January 27, 2012]

[145] OCCS project (Observation and Control of Collaborative Systems).
http://projects.aifb.kit.edu/effalg/otcqe/qe/phase2.htm
,[accessed, January 27, 2012]

[146] M. Mnif, U. Richter, J. Branke, H. Schmeck, C. Müller-Schloer. "Measurement and Control of Self-organised Behaviour in Robot Swarms". ARCS 2007, P. Lukowicz, L. Thiele and G. Tröster (Eds.): LNCS 4415, pp. 209–223, 2007, Springer-Verlag Berlin Heidelberg.

[147] N. Correll and A. Martinoli, "Collective inspection of regular structures using a swarm of miniature robots," in Proc. of the Int. Symp. on Experimental Robotics (ISER). Singapore: Springer Tracts for Advanced Robotics (STAR), Vol. 21, June 2006, pp. 375-385.

[148] Trianni V., Labella Th.H., Gross R., Sahin E., Dorigo M. and Deneubourg J.-L. Modeling Pattern Formation in a Swarm of Self-Assembling Robots. Technical Report TR/IRIDIA/2002-12, IRIDIA, Université Libre de Bruxelles, Bruxelles, Belgium, May 2002.

[149] Kurt Konolige , Charles Ortiz , Regis Vincent , Andrew Agno , Benson Limketkai , Mark Lewis , Linda Briesemeister , Dieter Fox , Jonathan Ko , Benjamin Stewart , Leonidas Guibas. "CENTIBOTS Large Scale Robot Teams". Artificial Intelligence Center, SRI International, Menlo Park, CA 2003.

[150] Curtis, S, A, Rilee, M, L, Truszkowski, W, Clark, P, E, "ANTS for the Human Exploration and Development of Space", Proceedings of the IEEE 2003 Aerospace Conference, Volume 1, March 8 – 15, 2003, Pages 1 – 7.

[151] M. Long, A. Gage, R. Murphy, and K. Valavanis, "Application of the distributed field robot architecture to a simulated demining task," in Proc. IEEE ICRA, Barcelona, Spain, Apr. 2005, pp. 3193–3200.

[152] CAS-wiki: Organic Computing.
http://wiki.cas-group.net/index.php?title=Organic_Computing
,[accessed, February 06, 2012]

[153] Kephart, J.O., Chess, D.M.: The vision of autonomic computing. IEEE Comput. 1, 41–50, 2003.

[154] Sterritt, R.: Autonomic Computing. Innov. Syst. Softw. Eng. 1(1), 79–88, 2005.

[155] Ian Jordaan. "Decisions under uncertainty: probabilistic analysis for engineerinjg decisions". Cambridge University Press, 2005.

[156] K. Decker, K. Sycara, and M. Williamson. Matchmaking and Brokering. Proceedings of the Second International Conference on Multi-Agent Systems (ICMAS-96), 1996.

[157] Robertson, D.I., and R.D. Bretherton. "Optimizing Networks of Traffic Signals in Real Time - The SCOOT Method." IEEE Transactions on Vehicular Technology, Vol. 40, No. 1, pp. 11-15, February 1991.

[158] Arthur G. Sims and K.W. Dobinson. "The Sydney coordinated adaptive traffic (SCAT) system - philosophy and benefits". IEEE Transactions on Vehicular Technology, 29(2):130–137, 1980.

[159] Bazzan, A. L. C. "A distributed approach for coordination of traffic signal agents." Autonomous Agents and Multi-Agent Systems, 10(2), 131-164, 2005.

[160] Roozemond, D. A. "Using intelligent agents for urban traffic control systems". In Proceedings of the International Conference on Artifficial Intelligence in Transportation Systems and Science, pp. 69-79, 1999.

[161] Balan, G., and Luke, S. "History-based traffic control". In Proceedings of the Fifth International Joint Conference on Autonomous Agents and Multiagent Systems, pp. 616-621, Hakodate, Japan, 2006.

[162] Halle, S., and Chaib-draa, B. "A collaborative driving system based on multiagent modelling and simulations". Journal of Transportation Research Part C (TRC-C): Emergent Technologies, 13, 320-345, 2005.

i want morebooks!

Buy your books fast and straightforward online - at one of world's fastest growing online book stores! Environmentally sound due to Print-on-Demand technologies.

Buy your books online at
www.get-morebooks.com

Kaufen Sie Ihre Bücher schnell und unkompliziert online – auf einer der am schnellsten wachsenden Buchhandelsplattformen weltweit! Dank Print-On-Demand umwelt- und ressourcenschonend produziert.

Bücher schneller online kaufen
www.morebooks.de

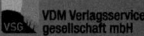

VDM Verlagsservicegesellschaft mbH
Heinrich-Böcking-Str. 6-8   Telefon: +49 681 3720 174   info@vdm-vsg.de
D - 66121 Saarbrücken   Telefax: +49 681 3720 1749   www.vdm-vsg.de

Printed by Books on Demand GmbH, Norderstedt / Germany